PRIME TIME

PRIME TIME

366 Devotions for Seniors

H. Robert Cowles

CHRISTIAN PUBLICATIONS
CAMP HILL, PENNSYLVANIA

Christian Publications
3825 Hartzdale Drive, Camp Hill, PA 17011

The mark of ✝ *vibrant faith*

ISBN: 0-87509-468-6
LOC Catalog Card Number: 91-73585
© 1991 by Christian Publications
All rights reserved
Printed in the United States of America

91 92 93 94 95 5 4 3 2 1

Cover Illustration: Step One Design, Brenda Wintermyer

Unless otherwise indicated, Scripture taken from the HOLY BIBLE: NEW INTERNATIONAL VERSION. Copyright © 1973, 1978, 1984 by the International Bible Society. Used by permission of Zondervan Bible Publishers.

INTRODUCTION

In case you have just arrived, welcome to the wonderful world of retirement! It is what you make it, and this year of meditations should help you make this year and all your future years the best possible.

Four sources comprise these daily meditations:
1. Bible texts that have particular application to seniors.
2. Bible seniors who continued to achieve.
3. My extensive research on retirement and aging.
4. My own experiences my first year of retirement.

You will find many Scripture quotations throughout (this *is* a devotional book). For your convenience I have included the references with the quotes in case you wish to look them up in your Bible. If you do not, simply skip the references as you read.

Each meditation ends with a prayer challenge. I have made these prayers mine; I hope you will make them yours.

You will find the book upbeat. In fact, you will soon begin to see a thesis: *Retirement is a great experience (1) if I let it draw me closer to God and (2) if I use these wonderful free days in God's service.*

So that the book can be an ongoing source of information for you, I have fully indexed it, both by subject and by daily Scripture text. You will find also a bibliography of books on retirement and aging that I have found helpful.

This book has been a big project, but it was fun. Maybe, five or 10 years down the way—if you and I are still around—we should pool our experiences and do another. If you wish to share with me what you have learned from retirement, address me in care of the publisher. I make no promises, but we will see what happens!

H. Robert Cowles
Garner, North Carolina
October 1991

JANUARY 1

Retired. Day One.

Give thanks in all circumstances, for this is God's will for you in Christ Jesus. (1 Thessalonians 5:18)

Retired!

Now that it has finally happened, a whole battery of emotions bombards me. *Apprehension*: Will I be bored? Will my retirement income be sufficient? *Joy*: I am finally self-employed—my own boss! *Fear*: What if I become ill? Incapacitated? *Satisfaction*: I have given full measure; I look back with no serious regrets. *Assurance*: The God who has led me until now will direct my tomorrows. The list goes on.

I have anticipated this day: new vistas, new direction, new challenges. The ability to set my own agenda, to do things I never had time to do before. A whole new chapter.

I empathize with those whom retirement caught by surprise, their hand forced by medical problems, company reorganization, an office shake-up. The suddenness of it all has left them winded. Worse, they may be unprepared financially for this moment. But my Heavenly Father's promise to clothe and feed me is equally valid for them. Therefore, I will give thanks *in everything*—even in a world that does not treat people evenhandedly.

I especially give thanks today for the God-given capacity to adjust—"in all circumstances." How well I adjust depends on my level of gratitude. If indeed God orders the details of my life, and He does, I can thank Him for retirement, and I do. In fact, I am determined to make every day of retirement Thanksgiving Day. Is that not God's will for me in Christ Jesus?

Father, I begin my retirement by saying "Thank You!" Amen.

JANUARY 2

Exclusive Privilege

You are not your own; you were bought at a price. Therefore honor God with your body. (1 Corinthians 6:19–20)

Thanking God for everything is a great attitude toner for the inevitable adjustments at retirement time. But it is more. When I thank God for everything, I tacitly admit that I do not belong to myself, but to Him. That indefinite stretch of free time suddenly on my hands is not mine to selfishly parcel out—or waste—as I please. It is God's time, given to me to invest in His kingdom work, and I am under constraint to invest it wisely.

Nowhere in the Scriptures is there any hint that my spiritual servanthood concludes upon retirement from the job force. All my days are to be dedicated to the God who bought me at great price and whose Lordship I acknowledge.

The fact is, retirement can be the beginning of a bold new chapter in my divine service. That is exciting! That is indeed cause for thanksgiving!

My generation may be the only one to retire en masse. It has never happened before in history, and with the aging of the baby boomers followed by a greatly diminished work force, retirement at age 62 or age 65 is a luxury that may not be available to the next generation.

So I have been granted an exclusive privilege! That is awesome. But with every privilege comes a responsibility, and this one is no exception. Will I take the money and run, selfishly doing my own thing, pursuing my own agenda? Or will I invest these free years in God's kingdom work?

Father, I belong to You, and so do these years ahead. Amen.

JANUARY 3

When Two Retire

*The Lord your God... will never leave you
nor forsake you. (Deuteronomy 31:6)*

In this day of two-income families, it is not unusual for both husband and wife to retire. Even wives who were not part of the labor force while their children were at home return afterwards to the job market for various reasons. The extra income may help with college expenses. Or they may want some extra spending money. Or they may be bored and relish the social contacts of an office or store environment.

By the same token, a woman tends to regard her job differently than her husband regards his. Her job is one of many interests that she tries to keep in balance. Its nature may demand regular hours and a certain level of priority, but she manages to find time for housework, social life and—if she is a Christian—church activities.

Her husband, in contrast, looks upon his job as his vocation. He has devoted 35–40 years to it, probably with a high level of dedication. He has lived and slept his work. Much of his social life may have revolved around his workplace.

It requires no great amount of insight to guess which partner will find it hardest to adjust to retirement. The wife, with her many other interests, can step out of the nine-to-five routine and hardly miss a beat. The husband, on the other hand, may be utterly at loose ends.

One purpose of this book of devotions will be to help walk that unfocused partner through the trauma of retirement.

Father, I shall prayerfully seek Your counsel. Amen.

JANUARY 4

"Jesus Loves Me"

This is how we know what love is: Jesus Christ laid down his life for us. (1 John 3:16)

I am grateful to God for the beautiful visit He allowed my daughter Esther and me to have with Aunt Hazel.

Aunt Hazel Yarnell. How thankful I am for the fond memories of Mother's school-teacher sister. Although she lived relatively far from us, it seems as if our lives have always been intersecting. When as a boy I needed surgery on my foot, it was Aunt Hazel who arranged for it in Cleveland. In 1943, while I was in military duty, it was Aunt Hazel who stood with us when Mother died. Aunt Hazel helped support Marge and me during our missionary service in the Philippines. Years later, Aunt Hazel gave us her spinet piano—a gift we continue to treasure.

It was fitting that Esther, on furlough from missionary work in Burkina Faso, West Africa, should be with me. She and Aunt Hazel share the same birthdate—66 years apart. Aunt Hazel, pushing the century mark, looked attractive as we entered her room at Holly Hill Nursing Home in Newbury, Ohio.

We talked together—loudly, for Aunt Hazel is hard of hearing. Then I read the most appropriate Scripture I could think of—Psalm 90. As I read, Aunt Hazel recited it with me by heart. After I prayed, Esther asked Auntie if she would like us to sing. Aunt Hazel immediately quoted the words of "Jesus Loves Me, This I Know," then joined us with strong voice.

What a testimony of God's activity in a life! What a model of practical, selfless Christianity!

Father, may I always live as generously as Aunt Hazel. Amen.

JANUARY 5

No Empty Days

Command them to do good, to be rich in good deeds. (1 Timothy 6:18)

"The secret of a good retirement," says Richard S. Emerich, writing in the *Detroit Sunday News*, "is in its essence no different than the secret of life at any other time. The advice to seek happiness directly always has been a fraud; happiness is a mysterious by-product of good battles, of having the wind in our faces, of getting out of bed because there is something God wants us to do. Emptiness and nothingness are the curse of a secular culture." He is right.

Our youth-oriented culture, as Mr. Emerich notes earlier in his article, would lead us to suppose that youth is the happiest of all times. Indeed, Emerich counters, it may be the *un*happiest. Youth often have not yet found themselves, and they may lack the perspective as well as the inner resources to cope adequately with life's problems.

But if youth is not the happiest of all times, neither may retirement be—unless I deliberately set about to make it such by continuing the "good battles," by facing the winds of adversity.

Emerich goes on to caution: "One of the dangers of retirement must be the danger of empty days. During our working days, the demands of office or factory forced a pattern upon us. Now we must create our own—and new friendships, too. . . . As there is a qualitative and an inner difference between loneliness and solitude, so there is an inner difference between hectic triviality and creative leisure."

Father, help me find that "creative leisure." Amen.

JANUARY 6

Never Lack Zeal

Awake, my soul!
Awake, harp and lyre!
I will awaken the dawn.
(Psalm 57:8)

When I became manager of my church's publishing house, I made a point to be the first one at work each business morning. Because we had several very dedicated workers who showed up close to an hour before starting time, that meant arriving by 7:00 a.m.

I happen to be a "morning" person, so rising at 5:30 in order to have time for personal devotions before work was not usually a chore. All the same, I relished the mornings when I did not have to set the alarm, when I could "sleep in" an extra hour or even two. But it did not require genius status for me to realize that I could waste a staggering amount of irreplaceable time lying between the sheets of a comfortable bed.

There is no particular virtue, of course, in early rising. Virtue is utilizing one's waking hours to best advantage. I have friends who struggle to get going by nine in the morning, but who far outdistance me in the evening.

Success, I once read, consists not so much in staying awake nights as in keeping awake during the day. Depriving myself of *necessary* rest is counterproductive; depriving God of the time due Him in worship and work is also counterproductive.

I have determined not to capitulate to laziness! More than ever, my days are numbered. Now, while I am still sound of mind, I will fix the habit of putting each day at God's disposal—to be lived for His purpose, not mine.

Father, I now give You what remains of this day. Amen.

JANUARY 7

Husbands, Wives - I

Husbands, . . . treat [your wives] with respect . . . as heirs with you of the gracious gift of life. (1 Peter 3:7)

God has made us so different—Marge and me, wives generally, husbands generally.

Built into me is the instinct to conquer; into Marge, the instinct to love. My interest is the whole world around me; hers centers on her home, her family, her friends.

I am objective; Marge is subjective. I tend to be impersonal; she, personal. My weakness is discouragement; hers is loneliness. I am future-minded; she is present-minded. I want to know the essentials; she wants to know the details. I am logical; she is intuitive. I am steady; she is changeable.

Despite these innate male-female differences, God says very emphatically to me as a husband that I am to love my wife (Ephesians 5:25, 28, 33; Colossians 3:19). By this time in life, I have come to realize that, essentially, love is not an emotion; it is an attitude—*an act of the will.* Love proceeds from the mind, not simply from the heart.

The physical beauty of youth has long since matured into a beauty of character and personality. Now at last I understand why a lengthy courtship—getting beyond the outward appearances to the inner character—is such an important precedent to a good marriage. But whether the union was carefully crafted or hastily thrown together, the "till death do us part" commitment is a vow no honest person dares void.

And most would not wish to.

Father, thank You for a priceless marriage partner. Amen.

JANUARY 8

Husbands, Wives - II

Guard yourself in your spirit, and do not break faith with the wife of your youth. (Malachi 2:15)

Most people coming into the retirement experience bring with them a background of 35–45 years of marriage. That for-better-or-for-worse commitment, made optimistically in the bloom of youth and good health, has been tested and proved.

The vows Marge and I took in 1947 in Waverly, New York, may be subject to new strains in Retirementville, USA. "Half as much money and twice as much husband" is how one experienced wife described retirement. Either circumstance can impose unexpected stress on the marriage relationship.

I am aware of some of my shortcomings. Marge is doubly aware of them. Now that retirement has thrown the two of us into perpetual proximity, I must be sure my deficiencies are not a perpetual irritant.

The problem is compounded by the fact that we have completed some of our traditional responsibilities. With the coming of age of our four children, my "protector" responsibilities greatly diminished. Until now, a major part of my time has been devoted to providing materially for my family. No longer is that the case. For Marge, child-rearing responsibilities that absorbed much of her time and energy for almost 30 years are behind her. Housekeeping and cooking take much less of her time now that we are only two instead of six.

Clearly, Marge and I need to be sensitive to the role changes involved in retirement and to adjust accordingly.

Father, help us adjust to our new circumstances. Amen.

JANUARY 9

"Love Your Wives"

*Husbands, love your wives and do not
be harsh with them. (Colossians 3:19)*

When I retired, my wife Marge retired. In facing my retirement adjustments, I must bear in mind that Marge is adjusting not only to retirement but to having me underfoot. I think I know which one takes the most grace.

For 40 years the house has been Marge's domain. To be sure, I did the repairs and occupied some of the space some of the time. But Marge ran the house, kept it clean and in order, programmed the periodic rearrangement of furniture. Suddenly this man who for four decades minded his own business and sometimes complimented his wife for the good way she minded the house is home 24 hours a day. It is enough to give any woman a sense of what Roslyn Friedman and Annette Nussbaum term "territorial invasion."

The wife feels threatened by this unreasonable man who now wants to tell her how the kitchen should be arranged for greatest efficiency and how she should grocery shop. And all this precisely at the time she is trying to cope with retirement.

If, as is often the case, there has to be a cutback on expenditures, the problem is compounded. With more time to shop and to do artful things in the kitchen and to the house, the wife finds herself frustrated by money restrictions. It is enough to drive her to the precipice.

Tomorrow I will suggest some ways retired husbands and wives can together work through these situations that are concurrently confronting them.

Father, help me to be considerate of my spouse. Amen.

JANUARY 10

Four Rules

She is your partner, the wife of your marriage covenant. (Malachi 2:14)

Marge is a great wife! And I think she considers me a reasonably good husband. But 168 hours of togetherness each week are a burden no marriage can long sustain.

So Rule One. We each need time on our own to do our own thing. For Marge it can be a visit with our daughter Rebecca, or a morning of shopping without me, or a women's meeting at the church. For me it can be an afternoon at the library or a work project at a friend's house.

Rule Two. We each need space we can call our own. In a small house that is not easy. The kitchen is principally Marge's domain. Also our bedroom—except for sleeping hours. My study (where I am writing this book) is my space. So sometimes is the living room if I am just reading.

Personal Rule Three. As an out-of-work male, I am tempted to feel set upon—to feel the need of someone to hold my hand and walk me through the dreadful experience. But I will not impose my childish need for nurture as an added burden upon Marge. I am *not* a child (by some 50 plus years); I can cope. Good husband-wife relations are adult-to-adult, not adult-to-child.

Rule Four. To the extent Marge is interested, I will be frank about our finances. She will know exactly what and how much our reserves are and how much monthly income we can count on. She will have input on our yearly budget. She will participate in all of our major spending decisions.

Father, help me to observe these rules. Amen.

JANUARY 11

Wives, Husbands

Wives, submit ... Husbands, love your wives.
(Ephesians 5:22, 25)

Submission and respect are the biblical pattern that God has set out for wives. "As the church submits to Christ, so also wives should submit to their husbands in everything" (Ephesians 5:24). "Wives, submit to your husbands, as is fitting in the Lord" (Colossians 3:18).

Words like that are jarring in an era that espouses sexual equality. But perhaps I as a husband need to review again the many times God commands—yes, *commands*—me to love my wife. I am to love my wife as I love myself (Ephesians 5:28–29). I am to "be considerate" of my wife (1 Peter 3:7). A husband like that is easy to submit to.

No matter how ideal the marriage, too much togetherness, as I noted yesterday, can be a strain on any relationship. Probably Marge and I, thrown together by the circumstance of retirement, need to give each other "breathing room." An outside part-time job can both accomplish this and provide additional income. There is the local public library, good for unlimited hours away from the house. There may be a college or other institution offering study courses of interest. Membership at the local "Y" will improve the body while providing a break from each other. Just a room apart, such as this one where I write these meditations, will isolate and insulate, even in a small house.

"Absence makes the heart grow fonder." If so, for my own sake as well as Marge's, I should give her a break *from me.*

Father, keep my marriage solid—Your way. Amen.

JANUARY 12

Priceless Treasure

*Our daughters will be like pillars
carved to adorn a palace.
(Psalm 144:12)*

Now that Esther is off to Alliance Theological Seminary to continue her studies, I did not suppose the house could be so empty. Marge and I are grateful to God for her successful first term of missionary service in Burkina Faso, West Africa. We marvel at her rapport with the Burkinabe—and her ability to move homeland audiences with her stories. All of our children have far exceeded their parents in achievement.

We hardly have seen Esther since her arrival home last July. First it was the seminar for furloughing missionaries (I am glad Marge and I could attend the concluding dinner with Esther and meet again so many of our friends). Then came six or seven weeks of deputation in the metropolitan New York area. Then three weeks in Malaysia. And Christmas. Christmas, delightful as it was, afforded us little quality time with Esther.

Now she is gone again, probably with scant chance of coming home for an extended visit before she again returns to West Africa. Studies, nursing (to pay the bills), and speaking engagements will soak up all her time.

Wryly I reflect that history is simply repeating itself. In my own younger years I, too, was a busy person. Probably *my* parents wished I might have had more time at home. If people in heaven have any residual interest in their past lives on earth, I hope God will let Mother and Dad know that I love them, and I look forward to quality time with them by and by.

Father, children truly are a priceless heritage. Amen.

JANUARY 13

Continuing Education

When you come, bring ... my scrolls, especially the parchments. (2 Timothy 4:13)

For the past 25 years, more of my waking hours have been devoted to reading than to any other one thing. The only caveat: the reading was not usually material of my choice.

I read letters, memos, reports, minutes, manuscripts, works in progress, newspapers, news magazines, selected other magazines, books. For years I have read through the Bible annually. Some of what I read was interesting. Some contributed to my useful knowledge. The Scriptures have instructed me. Much of the other reading I could have done without.

Now that the choice of what I read is mine, I am determined to concentrate on some of the good books I never got around to before. But I am already discovering that reading requires discipline. When the day becomes crowded with activities, I do not cut out lunch, or sleep, or socializing. Rather, my reading gets slighted.

Reading puts me in very good company. The Apostle Paul, "retired" in a Roman dungeon at probably age 62 (we are not at all sure when he was born), requested Timothy to bring his "scrolls, especially the parchments." Despite poor light and his long-standing eye affliction, Paul was determined to keep reading. Commentators suggest that the "parchments"—his special request—were the holy Scriptures. As schooled as he was in the Scriptures, Paul was determined to keep on learning.

It behooves me to be at least as diligent.

Father, discipline me to take the time to read. Amen.

JANUARY 14

God's Strength

"My power is made perfect in weakness."
(2 Corinthians 12:9)

As I prepare to sprint across that indefinite block of time labeled "retirement," certain enemies lie in wait to ambush me.

Sickness is well-known, but no less an enemy for its familiarity. I have tangled with sickness before. I respect its strength, its ability to surprise, its great power.

Physical weakness, allied to sickness, also lurks. Already I cannot do all I once did. A rigorous program of exercise may postpone some of the ravishes of physical weakness. But the odds are stacked against me.

Paul mentions four other specifics.

Insults. My Christian viewpoint is a minority perspective. Where it tangles with current humanistic philosophy, I can expect retaliation in the form of insults.

Hardships. They come to Christians and non-Christians. But when they come to Christians, the non-Christian likes to suppose they are religion-oriented.

Persecutions. The insidious kinds are always present. The more intense, physical varieties are not well-known in America, though they soon may be.

Difficulties. Like hardships, these difficulties strike indiscriminately. Christianity, however, gets blamed if they happen to the believer.

But God's promised strength comes precisely at the point of need. It is not necessarily physical strength that God promises. It is inner, moral strength—the most potent of all!

Father, I thank You for promised grace. Amen.

JANUARY 15

Senior Achievers

Consider Abraham... (Galatians 3:6)

Martin Sherwood reports an ambitious listing of the world's 400 most noteworthy men of all time. The list included statesmen, poets, painters, writers, warriors, historians, architects. Once the names were agreed on, each person's greatest contribution was also assessed and agreed on. By dating the work and noting when the person was born, the compilers could calculate when in life each one was at his best. The findings?

Thirty-five percent of these illustrious contributors were between 60 and 70 years old at the time of their greatest work. Another 23 percent were between 70 and 80. Six percent were above 90. *A full 64 percent of these notable achievers, at the time of their greatest work, had already passed their 60th year*!

The Bible is not without its roster of "senior achievers." Beginning tomorrow and periodically throughout these devotional meditations will be the accounts of nearly 70 of them—men and women who, by best estimates, were at least 60 years old at the time they made their significant contribution. Most of their achievements were positive. The few that were not are nevertheless instructive warnings for Christians today "on whom the fulfillment of the ages has come" (1 Corinthians 10:11).

The biggest surprise to those familiar with the Bible may not be what some of these people did, but that they were, in all probability, above 60 at the time. The names are in approximate chronological order. The first one—Adam—is the subject of tomorrow's meditation.

Father, use these "senior achievers" to inspire me. Amen.

JANUARY 16

Adam

Adam lay with his wife Eve, and she became pregnant and gave birth to Cain.
(Genesis 4:1)

The Scriptures offer but one chronological peg in Adam's long, 930-year life span. Adam was 130 when Seth was born. Clearly all the other known events of Adam's life—his expulsion from the Garden of Eden, the birth of Cain and Abel, Abel's murder by Cain—occurred prior to Seth's birth.

But how long did Adam and Eve live in Eden? How much time elapsed before Cain was born? and Abel? Were the boys twins, as some suppose? How old were Cain and Abel when they had that fateful, fatal altercation in the field?

Presumably Adam and Eve continued to have children as Cain and Abel grew. Cain got his wife from somewhere, and whence if not from among his own siblings?

It is reasonable to suppose that Adam, at age 60-plus, was still working, still involved with rearing a family. Seared across his memory would be the still-vivid details of the Punishment. He lived with the remorse of the What-once-was. He carried the regrets of the What-might-have-been.

Nor were Adam's personal tragedies all behind him. Abel's murder was a catastrophe yet to happen that would send shock waves throughout the clan.

Adam's life was overbalanced with disappointment. But he had a willingness to hang in there, no matter how great the tragedy or how unrelieved the future might appear to be. That trait of Adam is one I could well emulate.

Father, though You slay me, yet will I trust You. Amen.

JANUARY 17

Eve

[Eve] gave birth to a son and named him Seth, saying, "God has granted me another child in place of Abel." (Genesis 4:25)

The name *Eve* appears just four times in the Bible. Her name is mentioned with two factual statements in Genesis (3:20 and 4:1). Twice Paul makes uncomplimentary references to Eve in the New Testament (2 Corinthians 11:3 and 1 Timothy 2:13). Everywhere else she is simply Adam's "wife" or "the woman."

Poor Eve! It is good she did not live in this era of women's affirmation. She would have groveled in inferiority all her life. I cannot—dare not—gloss over the enormity of Eve's sin and its awful consequences not only for her family but for the whole race. But if not Eve, it would have been Adam. Adam, too, was deceived. Adam, too, was tempted. Adam, too, sinned.

Probably by the time Eve's son Abel was murdered by his brother, Eve had outdistanced all of this generation in age. Yet it was still later when God granted her another son, Seth, to help fill the void left in her life by Cain's delinquency and Abel's untimely death.

Within a generation "men began to call on the name of the Lord" (Genesis 4:26). But before that happened, Eve, like Adam, lived through many lean years when every hope became a disappointment and every sweet morsel turned bitter.

Does Eve's life sound familiar? *I must have faith in God!* The past is past. There is no benefit in morbid remorse or in self-flagellation. A loving, merciful God promises comfort (Isaiah 40:1–2) to those who have endured His discipline.

Father, I believe You. I seek You. I love You. Amen.

JANUARY 18

Enoch

When Enoch had lived 65 years, he became the father of Methuselah. And after he became the father of Methuselah, Enoch walked with God 300 years. . . . Enoch walked with God; then he was no more, because God took him away. (Genesis 5:21–24)

The whole lineage of patriarchs from Adam to Noah qualifies for inclusion in any survey of Bible seniors. Enoch, the youngest, lived 365 years. Methuselah, the oldest, lived 969 years. Aside from their longevity—and the fact that they produced children—the chronicler says little about most of them.

Enoch is the exception. Enoch walked with God. Then, after 365 years, Enoch was no more because God took him away. The two statements are not necessarily related, but the writer at least implies a connection. Because of Enoch's close walk with God, God translated Enoch directly to heaven, sparing him the route through death that has come to all others except Elijah.

Enoch was not the only one of that era to walk with God. Noah also walked with God. Walking with God does not necessarily exempt a person from dying.

What transferable lesson, then, can I gain from Enoch? The term "walked with God" replaces the word "lived" in the reports of all the other patriarchs, except Noah. There is a difference between just living and walking with God. It is possible to rise above the level of merely living to actually walk with God.

How? Well, what are my waking thoughts about? Money? People? Things? The house? Travel? Shopping? I am "living," but I have not attained Enoch's favored status.

Father, I too want to truly walk with You. Amen.

JANUARY 19

Noah

Noah was a righteous man. . . . God said to Noah, . . . "Make yourself an ark." . . . Noah did everything just as God commanded him. (Genesis 6:9, 13–14, 22)

There is no question that Noah qualifies as a senior achiever. After he was 500 years old, he became the father of three sons. Sometime still later he began construction of the ark. He was 600 years old when the Flood came.

A senior indeed!

In the New Testament Noah is among those singled out for their faith: "By faith Noah, when warned about things not yet seen, in holy fear built an ark to save his family" (Hebrews 11:7).

Those who read the Bible tend to overlook something that is rather obvious: the close relation between obedience and faith. God said to Noah, "Make yourself an ark." The Scriptures report: "Noah did everything just as God commanded him." The New Testament says, "By faith Noah . . . built an ark."

Nothing could have seemed less appropriate than God's command to Noah to build an ark. Noah was in high country, distant from even a lake that could accommodate a monstrous, 450-foot-long barge. Some scholars doubt that there had been rain on the earth up to that point. But Noah in obedience went ahead. With the assistance of his three sons he built the ark.

If faith is acting on what God says, two corollaries seem evident: (1) Others will know my level of faith in God by my level of obedience to God, and (2) I had better study the Scriptures so I know what God wants to say to me.

Father, help me translate faith into obedience. Amen.

JANUARY 20

They Walked with God

Enoch walked with God.
(Genesis 5:24)
Noah ... walked with God.
(Genesis 6:9)

Two senior citizens from the dim recesses of the antediluvian world had something in common not said of anyone else in all the Bible: they walked with God.

Enoch was seventh in the godly lineage of patriarchs from Adam to Noah. Enoch and Noah would have been contemporary except for Enoch's unexpected departure when God "took him away" (Genesis 5:24). As it is, less than 70 years separate the two.

Walking with God for Enoch and Noah was no ascetic life lived in the seclusion of a desert monastery. They did their walking along with fathering children and likely providing for their families. Noah did his walking while building an ark and caring for the details of getting family, animals and fowls settled for an extended stay on the face of the deep.

The course of their lives is an interesting contrast. "God took [Enoch] away." Noah, far from being raptured, had to ride out the earth's destruction by flood, had to begin with his sons the laborious process of founding a new civilization on a very changed, very empty earth.

It stretches the analogy to see in these two men the current controversy concerning the coming tribulation and whether Christians will be raptured to escape it or, as others insist, forced to go through it. It suffices to aspire to what both Enoch and Noah achieved: a day-by-day walk with God—in His presence, enjoying His fellowship.

Father, let me also walk with You. Amen.

JANUARY 21

Where? Why?

"See, I have placed before you an open door."
(Revelation 3:8)

For a person newly retired, most of the who?-what?-where?-when?-why? questions have rather obvious answers. But the *where?* and *why?* will be major considerations for me.

The only immediate thing to say about the *where?* question is this: I should not be in a hurry. I need to take time to explore all my options. I need to weigh carefully all the pros and cons. Repeat: *I must not be in a hurry*.

That leaves the all-important *why?* question.

The philosophy that permeates these devotions is this: Retirement for the Christian should not be unrelieved play. Life is too precious, too serious to squander it on fun and games. That is not what I was put here for.

Does that mean I should keep my nose to the grindstone, eschewing all pleasure? Of course not. Life should be enjoyable. But who said only play was pleasurable? Did I not get pleasure from my work? Frankly, a person who found no pleasure in work may find little in retirement, no matter how the time is spent.

Jesus is the source of joy. Life lived with Him is fulfilling. Just as in the working years past, so now. My greatest satisfaction (translate that *pleasure*) will come in serving Him—not in serving myself.

There is a church that can use me. There are people who need my friendship. God invites me to be an intercessor for His kingdom work the world around.

The possibilities are unlimited!

Father, I dedicate myself anew to Your service. Amen.

JANUARY 22

No Place like Home

Live as free men, but . . . live as servants of God. (1 Peter 2:16)

Quite probably Americans' overwhelming decision to stay put when they retire is tied as much to finances and lethargy as to anything else. Selecting a new location requires planning, and a large percentage of people coming to retirement have made no plans and seem uninterested in making any.

Moving also requires money. Frequently, but not always, the sale of a larger or costlier residence can be "traded" against a less expensive retirement home with money left over for moving and resettling expenses. But I need a sharp pencil. The sale money may not be all free and clear (certainly not if the present house still carries a mortgage). And the new place, quite apart from closing costs, is sure to require much more money than the figure the seller and I have agreed upon.

I can be sure the banker who made it possible for me to buy my present house will not be as willing to help me buy another now that my income is reduced to Social Security and a modest pension. This time it must be cash on the barrel head.

In the final analysis, I may have no option but to stay where I am. At least, I have plenty of company. And I have the security of waters that are well charted and a lifestyle that is both familiar and comfortable.

There is biblical precedent—though no biblical command—for staying where I am. As the years mount and vitality wanes, I will be thankful for my network of family and friends.

Father, I am ready to go, ready to stay. Amen.

JANUARY 23

Staying Put

"Let your servant return, that I may die in my own town near the tomb of my father and mother." (2 Samuel 19:37)

What are the arguments for staying put, either in my present residence or in another nearby?

Family is the most compelling reason. Still-living parents are not uncommon. Children and grandchildren, extended family members need my support and I need theirs.

Friends can mean as much as family. I do not lightly walk away from strong friendships. Distance will not necessarily snuff out friendship's flame; in practice it often does.

Church, if it has been an especially meaningful part of my life, cannot be quickly dismissed. Only time will tell if I can find another as compatible. Even within denominations, there are wide differences between churches.

Climate. I have managed to survive the climate thus far. Probably I can survive a while longer. Besides, every climate has its trade-offs. In seeking milder winters I will also find hotter summers. Sunny skies promise cheerful warmth, but they also may mean parching drought.

Service networks. I have a good working relationship with doctors, dentist, auto mechanic, barber, clothiers and an almost infinite number of other suppliers. If I move, I must begin at square one to rebuild.

A scant five percent of retired people leave the locale of their adult years. Certainly I should think long and thoroughly before I make plans to defy the trend and move elsewhere.

Father, if ever I needed Your wisdom, it is now. Amen.

JANUARY 24

Weighing a Move

"Leave your country, your people and your father's household and go to the land I will show you." (Genesis 12:1)

Just reading the words is enough to make me want to reconsider. *Should* I leave the locale in which I was reared and what remains of my "father's household" to venture into some remote, untried-by-me region? I cannot really answer that question without asking and answering some related questions:

1. How much isolation from long-time friends can I stand? How far from family is too far?
2. What kind of a climate do I really want?
3. Can I afford to stay where I am? Can I afford to move?

If moving seems to be an option worth considering, then I need to investigate the top several possibilities with another series of questions:

1. Do climate or terrain pose special problems?
2. Will I "fit" into the prevailing spirit of the region?
3. Can I expect to find the church of my choice?
4. How much are taxes? Will area growth push them up?
5. What about other living costs? How do they compare with where I now am? with other retirement regions?
6. Can I expect to cultivate congenial friends?
7. What are the public transportation facilities?
8. Does the area offer the social services I may need?
9. What about part-time jobs should I need one?

There will be more questions—probably many more questions—when I settle on a region and begin looking at specific communities.

Father, questions, questions. Help me do my homework. Amen.

JANUARY 25

Where to?

*Abram said to Lot, . . . "Is not the whole
land before you?" (Genesis 13:8–9)*

When it comes to searching the country for the ideal places to retire, I can facilitate the process several ways.

1. Unless I am really adventurous, abundantly rich and totally untied to family or friends, I probably will limit my research to places within 1,000 to 1,500 miles of where I now live.

2. There may be other extenuating factors: friends who have discovered the "ideal" retirement locale or family members living in a particular area. (I am cautioned against moving near my children; in our mobile society, a job transfer for them could leave me very alone.) Hobbies or recreational interests might tip the scales one way or another.

3. Although ideally I should personally visit each of the possible places I have selected, I can judge all but the top two or three at far less cost. I should buy short-term subscriptions to their local newspapers, request a demographics report from their chambers of commerce and get information from real estate agencies (I will need to be as specific as possible concerning the type of housing I want).

Much of this legwork has already been done for me. In a large-size paperback entitled *Retirement Places Rated* (Rand McNally), Richard Boyer and David Savageau have gathered data on what they consider the top 131 retirement locations in the United States. Using a system of numeric values, they have rated each one. Frequently the book is available in local libraries.

Father, after all the data, I still need Your help. Amen.

JANUARY 26

Close Inspection

Moses ... said, ... "See what the land is like." (Numbers 13:17–18)

Once I have focused on a particular location, one or more trips to the area are essential. It is much less costly than backing out after my furniture arrives at the house I have bought.

Annual rainfall sounds ideal, but does some of it come down every day? What about the humidity? The tax rates seem favorable, but how does a typical grocery order compare in price with the same items back home? Is housing affordable because of a market glut? That helps me now, but what if I want later to sell? How does the market look five years from now? Ten?

Are utility costs in line, or has an expensive new system escalated the charges? What are the possibilities for part-time employment should Marge or I want it? And that all-important question: What about the church?

How does the community regard retired people? What medical facilities are there, and how accessible are they? What colleges or universities are within easy distance should I want to take some classes? Are there affordable recreational facilities of the kind I want? What about shopping centers?

These are considerations that can only fairly be sized up by an on-site look. James H. Hutchinson, in *Ten Steps to Successful Retirement*, advises the "acid test":

> Visit the place for a week in the worst weather, talk to as many as possible and attend as many functions as possible.

And even then, it may pay to rent first, buy later.

Father, give me ability to assess the total picture. Amen.

JANUARY 27

The Moving Ship

You guide me with your counsel. (Psalm 73:24)

Back when retirement was farthest from my thinking, I had a godly professor at Nyack (New York) College who had come to that point in life. Harold M. Freligh, a saintly man if there ever was one, had made his retirement a matter of much prayer and thought. Of several viable options before him, he wanted to be sure he was in God's will. But he could get no clear inner leading from heaven or from the Bible. God was silent.

At that point, Harold Freligh remembered an adage he once had heard: *It is the moving ship that can be steered.* He applied it to his own circumstances. "God," he prayed, "I have sought Your mind; I am open to Your will; I desire to walk in Your ways. I am going to set out, trusting You to steer me."

For Harold Freligh, it became a journey all the way to Seattle and what was then King's Garden—a Christian retirement community where Mr. Freligh and his wife were lovingly and comfortably cared for. Harold Freligh was satisfied that the decision was the right one, the best one for him and his wife.

"You guide me with your counsel." God did not intend me to be a robot, my every movement mindless. I am not "like the horse or the mule,/ which . . . must be controlled by bit and bridle" (Psalm 32:9). God has given me ability to think, to reason, to make judgments. He has given me a Book of moral directions. And He has offered to guide me. But God cannot guide me if I am sitting still. I have done my best to sort out the options; now I must get myself in motion.

Father, I am trusting You to guide me. Amen.

JANUARY 28

Slave or Master?

"The Son of Man did not come to be served, but to serve." (Matthew 20:28)

Retirement marks the terminus of some forty years of slavery. *Slavery?* Not real slavery, of course. Most retired Americans can look back to a fair degree of comfort in the job place: five-day work weeks, 10–15 paid holidays, two to four weeks of paid vacation annually, coffee breaks twice daily.

Still, the responsibility of the job kept them tied down. They were not free to take off at will, to be away for any extended period of time, to live in some other region of the country. Even their dress was dictated by their job.

Now, suddenly, freedom! No more restraints. Sleep late. Travel at will. Live anywhere. Dress any way. Restaurants, motels, even some stores offer them discounts. Communities erect senior citizen centers for them.

And subtly, an attitude begins to gestate: The years of serving are behind me; I am now in a position to be served. I am no longer a slave; I am now the master.

That may be the case for the pagan. It certainly is not true of the Christian. My surrender to Christ was unconditional. His Lordship over me is eternal. Retirement does not change my status with God. It may free me to serve God in new ways and new places, but my servant status remains as it was.

Even as Jesus, my Example, did not come to earth to be served but to serve, so I am on this earth not to be served but to serve. And, if need be, to give my life in that service.

Father, retirement has not changed my commitment to You. Amen.

JANUARY 29

Satisfied

Be content with what you have. (Hebrews 13:5)

Has anyone faced retirement without wishing that he or she had saved a little more, prepared a little better? I take comfort in the knowledge I am not alone!

But such knowledge does not put bread on the table or periodically update the car or cover the medical crisis I hope will not happen.

All our lives, Marge and I have lived relatively simply. As "planters" of a new church in Bennington, Vermont, and later as missionaries in the Philippines, we had to. Necessity became habit. If we have been lavish in any area, it has been in our support of the church and its worldwide mission. I do not for a minute regret that generosity. Jesus said concerning our daily necessities, "Seek first [God's] kingdom and his righteousness, and all these things will be given to you as well" (Matthew 6:33). Marge and I took our Lord's words at face value, and thus far the promise has not failed!

Thankfully, I have Social Security and a modest pension from my church denomination (my "employer" most of my working years). Thankfully, also, I have good health. I have neither intention nor desire to spend the next however-many years fishing, playing—or even rocking. Until I am no longer able to be productive, Marge and I should manage without tapping our reserves. Meanwhile, I intend to be content with what I have. I have long since discovered the difference between needs and wants. The needs God has promised to supply.

Father, may Your work always be a priority with me. Amen.

JANUARY 30

Musical Praise

Speak to one another with psalms, hymns and spiritual songs. Sing and make music in your heart to the Lord, always giving thanks to God ... for everything. (Ephesians 5:19–20)

Here is that thanksgiving theme again! It recurs so often in the Bible that I cannot escape the conclusion that God is serious about expecting His children to praise Him.

This time the Scriptures relate praise to music—to singing and to making "music in your heart."

I have always suspected that "make music in your heart" was directed to those like me whose singing voice leaves much to be desired. But as an amateur pianist, I delight—really!—to sit down at the keyboard and play not only the grand old hymns of praise but the popular new praise choruses, the words of so many of them lifted verbatim from the Bible.

Not likely will we ever in this life know exactly what Paul and the Holy Spirit had in mind in their three categories of "psalms, hymns and spiritual songs"—or how they were to be employed in "speak[ing] to one another." My own simplistic opinion: "psalms" are the Psalms, sung for centuries by Israel; "hymns" are praise and prayer songs directed to God; "spiritual songs" are praise songs about God; "speaking to one another" is the use of these three in corporate worship.

Nothing lifts me more than a joyous, sincere congregational hymn sing. And judging from the many Bible exhortations to such singing, nothing delights the Lord God more.

Father, thank You for giving Your people song. Thank you for putting a song in my heart. Amen.

JANUARY 31

No Favoritism

There is no favoritism with [God]. (Ephesians 6:9)

The words were spoken in the context of slaves and masters and how each should treat the other. Paul turns to the masters, saying: "And masters, treat your slaves in the same way [that is, fairly, honestly]. Do not threaten them, since you know that he who is both their Master and yours is in heaven, and there is no favoritism with him."

There is no favoritism with God. The Bible very plainly declares it. But I think of Abraham, Jacob, Moses, David, Daniel, Peter, James, John—even Paul himself. Did not God choose these for special assignments and permit them to get closer to Him than the rank-and-file? Yes, He did. But that is the mystery of free will and predestination. A sovereign God knows in advance who has the capacity and the will to love Him supremely and to obey Him without reservation. There is no favoritism with the Lord. I may be a slave or a master, poor or rich, handicapped or perfect; at Calvary the ground is absolutely level. It is the disposition, the attitude I bring to my relationship with God that determines how high I rise in the arms of faith.

Clearly, then, the next move is mine. However close or distant my past relationship with Deity, God is giving me new opportunity today—now—and maybe in the tomorrows—to draw near. The One who has no favorites makes an open, unconditional promise to me and to every one of His children: "Come near to God and he will come near to you" (James 4:8).

Father, I come. I purpose to take time to be holy. I want our relationship to be close, satisfying. Amen.

FEBRUARY 1

Self-discipline

*God ... [gave] us ... a spirit of power, of love
and of self-discipline. (2 Timothy 1:7)*

Self-discipline is not popular. Now that I am retired, it is easy to take the attitude that I have earned the right to sleep in, to snack at will, to pamper myself a bit. But the Scriptures read otherwise. God gave me a spirit of self-discipline.

The kind of self-discipline that allowed John Wesley to ride horseback 5,000 miles a year, preach four or five sermons a day, write a journal, edit a monthly magazine and translate numerous works from Greek, Latin and Hebrew is probably irretrievable. Nor am I sure that Wesley's breathless pace is to be emulated. Not so surprisingly, he had a very unhappy home life. His long absences from the hearth may have been both the cause and the result of his wife's irritability.

But I am far, far from approaching John Wesley's excessive self-discipline. In fact, self-discipline is something I could use much more of.

Paul goes on to say to Timothy that undisciplined living will be a sign of the last days (1 Timothy 3:1–3). I need only look around to be convinced that that time has come. A quick scan of the ads in the local paper or the national magazines is clear evidence that Americans are motivated by pleasure, the love of luxury, the desire for easy living.

In an appropriate climax, Paul adds his personal testimony: "I have fought the good fight, I have finished the race, I have kept the faith" (4:7). What an example!

Father, the flesh is weak and getting weaker. Help me! Amen.

FEBRUARY 2

Crowned!

*Gray hair is a crown of splendor;
it is attained by a righteous life.
(Proverbs 16:31)*

It is happening! Advertisers are beginning to acknowledge that among the American populace there may be more than just youth. As the baby boomers age and the seniors multiply, an increasing number of gray heads are suddenly appearing on the television screen and in the consumer magazines.

To be sure, the advertisers will limit their "gray heads" to the best-looking, youngest of my genre. At age 67 I need not apply. To sell their products, advertisers need attractive models to testify to the virtues of Scope, Dial soap, retirement living in Phoenix and Buick Park Avenues.

One plus: If gray hair really achieves a comeback in America, all the women—and men—who have been addicted to Grecian Formula and Clairol Hair Rinse will have a sudden windfall to divert to more worthy causes.

With considerable help from the media, America has strayed far from the biblical exhortations to honor old age. Until recently, industry has dismissed both its leaders and workers at age 65—often earlier. American government—to its credit—continues to seek the advice of its elder statesmen, though relatively few remain in active roles much beyond age 65 or 70.

Why is gray hair a crown of splendor? Because, says the Bible, "it is attained by a righteous life." That may not always be the case, but the principle is intact. Gray hair culminates a lifetime of godliness.

Father, help me to live up to my status. Amen.

FEBRUARY 3

Job

*The Lord blessed the latter part of Job's life
more than the first. (Job 42:12)*

The Old Testament patriarch Job has an important message for any believer who is at wit's end because of physical suffering or a plaguing personal problem.

Job's three friends were sure they had the answer. Obviously, God was punishing Job for some secret sin. How else to explain Job's financial reverses, his physical suffering, his sudden and devastating bereavement of all 10 grown children?

Yes and no. Job was no exception to Paul's later statement that "all have sinned" (Romans 3:23). And, yes, Job at the moment was engaged in a prideful attempt to justify himself at God's expense. But that was not really the point. God's intent was to do a deeper work of perfection in the righteous life of His servant Job. In order to accomplish His purpose, He had to get Job to the end of himself.

After Job's friends exhausted their patience, if not their arguments, God began to speak. When He finished, a chastened, silenced Job admitted, "My ears had heard of you/ but now my eyes have seen you./ Therefore I despise myself/ and repent in dust and ashes" (Job 42:5–6).

God's fires of affliction are for my spiritual refinement. He wounds in order to work in me a greater healing. "The Lord disciplines those he loves,/ as a father the son he delights in" (Proverbs 3:12). "Discipline . . . produces a harvest of righteousness and peace" (Hebrews 12:11). I can take courage!

Father, You love me, and I am Your child! Amen.

FEBRUARY 4

Eliphaz & Co.

When Job's three friends, Eliphaz the Temanite, Bildad the Shuhite and Zophar the Naamathite, heard about all the trouble that had come upon him, they set out . . . to go and . . . comfort him. (Job 2:11)

I would as soon forego the brand of comfort meted out by Eliphaz, Bildad and Zophar—those three senior friends of Job!

Each person came at Job's problem from a different perspective. Eliphaz drew from "dreams in the night,/ when deep sleep falls on men" (Job 4:13). Bildad appealed to history: "Ask the former generations/ and find out what their fathers learned" (8:8). Zophar relied on his intuitive knowledge; "My understanding inspires me to reply," he said (20:3).

Whatever their approach, the conclusion was the same: Job had sinned, and Job was being punished for his sin.

The three "comforters" kept up their barrage of advice until Job froze. "These three men stopped answering Job, because he was righteous in his own eyes" (32:1).

After a fourth, younger man—Elihu—had his say, it was God's turn. He began by asking, "Who is this that darkens my counsel/ with words without knowledge?" (38:2). Later he confronted Eliphaz and said to him, "I am angry with you and your two friends, because you have not spoken of me what is right, as my servant Job has" (42:7).

Should I refrain from giving any counsel? Not necessarily. But I must know God's Word, and I must be in close touch with the God of all wisdom.

Father, keep me supersensitive to You and Your Word when I am called on to advise others. Amen.

FEBRUARY 5

Living Carefully

"Man looks at the outward appearance." (1 Samuel 16:7)

God looks on the heart. But my fellow beings tend to look on the outward appearance. If they look at me, what do they see?

It is important that I keep up my outward appearance. A daily shower, shave and change of fresh clothes. Brushed (and flossed) teeth and combed hair. Regular haircuts. That shuffle I am developing, the hallmark of older people, can be avoided—or at least postponed—by a little attention on my part. So can the slouch that takes inches off my height and adds the ugly bulge to my abdomen.

Since I am married, I need to be extra attentive and courteous to my wife. I am spending considerably more time with her. I do not want familiarity to breed contempt. My wife's personality, as well as her appearance, is largely a reflection of me, her husband. If she becomes as dull as dishwater (to borrow another's expression), I am the ultimate loser.

Says Oscar H. West, "Nobody grows old merely by living a number of years. People grow old because they forsake their ideals, smother their enthusiasm, deny the challenge of 'What's next?' and cease to love the joy and game of life. Years may wrinkle the skin; they need not wrinkle the soul."

What are the factors that contribute to a good outward appearance? Not so surprisingly, the same ones that contribute to a good personality: patience, purpose, the willingness to work hard, a sense of humor, an interest in others, good curiosity, a positive attitude, serenity.

Father, let me not forget that I represent You. Amen.

FEBRUARY 6

"It Is to Be"

You have taken off your old self... and have put on the new self. (Colossians 3:9–10)

"If it is to be, it is up to me." Those 10 two-letter words at first sound arrogant—an almost "I-am-the-captain-of-my-fate" decision to transfer things from God's hands to mine.

But they suggest a spiritual truth that is inescapable. The discipline that transforms me from the worlding I once was to the saint God intends me to be is my responsibility. "If it is to be, it is up to me."

I personally am to put off sexual immorality, impurity, lust, evil desires, greed—five things that will be bringing God's wrath upon this world (Colossians 3:5). But there is more. I am also to put off anger, rage, malice, slander, filthy language, lying. I had supposed these were "defects" in my character that only God in grace could deal with. Here He is asking *me* to deal with them! I am to put them from me.

I am also instructed to put some things on: specifically compassion, kindness, humility, gentleness, patience, forbearance, forgiveness, love.

If there is consolation in the shock of discovering that these subtractions and additions are up to me, it is in the fact that God never tests me above my ability. If He tells me to put off and to put on, then I can be sure it is possible to do so.

It is easy to push the responsibility onto God and blame Him if I fall short of His purpose for me. But God is telling me "if it is to be, it is up to me."

Father, I accept the challenge. I will start today. Amen.

FEBRUARY 7

Agent of Change

*... to be made new in the attitude
of your minds. (Ephesians 4:23)*

In "A Light in the Toolbox," Richard Bach, the author of *Jonathan Livingston Seagull* and an experienced pilot, tells how for years he insisted, "I'm no mechanic." He alleges he did not even know "which end of the screwdriver to hit the nail with."

But Richard Bach bought "a crazy old biplane"—a plane with a "mind of its own" that did not object to quitting at odd times, leaving Bach stranded in farmers' pastures and other inappropriate places.

"That was how the rarest event in life came to me," Bach remembers. "*I changed the way I thought.* I learned the mechanics of airplanes."

Commenting on Bach's transformation, Martin A. Janis in *The Joys of Aging*, says, "Most adults don't even think that's possible. But Bach shows us . . . that, by making a conscious decision to change, many things are possible.

" 'I can't paint,' says a senior citizen. . . . 'I couldn't possibly walk a mile,' says another. . . . But to the individuals who change the way they think, painting a picture, walking a mile, or doing whatever they choose is possible."

"How should you begin to assert the 'new you'?" Janis goes on to ask. "By smiling. This will have an effect upon whom you smile and on you." And he adds, "When was the last time you complimented anyone? . . . Multiply these actions by everyone in the New 65+ Generation and you will realize how successful we would be in bringing about change."

Father, I am only one, but I am one. Amen.

FEBRUARY 8

Have a Minute?

. . . making the most of every opportunity. (Ephesians 5:16)

There are 1,440 minutes in each day, more than 10,000 in each week. The person who retires at age 65 has gone through *34 million minutes*. I once bartered with minutes for material things like food, shelter, clothing. I depended on them for esthetic and spiritual intake. Had the supply run out, I would be dead.

If minutes were priceless when I was part of the work force, they are still priceless. Yet no commodity of equal value is treated by people so contemptuously.

Bishop Hugh Latimer, in his sermon, "The Ploughers," remarked on the devil's diligence, saying, "He is no lordly loiterer." Neither should I be—even in retirement. God has given me those 1,440 minutes each day, and my accounting of the deeds done in the body will certainly include my utilization of the minutes God has lent me.

I should also use those minutes to draw closer to God. In his little book, *Christ Liveth in Me/Game with Minutes* (Fleming H. Revell Co.), Frank C. Laubach, the late literacy expert, tells how he made a point of consciously thinking about Christ for at least one second each minute. As he passed strangers on the street, he breathed a prayer for them. In conversation he silently asked God for the words to say. When reading the newspaper, he read it to God. As he fell asleep at night, he let the name of Jesus be his last thought.

The result, Laubach said, was what Thomas à Kempis calls "a familiar friendship with Jesus."

Father, let me make the most of today's 1,440 minutes. Amen.

FEBRUARY 9

My Ever-Present Help

God is our refuge and strength,
an ever-present help in trouble.
(Psalm 46:1)

Retirement, I discover, works some subtle psychological changes in me. From a financial viewpoint, it tends to shift my mind-set from self-sufficiency to dependency, from paying my own way to relying on outside help.

For most of nearly 50 working years, money came in regularly—the product of my diligence and effort. The rent or the mortgage and the other recurring bills got paid. There was always food on the table. And clothes to wear. Being a Christian, I bowed my head before each meal to thank God for His provision. Family needs were regular subjects in my other prayer times. At the same time, not usually did I feel a sense of utter dependence on God for temporal provisions, an if-You-don't-supply-we-won't-make-it kind of desperation.

My family had its share of health emergencies. Again, there usually was medical insurance to cover the expense.

Retirement has ushered me into a changed environment. It is not that what Marge and I have is insufficient—probably we are better off than the average retired couple. It is just the hard-to-define worry that I may not be able to make it on my own—that Marge and I could end up having to accept government aid or some other form of charity.

Did I say "worry"? That is precisely what the Bible tells me not to do. God is my refuge and strength. He is "an ever-present help in trouble." Therefore I must not fear.

Father, forgive me for doubting Your promises. Amen.

FEBRUARY 10

Unashamed Giving

If the willingness is there, the gift is acceptable according to what one has. (2 Corinthians 8:12)

One of my spiritual delights over the years has been the financial support God by His grace enabled Marge and me to give to our local church and our denomination's missionary work worldwide. I say that not to brag—many people doubtless give proportionately more—but to register my sense of frustration as I realize we no longer can be as generous.

I need to recognize some Bible principles: First, God, who owns everything, nevertheless does rely on the largess of His people for the support of His work. Second, when God financially prospers a believer, it is so he or she can more generously support His kingdom work. Third, God is reasonable; He does not expect that we should be pressed so that others might luxuriate (2 Corinthians 8:13). Fourth, it is our attitude that counts: "If the willingness is there, the gift is acceptable according to what one has."

And there is yet another principle. The adage "Time is money" applies to the retirement years. I have less money. But I have more time. Just as the financial investor may shift his assets from stocks to bonds to money market instruments according to the state of the economy, so retirement is an opportunity for me to shift from a dollar intensive investment to a time intensive investment. I can donate time to my local church. I can donate quality prayer time to the church worldwide. My stewardship of resources is unchanged; only the emphasis has changed.

Father, I am still a member of the team! Amen.

FEBRUARY 11

The Necessities

[The money] was distributed to anyone as he had need. (Acts 4:35)

Anyone who has lived more than 60 years certainly has discovered the difference between necessities and wants. I happened to grow up in northwestern Pennsylvania during the depression of the '30s, when $25 a week paid the rent and fed and clothed our family of five—and supported the church and ministered to the needs of less fortunate families that did not have $25 dollars a week for living expenses.

We walked wherever we went. We hauled our groceries home in a toy wagon. Ice cream cones, even at five cents each, were a rarity. I wore my share of patched pants.

But there were compensations as well: physical stamina from all the exercise, home-baked bread because it was cheaper than "boughten" loaves, a certain camaraderie within the community because many were in similarly straitened circumstances.

Life could end up for me as it began—in a considerably less than lavish style. I leave that matter in God's capable hands. I have His promise that He will meet all my *needs*. He who feeds the birds of the air and dresses the lilies of the field will assuredly take care of me. "The Lord is my Shepherd, I shall not be in want" (Psalm 23:1).

Once I put the material concerns behind me—actually put them above me!—I am released in spirit to concentrate on the important business at hand: bringing glory to God in all I do, all I say and all I think.

Father, I shall continue to let You determine my needs. Amen.

FEBRUARY 12

Credit Cards

Let no debt remain outstanding. (Romans 13:8)

I am thankful for my credit cards. I am also thankful for the discipline to use them wisely.

Ever since our first store card back in 1962, the year we returned from the Philippines, Marge and I have observed one cardinal rule: Never buy more on a credit card than you can pay for *in full* when the charges come in.

Credit cards have made it easier to systematize my financial accounting. Because we have an interest-bearing checking account, credit cards have extended 10–30 days the earning power of our money. Credit cards have greatly reduced the need to carry large amounts of cash, both on trips and every day.

Over the years, federal and state regulations have limited my liability should a lost or stolen card be used fraudulently. They have also protected me, as a card user, against merchants who misrepresent the worth of their wares.

The two-cards-twice-the-credit pitch that banks routinely make to me falls on deaf ears. My credit limit on one card is well beyond my self-imposed buying limit. Department stores that promote their own cards will not usually refuse MasterCard or VISA. So life is simple. One check and one postage stamp each month care for practically all our credit purchases.

Do credit cards violate God's "Let no debt remain outstanding" principle? Under terms of the contract, I have no outstanding debt unless I default on the terms of payment.

Father, help me use credit wisely, advantageously. Amen.

FEBRUARY 13

Remember the Poor

He who mocks the poor shows contempt for their maker. (Proverbs 17:5)

Statistics indicate there are fewer impoverished among retired people than the general public supposes. That is of course hollow comfort to any of the exceptions.

It is by God's favor that I have been provided for. Marge and I made His righteousness and His kingdom our first objective, and true to Jesus' promise, "all these things" have been "given to us as well" (Matthew 6:33). Not that we had no role in the outcome. We tried to be prudent with what God allowed us to have. And He sovereignly orchestrated the favorable circumstances that multiplied our efforts.

In both the Old Testament (Deuteronomy 15:11) and the New (Matthew 26:11), God declares there will always be poor people. God charged Israel's kings to see that the poor received just treatment (Proverbs 29:14). He directed the Israelites to allow the poor to glean their fields and benefit from the sabbatical year when the fields lay uncultivated (Exodus 23:11; Leviticus 19:10). He prompted the New Testament church to take a special interest in the poor (Galatians 2:10).

Paul called himself poor (2 Corinthians 6:10). Jesus "became poor" for my sake (2 Corinthians 8:9). Honest poverty is no disgrace and deserves our remedial efforts. Lazy poverty is intolerable. Paul wrote the Thessalonians, "When we were with you, we gave you this rule: 'If a man will not work, he shall not eat' " (2 Thessalonians 3:10).

Father, give me honest concern for the honestly poor. Amen.

FEBRUARY 14

Rise and Shine!

*Satisfy us in the morning with your
unfailing love,
that we may sing for joy and be glad
all our days. (Psalm 90:14)*

There are "morning" people who hit the deck running, and there are "evening" people whose best hours happen around midnight. With deference to retired people who find themselves in the latter category, I must nevertheless be faithful to the many Bible references extolling the morning hours.

The manna was waiting for Israel in the morning (Exodus 16:8). God summoned Moses to "be ready in the morning" to meet Him on Sinai (Exodus 34:2). David laid his requests before God in the morning (Psalm 5:3). He said to God, "In the morning I will sing of your love" (59:16). He wanted "the morning [to] bring [him] word of [the Lord's] unfailing love" (143:8).

Mark recounts how "very early in the morning, while it was still dark," Jesus went to a solitary place to pray (Mark 1:35).

Early risers can claim company with Abraham, Jacob, Moses, Joshua, Gideon, Samuel, David, Job, the women at Jesus' empty tomb. The apostles, miraculously freed from incarceration and in obedience to the Lord's command "at day break . . . entered the temple courts" (Acts 5:21) to tell the people the full message of this new life in Christ Jesus.

Little wonder David prays, "Satisfy me in the morning with your unfailing love." Then, he says, "we may sing for joy and be glad all our days."

Father, I would meet You in the morning before the demands of the new day begin to crowd in. Amen.

FEBRUARY 15

Faith all the Way

Abraham believed God, and it was credited to him as righteousness. (Romans 4:3, quoting Genesis 15:6)

It has been 49 years since God saved me through Jesus Christ. It was during evangelistic meetings with Nathan Cohen Beskin at the First Church of the Nazarene, Warren, Pennsylvania—the church I still fondly consider "home."

I had gone forward to pray for friends who had responded to the evangelist's invitation. And while I was there praying, God cut through my past ignorance with understanding. He told me that He loved the world (translate that *Robert Cowles*) so much "that He gave his one and only Son, that whoever believes in him shall not perish but have eternal life" (John 3:16). Light dawned! *I* believed in Jesus Christ; therefore, I had life. All my previous efforts in pursuit of salvation were swept away in the marvelous realization that God had already done it all.

Writing to believers in Rome, Paul differentiates between Jews and Gentiles in respect to judgment. "All who sin apart from the law [Gentiles] will also perish apart from the law, and all who sin under the law [Jews] will be judged by the law" (Romans 2:12). But when it comes to salvation, he declares there is just one way—the faith way: "There is only one God, who will justify the circumcised [Jews] by faith and the uncircumcised [Gentiles] through that same faith" (Romans 3:30).

Forty-nine years! And the righteousness credited to me by faith that night in Warren, Pennsylvania, is what I am still counting on as I face an ever-closer eternity.

Father, thank You for such a great salvation! Amen.

FEBRUARY 16

Path of Life

You have made known to me the path of life.
(Psalm 16:11)

"Lord, give me some word of comfort," I prayed. Minutes before, late on that Friday night, I had had the chilling call from Liz, my sister, in Warren, Pennsylvania.

"Norm's gone!" Liz exclaimed. Norman Huck—brother-in-law, college roommate, prayer warrior, benefactor, friend. Struck down by a car as he was walking the snow-covered four-lane road a block from his house. Killed instantly.

"Lord, give me some word of comfort," I prayed. And almost that promptly it came to me:

> "You have made known to me the path of life;
> you will fill me with joy in your presence,
> with eternal pleasures at your right hand."

The world would look upon that fateful accident as a path of death, the oncoming car in the snowy roadway unable to stop or swerve. But a sovereign God viewed it differently.

God viewed it from eternity, and from that vantage point it was a path of life. Absent from the body, present with the Lord. Out of His victorious encounter with death Jesus carved a path of life. That is the triumphant good news: death has been conquered at last, life can be unending.

The deep wound of bereavement heals slowly. But the Christian has faith in the One who overcame death. God's way to immortality is not to keep His children from dying; it is to make them live again—eternally—in His presence.

Father, give me Your attitude toward death. Amen.

FEBRUARY 17

Destiny: Death

Man is destined to die once. (Hebrews 9:27)

It is an American custom—maybe a human, universal custom—to treat unpleasant subjects as though they did not exist. Death heads most people's list of unpleasant subjects.

For Christians, the eternal physical presence of Jesus and the glories of heaven should be exciting prospects. But Christians are as reluctant as everyone else to face the only current means of attaining those priceless goals.

If mortality is a fact of life, it is more so for me now that I am old enough to retire. Thus far, I have escaped death by

> heart attack (2,113 deaths per day in America)
> cancer (1,265 deaths per day in America)
> stroke (419 deaths per day in America)
> accidents (256 deaths per day in America)
> all other causes (1,884 deaths per day in America).

But not forever will the Grim Reaper ignore me. Sooner or later I can expect his knock.

For those bereaved, death seldom has happy connotations. Very frequently it is associated with the most traumatic experiences of earthly existence. But for the Christian, death ushers him or her into the very presence of God—the goal toward which all of life should be pointed.

As a retired person, I need to change my attitude toward death. An enemy? Yes, death is an enemy. But it is a conquered enemy. And God can and does use even the work of an enemy to fulfill His purposes for His children.

Father, I will fear no evil, for You are with me. Amen.

FEBRUARY 18

How Describe It?

So we will be with the Lord forever.
(1 Thessalonians 4:17)

What will it be like to slip from the shackles of mortality into the wonder of God's presence? Thankfully, I am not left entirely to my imagination.

The Bible declares, "We know that if the earthly tent we live in is destroyed, we have a building from God, an eternal house in heaven" (2 Corinthians 5:1). In my human assessment of dying, life is swallowed up by death. From God's perspective, death is swallowed up by life (1 Corinthians 15:54). For the Christian, as the song says, "it is not death to die."

"To be away from the body" is to be "at home with the Lord" (2 Corinthians 5:8). What a comforting hope for creatures who enjoy close relationships! David declares, "I will dwell in the house of the Lord/ forever" (Psalm 23:6). Paul says, "So we will be with the Lord forever" (1 Thessalonians 4:17). Jesus Himself assures His followers, "I will . . . take you to be with me that you also may be where I am" (John 14:3).

What will it be like suddenly to be in God's very presence, as another song puts it, "standing before Him at last"? What will it be like, in the words of John's description (Revelation 4:8-11), to hear the four "living creatures" chanting "Holy, holy, holy"? to see the 24 elders "fall down before him who sits on the throne, and worship him who lives for ever and ever"? What will it be like to hear them say, "You are worthy, our Lord and God,/ to receive glory and honor and power"?

What indeed will it be like!

Father, sometimes I can hardly wait! Amen.

FEBRUARY 19

Living Wisely

Be very careful... how you live—not as unwise but as wise. (Ephesians 5:15)

How can I obey this scriptural injunction to live wisely? Exactly what did God have in mind when He commanded that I "be very careful... how [I] live"?

Ephesus was a pagan, idolatrous city. The citizens of Ephesus, "darkened in their understanding" (Ephesians 4:18), had "given themselves over to sensuality so as to indulge in every kind of impurity, with a continual lust for more" (4:19).

The believers in Ephesus were a people apart. They had been "made new in the attitude of [their] minds" (4:23). They had "put on the new self, created to be like God in true righteousness and holiness" (4:24).

Out of the "darkness" of pagan idolatry, these believers had emerged, like white lilies in a slag heap, transformed by the resurrection power of Jesus Christ. They stood as "children of light" (5:8). Among them there "must not be even a hint of sexual immorality, or of any kind of impurity, or of greed" (5:3). They were to have "nothing to do with the fruitless deeds of darkness, but rather expose them" (5:11).

The wisdom Paul wished for these Ephesians was to "understand what the Lord's will is" (5:17). They were to be surrendered to the control of God's Spirit even as they had once surrendered to wine's intoxication (5:18). Spirit control would put a song in their hearts and praise on their lips (5:19–20). Reverence for Christ would make them submissive to one another (5:21).

Father, I wisely surrender to the control of Your Spirit. Amen.

FEBRUARY 20

Joyous Long Life

"Honor your father and mother"—which is the first commandment with a promise—"that it may go well with you and that you may enjoy long life on the earth." (Ephesians 6:2–3)

Not too many retirees have living parents—or a parent—whom they can honor. I have buried a mother, a step-mother, a father, a father-in-law and a stepfather-in-law. Marge's mother, born in 1900, is still alive.

Alma Dailey Fisk has been anything but the proverbial mother-in-law. Her presence in our home for several years after Marge's dad died was a priceless blessing to us all. Our four children revere her as a combination saint-matriarch-benefactor. Her range of interests is worldwide. We count on her prayers and keep her informed of all household crises.

"Honor your father and mother." All my years I have tried to be faithful to the spirit of that commandment. Marge and I have been blessed by loving, gracious parents whom it was easy to honor. We hardly deserve reward for what has been a natural response to these godly progenitors. Nevertheless, the promise is there: ". . . that it may go well with you and that you may enjoy long life on the earth."

I have had contemporaries whose honor of parents seemed as genuine as mine whose lives were snuffed out prematurely. But a promise is a promise. And I claim this one. The phrase *enjoy long life* holds special interest. Some who have length of years find them odious by reason of pain or incapacity. God's promise is long life that is enjoyable!

Father, You gave the command. Help me to obey it. Amen.

FEBRUARY 21

Today

"Today, if you hear his voice..." (Hebrews 3:7)

If, as seems quite certain, Moses wrote Psalm 90, it was from the perspective of long experience, for Moses lived 120 years. And he prayed, "Teach us to number our days aright,/ that we may gain a heart of wisdom" (90:12). I think I am seeing more clearly than before the importance of *today*.

As a child I dreamed of what I would do "when I grow up." As a young man, I refined those dreams considerably and added some more. But the tense of my ambitions was always future. And for reason. Achievement takes time, and goals too readily reached are unworthy of lifetime effort.

Now, squarely in the clutches of retirement, I can look back—if I dare—and see the route I have come. I can know how many of those earlier dreams have been realized. And, like it or not, I must face raw reality. Those youthful dreams either have or have not been realized. If they have not, then hope of attaining them is dimming. Time is running out.

I am an inveterate futurizer. Tomorrow. Next year. When such and such conditions prevail.

This is not to say that at 60 or 70 I should forget about goals and concentrate only on today. The Scriptures *do* speak of Spirit-filled old men dreaming dreams!

But neither dare I lose sight of the value of today. This day has been given me from God to savor, to enjoy, to use for His glory. Today is the first day of the rest of my life. It *may* be the final day of all of my life.

Father, help me to make today count. Amen.

FEBRUARY 22

Ransomed

"The Son of Man [came] . . . to give his life as a ransom for many." (Matthew 20:28)

Ransom is the key word in that text. Ransom—the redemption price of a slave. Once I was a slave to sin. But Jesus ransomed me, paid the price of my redemption.

There was, however, a catch of sorts. In order to be ransomed from my slavery to sin, I had to agree to a new slavery. I had to make Jesus Christ the new Master of my life.

Salvation from sin's claims on my life involved a new Lord, a new allegiance: "If you confess with your mouth, 'Jesus is Lord,' and believe in your heart that God raised him from the dead, you will be saved" (Romans 10:9). I became Jesus' property. He became the new Lord of my life.

That, at least, was my standing. In practice, however, I too often tried to reverse the roles. *I* wanted to be lord and make Jesus my slave. Even my petitions frequently betrayed my heart: "Supply my needs." "Protect my loved ones." "Help me in my work today." The prayers were not necessarily faulty, but they reflected what sometimes was my faulty attitude.

Here near the threshold of my retirement, it is important that I reaffirm Jesus' rightful place as Lord and my obligatory place as slave, His role as Master and mine as servant. Jesus is Lord—Sovereign. I am His slave, bought with a price, devoid of personal "rights," obligated to obedience, sentenced to service. *And in my heart of hearts I want it no other way!*

Father, thank You for sending Jesus to redeem me from Satan's slavery. With my heart I say it: "Jesus is Lord!" Amen.

FEBRUARY 23

Uneven Exchange

They exchanged the truth of God for a lie. (Romans 1:25)

It would be advantageous if years produced an immunity to temptation and to doubt—like the immunity most older people have from the so-called childhood diseases. But it does not exactly happen that way.

In a sense, my experience with God has built confidence. God who answered prayer about the kids and the job is not about to abandon me now. But I need to take heed lest experience breed presumption and a certain carelessness about truth.

If I sin deliberately, I do so by suppressing God's truth (Romans 1:18). Sin and truth cannot occupy the same space. Sin clouds my thinking (1:21). It scrambles my perspective.

Moreover, God does not strike with lightning those who sin in flagrant violation of his truth—usually. That is not His normal method of operation. Rather, He simply "gives them over" (1:24, 26, 28) to the very sins they espouse. Those sins become their own judgment on the perpetrator. I doubt that there is a happy adulterer. Or a joyful thief.

So what are the lessons for me? *I must be vigilant*. My adversary still "prowls around like a roaring lion looking for someone to devour" (1 Peter 5:8). *I must be steadfast*. "[God] is able to guard what I have entrusted to him" (2 Timothy 1:12). *I must be prayerful*. God alone "is able to keep [me] from falling and to present [me] before his glorious presence without fault and with great joy" (Jude 24).

Father, at this chronological point in my life, help me not to fall for Satan's lies. You are the truth. Amen.

FEBRUARY 24

Abraham

"Your name will be Abraham, for I have made you a father of many nations." (Genesis 17:5)

As familiar as I am with Abraham's story, it still seems almost incredible. To think that God would speak those words to a 99-year-old man, whose son through whom God intended to accomplish much of His promise had not yet been born!

But the outcome is well known. Abraham and Sarah *did* have a son—at ages 100 and 90, respectively. Isaac, their son, eventually had twin sons—Esau and Jacob. Jacob had 12 sons, and the nation Israel was on its way.

Abraham is especially remembered for two reasons. He was a man of great faith. He believed what God told him. So sure was he of God's word that when he was in the act of sacrificing his beloved son Isaac at God's command, he reasoned that God would raise Isaac from the dead rather than to turn from His promise concerning the boy (Hebrews 11:19). That is implicit faith! Abraham is indeed the father of the faithful.

Also, Abraham is remembered for his friendship with God. Centuries later, King Jehoshaphat, in a public prayer, asks: " 'O our God, did you not drive out the inhabitants of this land before your people Israel and give it forever to the descendants of Abraham your friend?' " (2 Chronicles 20:7). And New Testament James says Abraham was called "God's friend" (James 2:23). Abraham enjoyed God's company, and God enjoyed his. Few others have achieved so close a relationship with God—probably because few others have given it so high a priority.

Father, I would pattern my life after Abraham's. Amen.

FEBRUARY 25

Sarah

"As for Sarai, ... her name will be Sarah. I will ... surely give you a son by her." (Genesis 17:15–16)

Today's women might well wish they had Sarah's quintessential beauty. At age 65 she caught the eye of Egypt's officialdom and was actually taken into Pharaoh's harem—though God kept the king from transgressing (Genesis 12:14–19). Twenty-four years later, at age 89, history repeated itself, and Sarah's charm attracted a Philistine chieftain (20:1–5).

But Sarah would have traded all her natural beauty for the one thing denied her: a baby. It was that long-term frustration that may have made Sarah somewhat hard to get along with. Her original name, Sarai, means "contentious," and there is between-the-lines evidence that Sarah lived up to her name.

But God mercifully altered all that. He changed her name to Sarah ("a princess") and promised her the child she had longed for all her life. And a year later Isaac was born to Abraham and Sarah—a miracle gift of God to this aging couple. He was the "child of promise" (see Galatians 4:23, 28)—as are all believers whom Christ Jesus has freed from sin's slavery.

Some people enter retirement as frustrated as Sarah—though probably for different reasons. The frustrations have caused them to be contentious, hard to live with. As a result, they may have a severely limited circle of friends.

Sarah found help in a personal encounter with God Himself. God changed not only her name, He changed *her*. God is still in the business of changing people. Even older people.

Father, be the Agent of Change in my life. Amen.

FEBRUARY 26

Lot

Lot ... pitched his tents near Sodom. (Genesis 13:12)

Lot, nephew to Abraham, like some other Bible personalities, is an example of how *not* to live.

Already advanced in years and a very wealthy herdsman, Lot's choice of the well-watered Jordan plain (Genesis 13:10–11), leaving Abraham to fend in the bleak Canaan hills, was patently selfish. It turned out to be a bad decision all around.

The Scriptures tersely comment about Sodom's populace: "The men of Sodom were wicked and were sinning greatly against the Lord" (13:13). What began with Lot pitching his tents *near* Sin City ended with Lot "sitting in the gateway of the city" (19:1) as a principal citizen.

There is no slightest hint that Lot stooped to the city's entangling sin. Peter refers to Lot as "a righteous man, who was distressed by the filthy lives of lawless men" (2 Peter 2:7). Perhaps Lot thought he might be a good influence on the people of Sodom. But it worked the opposite way. Lot would have been better off had he shunned the area entirely.

The men of Sodom who married Lot's two daughters refused to leave the city. Lot himself, mesmerized by his surroundings, was in no hurry to escape God's flaming vengeance. Lot's wife "looked back" (Genesis 19:26) in disobedience and died.

Lot and his two daughters became refugees in a cave in the hills Lot once had scorned. There he became the unwitting progenitor of two clans of people—the Moabites and the Ammonites (19:36–38). Both would be perpetual antagonists to Israel.

Father, deliver me from a selfish spirit. Amen.

FEBRUARY 27

Ishmael

"You shall name [your son] Ishmael, for the Lord has heard of your misery." (Genesis 16:11)

By retirement, I should have worked through all those sinister episodes that may have warped my childhood and distorted my adult personality. But not necessarily.

Ishmael never quite outgrew the sense of rejection that dogged his childhood.

Ishmael was Abraham's attempt—at his wife's suggestion—to help God answer the childless couple's prayer for a son. Sarah, jealous of her pregnant servant, Hagar, made life so miserable for her that Hagar ran away. But God caught up with Hagar and told her to return and submit to Sarah. He instructed Hagar to name her baby Ishmael, meaning, "God hears."

Ishmael was probably 13 when Isaac was born to Abraham and Sarah. The tents became too small for both "families," and Abraham sent Ishmael and his mother off into the harsh desert. Just when it looked as though both would perish, God heard their cries and intervened.

Ishmael grew up in the desert, produced 12 sons and a daughter and lived his life with "his hand . . . against everyone/ and everyone's hand against him" (Genesis 16:12)—not exactly the life of tranquility that I covet in retirement.

Do feelings of rejection plague me? *Ishmael*—"God hears!" Loved ones pass away. Friends find other interests. Children have their own lives to live. God cares. He may not remove the scars—or the wounds—but He promises me His grace!

Father, thank You for being here when I need You! Amen

FEBRUARY 28

Isaac

Isaac was sixty years old when Rebekah gave birth to [Esau and Jacob]. (Genesis 25:26)

Isaac lived somewhat longer than people today can expect to—he died at age 180 (Genesis 35:28). But that fact does not change another: Isaac was in his sixties as Esau and Jacob, his twin boys by Rebekah, were in their childhood. *Grand*children in retirement are a great idea. But I would not relish beginning a family at age 60!

Perhaps it was only natural that these two parents—Isaac and Rebekah—themselves so different in background and temperament, should have allowed themselves to be polarized over their equally different sons. Esau was like Isaac: a skilled hunter, a man of the fields. Jacob favored Rebekah. He was "quiet" and preferred "staying among the tents" (25:27). Since there were two, why not divide the children, one son for each?

But favoritism is dangerous when it comes to children—or grandchildren. It tends to foster unhealthy competition. It can leave emotional scars as well. Happy are the offspring who do not have to live under such a disadvantage.

It must not have been a pleasant household for Isaac and his wife—each pitted against the other, each pitting *his* or *her* son against the other's.

And for Isaac's two sons, the outcome nearly led to homicide—when Jacob by deception stole the birthright blessing from his brother. Even after the celebrated reconciliation some 20 years later, there was never real rapport between the two brothers. Each went his own way; each kept to himself.

Father, guard me from the trap of favoritism. Amen.

FEBRUARY 29

Faith Is Obedience

"The righteous will live by his faith."
(Habakkuk 2:4)

It is not news to Christians that faith is the number one ingredient of their spiritual walk.

God did the saving work. It was He who sent His Son to die for mankind (John 3:16). It was He who raised Jesus from the dead (Acts 2:24) and exalted Him (Philippians 2:9) to His present place of intercession for all believers (Hebrews 7:25). Through God Christ Jesus has been made the Christian's "righteousness, holiness and redemption" (1 Corinthians 1:30). But the work God did becomes effective personally through faith.

And what, exactly, is faith? It is not a nebulous nothing on which I begin to build my spiritual house. It is not in the strict sense an object. It is a means. *Faith is believing what God says.* In the case of Abraham or Moses or any of the other faith heros of Hebrews 11, wherever the Bible details their lives, their "faith" was simply obedience to what God was saying to them.

God told Abraham to go to the land He would show him. Abraham went. The Bible says, "By faith Abraham . . . obeyed and went" (Hebrews 11:8). God told Moses how to avoid the death of Israel's firstborn males as the final plague struck Egypt. Moses acted on those words. The Bible says, "By faith he kept the Passover . . . so that the destroyer of the firstborn would not touch the firstborn of Israel" (11:28). That is the pattern.

Faith is believing/obeying what God says.

Father, I have hidden Your Word in my heart that I might not sin against You. Keep me continually obedient. Amen.

MARCH 1

Of Some Value

Physical training is of some value. (1 Timothy 4:8)

I find very little in the Word of God concerning a subject that has irresistible fascination for modern Americans: physical exercise. Even Paul's comment to chronically ill Timothy was set alongside the observation that godliness is of far greater worth: "Godliness has value for all things, holding promise for both the present life and the life to come."

First century people, whether young like Timothy or elderly like Paul, did not have to rely on physical workouts to keep fit. They were not desk bound, like so many of my generation were and are. They had no televisions to immobilize them for hours, no automobiles to whisk them from place to place in effortless luxury. Everything from a drink of water to the clothes on their backs involved physical labor.

But I came almost 20 centuries later. I am used to a padded swivel chair and an upholstered car interior. I am given to little more exercise than clearing the occasional winter snowfall or walking behind my self-propelled lawn mower. Is there hope that I can "turn back the clock," that I can undo the negative effects of years of sedentary living? Many doctors say there is. They say I can reverse the aging process by as much as 15 years through good diet and prudent exercise. But these doctors add a precaution: it must be done under their supervision!

If I am to serve God to the maximum in these retirement years, I need to pay much more attention to exercise and the rules of good health than I have in the past.

Father, it will not be easy, but You will help me. Amen.

MARCH 2

Is This My God?

Many live as enemies of the cross of Christ.... Their god is their stomach.... Their mind is on earthly things.
(Philippians 3:18–19)

Saying no to too much food does not get easier in retirement. In fact, being around the house more of the time brings me face to face with the same temptation housewives have battled all their lives. Moreover, to the extent my physical activity is lessened, to that extent I need fewer calories to keep me going. So it is a war on two fronts.

I have discovered that food is habit-forming. My body does not now "ask" me for mid-morning and bedtime snacks because I have told it there will be but three meals a day. (I find biblical precedent for three meals, but no rule. Other cultures vary their eating routine, seemingly with no ill effects. I conclude that consistency is more important than any set pattern.) My routine of a cereal-and-orange-juice breakfast, a light lunch and a main evening meal about 5:30 works well for me. Plus my bedtime orange juice and a daily multivitamin, included with breakfast, to cover any nutritional lack.

Like my other activities, eating has spiritual dimensions. When I eat, I am to do it for God's glory (1 Corinthians 10:31). God has warned me not to let my stomach be my god. Recognizing the spiritual dimension of food is probably the best assurance that I will not abuse with too much food this body that has been God's good gift to me.

Father, in the matter of food and its intake, I recognize Your Lordship over my life. Amen.

MARCH 3

Living Bodies

Offer your bodies as living sacrifices. (Romans 12:1)

I doubt that I am straining the intent of God's inspired Word when I presume this exhortation may apply to the way I treat this "living sacrifice"—my body—that I have offered to God. In Old Testament times, God expected the best that an Israelite could offer: the unblemished lamb, the perfect goat. Surely His requirements remain unchanged.

By the time of retirement, many can offer God only an overweight, malfunctioning, disease-prone body. That is a pity and certainly not what He intended.

God designed these bodies of ours to need three kinds of exercise: *stretching*, to keep them limber; *movement*, to increase muscle strength, and *endurance*, to quicken the heartbeat and strengthen the whole circulatory system.

Dr. Laurence E. Morehouse, who helped develop the exercise system used by astronauts in space, says most people can improve their bodies by five simple, every-day exercises:

1. Limber up by reaching with the arms, twisting the trunk, bending the waist.
2. Stand at least two hours (it helps circulation).
3. Lift something unusually heavy for five seconds.
4. Walk briskly for at least three minutes.
5. Burn up 300 calories in physical activity (the equivalent of walking three miles).

I have an obligation even now to make this living sacrifice of mine as perfect as it can be.

Father, I commit myself to daily exercise. Amen.

MARCH 4

Lord of Every Area

Offer your bodies as living sacrifices, holy and pleasing to God—this is your spiritual act of worship. (Romans 12:1)

God wants all of me. This total signing over of myself to Him He calls my "spiritual act of worship."

The offering of myself to God took place at a point in time. It was deliberate on my part as well as His. It is not to be annulled by either of us. But the working out of that dedication is a process that will continue throughout these years of retirement to my dying day.

Paul's letter to the Romans is remarkable for its systematic teaching regarding salvation and sanctification. In all the Scriptures there is no finer theological treatise than this. But Paul is too much a "people person" to make any of his letters simply cerebral. Theory untranslated into practical life is of little value. Faith unexpressed in obedience is suspect. Paul is practical. He elicits action from those who read him.

Not only am I to discover God's will for me (Romans 12:2), but I am to determine and begin exercising my gift or gifts (12:3–8). I must love people sincerely (12:9–21; 13:8–10; 14:1–4; 15:1–7). I must submit to constituted authority (13:1–7).

If sound doctrine does not result in exemplary relations with my fellow beings in and out of the church, something is the matter. I dare not blame it on the other person or on God. That narrows the field to just one person: me. Either my surrender was insincere or my outworking of it is faulty.

Father, You have me—body, soul, spirit. Help me as I work out what You by Your grace have worked within me. Amen.

MARCH 5

Spirit Power

*"Not by might nor by power, but by my Spirit,"
says the Lord Almighty. (Zechariah 4:6)*

The growth of the New Testament church was amazing. One hundred twenty people were present at its birth. Before the day was out, the membership was 3,000! Opposition served only to spread the new religion. In the first three centuries of Christianity an estimated 5 to 10 percent of the entire Roman Empire was nominally Christian. In some parts, such as Asia Minor, Thrace and Cyprus, the ratio was nearly one to one.

Tertullian did not exaggerate much when he remarked to the Romans, "We [Christians] are but of yesterday, and yet we already fill your cities, islands, camps, your palaces, senate and forum. We have left you only your temples."

How do we account for such a phenomenal accomplishment? Acts 2:1–4 provides the clue. Those initial 120—and surely a great number of their converts—were "filled with the Holy Spirit."

It was never God's intention that I should work in my own strength, achieving through my own efforts. That fact is all the more timely in the retirement years as physical energy wanes and tasks require increasing effort.

Granted that truth, how do I avail myself of Spirit power? First, I need to recognize that if I am a believer, God's Spirit *already* indwells me (Romans 8:9). From there it is simple logic. A container 9/10ths full of water can be but 1/10th filled with milk. But if I empty out the water, the same container can be totally filled with milk. The application is patent.

Father, I empty myself that Your Spirit may fill me. Amen.

MARCH 6

Walking Temples

We are the temple of the living God. As God has said: "I will live with them and walk among them, and I will be their God, and they will be my people." (2 Corinthians 6:16)

God must have meant it. He made the statement first to Israel in the desert: "I will walk among you and be your God, and you will be my people" (Leviticus 26:12). And He twice repeated it through His prophets (Jeremiah 32:38, Ezekiel 37:27).

Were it not God's own pronouncement, I would consider the idea incredible, even ludicrous. If here the apostle seems to have in mind the corporate church (the "them," "their" and "they" are plural), in his earlier letter to the Corinthians he individualized the statement: "Your [singular] body is a temple of the Holy Spirit" (1 Corinthians 6:19). Think of it! *I*—bearing the unmistakable marks of age—am a temple of the Living God of the universe. Could any scenario be less likely?

Of course, having God resident within human flesh is not a phenomenon reserved for retired people—after the passions of youth have played themselves out and the struggles of bread-winning presumably are over. *Any* child of God through faith in Christ is a temple indwelt by God. But in the less demanding pace of retirement, I have the leisure to more fully enjoy my resident Priest, the God of creation.

It behooves me, as a walking temple of Deity, to give myself over to the divine Tenant. He redeemed me, else I would be dead in trespasses and sins. I owe Him full allegiance.

Father, here I am—body, soul, spirit. Make this human temple all You want it to be for Your purposes. Amen.

MARCH 7

Time to Houseclean

Let us purify ourselves from everything that contaminates body and spirit, perfecting holiness out of reverence for God. (2 Corinthians 7:1)

Incredible though it seems, I am "a temple of the Holy Spirit" (1 Corinthians 6:19). After saying it again (2 Corinthians 6:16), the Apostle Paul draws his conclusion: It is time to houseclean. My resident Priest is holy; I am to keep His temple holy.

Not that I have never housecleaned before. There have been numerous times when in contrition I acknowledged my sin before God and repented of it. But, as my wife, Marge, keeps insisting, clean houses do not stay clean. They must be cleaned again and again. *I* may not see the dust, but *she* does. (She is vacuuming right now.) So at this juncture in life, it is appropriate that I houseclean.

Have I allowed anything impure to enter the temple? Have I made any compromises with sin in the recent past? Now that I have a bit more leisure time, is my resolve firm to police what I read, what I listen to, what I watch on TV (including the ads)? Do I consciously focus my waking thoughts on Jesus? When I look at people, do I see them through the eyes of Jesus?

If I have any doubts concerning the value of such discipline, they are dispelled by God's overwhelming promise to me and to all who separate themselves from this world's evil influences:

> "I will be a Father to you,
> and you will be my sons and daughters." (6:18)

Father, I forsake everything that would make me unholy. Amen.

MARCH 8

Gray Matter, Power

Be transformed by the renewing of your mind. (Romans 12:2)

Something is missing! Between age 30 and age 60 I lost half my lung function and half my muscle function. Before I am 70, I will have lost a quarter of my heart function. (Not to worry. God in His wise providence saw to it that my body at birth had two to seven times the capacities it would actually need.)

In contrast, my mental powers are holding their own. Even if I should live to age 80, my brain will have lost only 10 percent of the functional capacity it had when I was age 40!

"A mind is a terrible thing to waste," ran the TV public service ad. If it is true for disadvantaged kids in the inner cities, it is true as well for all the older people with their wealth of experience-based wisdom.

I am just one of some 32 million Americans over age 65. What about me? How can *I* "renew" my mind to better contribute to society generally and God's work particularly?

1. Colleges and universities offer adult education courses in a number of fields. I might choose studies that enhance my present specialties—or I could strike out in a totally new direction of interest to me.

2. The world of books offers the same benefits at an even lower price—especially when there is a good lending library within easy distance. An hour or two every day, or a morning or two every week, can work wonders.

The potential for good is almost limitless if I am willing to work at renewing my mind.

Father, I accept the challenge You put before me. Amen.

MARCH 9

Second Wind

Even youths grow tired and weary, ...
but those who hope in the Lord
will renew their strength.
They will soar, ...run, ...walk ...
(Isaiah 40:30–31)

Anyone who has ever jogged knows the phenomenon of the "second wind." Those exhilarating first paces quickly degenerate to a point where only sheer willpower keeps one heavy foot pounding in front of the other. But precisely at that point, the body makes an internal shift of gears and the pace goes better.

Retirement can be a "second wind." The 40-year struggle to achieve, to serve, to bring children to maturity was an effort that at times left me winded. Sheer willpower (and the desire to eat) kept me competing.

These senior years, far from being the end, are, as Browning put it, "the rest for which the first was made." Even discounting the romanticism of his line, retirement does have its advantages. The largest one is time. Pitiable is the man or woman who wastes this priceless commodity.

Like the runner's second wind, retirement is a shifting of gears, a time of renewal of strength and purpose.

God's three-fold promise is scaled to the stages of life:

"They shall soar"—connoting youth's energy and strength.

"They shall run"—the steady down-to-earth, still-enviable pace of middle age.

"They shall walk"—the slower steps of those in their senior years who trust God to keep them from weariness.

Father, even in the "walking" stage, I can count on You. Amen.

MARCH 10

Plain Talk

Do not let any unwholesome talk come out of your mouths, but only what is helpful for building others up according to their needs, that it may benefit those who listen. (Ephesians 4:29)

"If anyone is never at fault in what he says," James comments, "he is a perfect man" (James 3:2). Alas! The Lord has had to dispense few awards for perfection.

James admits that the tongue is a hard member to tame. He calls it a "fire, a world of evil among the parts of the body." He says, "No man can tame the tongue. It is a restless evil, full of deadly poison" (3:6–8).

Paul warns me against letting "any unwholesome talk come out of [my] mouth." Later in his same letter he is more pointed: "Obscenity, foolish talk or coarse joking . . . are out of place" (Ephesians 5:4).

I hear You, Father. And the best way to keep these things from my lips is to keep them from my thoughts.

A couple of years ago Marge and I counseled with a heartbroken mother who in the midst of some "words" with her daughter-in-law, had called the younger woman "a bad name," irretrievably worsening an already shaky relationship.

"I *never* say that word," the mother remarked incredulously. But could she have harbored the word in her mind, only to have it pop out at an unguarded moment?

Reflecting on God's mercy and goodness is one powerful way to keep my tongue disciplined. It is also the best way to "build others up according to their needs."

Father, keep my thoughts holy; then my speech will be. Amen.

MARCH 11

True Riches

*... poor, yet making many rich; having nothing,
and yet possessing everything. (2 Corinthians 6:10)*

Depending on just when he was born, the Apostle Paul may have been a senior citizen when he wrote those words in A.D. 55. I certainly cannot consider myself penniless, but the point Paul is making is the very one God has kept reminding me of all through life: *Money is not the key to happiness—or even to an effective ministry to my fellow beings.*

One of the most generous persons I ever knew was Annetta M. Holsted. By the time Marge and I reached the Philippines, Miss Holsted was already a living legend. That elderly little missionary, intense, earnest, tramped the trails of southern Cotabato and Davao provinces. New Testament in hand, she mixed the good news of Jesus Christ with literacy lessons for the populace and conferences for pastors and lay workers. She existed on a subsistence-level missionary's allowance—and even gave a good share of that away to meet the temporal needs of the people to whom she ministered. Although she had little money, she enriched many through her gospel witness and her deeds of kindness. Annetta Holsted possessed all that really mattered—the living God who never leaves His people.

My ability to help others is not dependent on my financial status. Neither should my well-being be measured by financial net worth. If I have God, what else really matters? And if I use the resources I have as I minister in His name, can I not expect Him to supply any lack?

Father, help me to share my true riches in Christ Jesus. Amen.

MARCH 12

Confidence

... confident ... that he who began a good work in you will carry it on to completion. (Philippians 1:6)

Although I like to think I am not given to worry, in fact I tend to be apprehensive, especially if the anticipated experience is new or out of the routine. Like, for instance, being father of the bride in a wedding, or speaking to a large group.

Since my remaining time on earth is, from my perspective, both unknown and uncharted, I regard it somewhat apprehensively. Will my mind fail me? Will I end as a physical invalid? Will I undergo intense suffering to the point of mental derangement? Will I be bereaved of the wife who has been my faithful, loving helpmate these past decades?

God mercifully veils the future from me. But I am not "left hanging." God promises to complete His good work in me. Although Paul's confidence was for a specific church—the believers in Philippi—it was certainly applicable to individual Philippians. By extension (since God is both consistent and evenhanded) it is also applicable to me. He who began a good work in *me* will carry it on to completion.

But what if I get Alzheimer's disease? What if I become bedfast? What if I undergo a baptism of physical suffering? What if Marge is taken from me? He who began a good work in me will carry it on to completion.

I can be confident that nothing, absolutely *nothing* "will be able to separate [me] from the love of God that is in Christ Jesus [my] Lord" (Romans 8:39).

Father, I put my future in Your capable hands! Amen.

MARCH 13

"Childrenized"

People will be ... lovers of pleasure rather than lovers of God. (2 Timothy 3:2–4)

I am not sure this phenomenon called retirement has divine approval. And, as I said, if a shrinking labor force must support too many millions more, as the statistics promise, it may not have American approval very long, either.

Retirement could be a one-generation aberration in the democratic experiment.

If I understand the Bible's main thrust, God never intended that people would retire to a life of leisure. As Alex Comfort said: "Leisure should occupy an occasional afternoon, not 20 years.... Leisure in our culture means activity which is by definition godless and irrelevant, and our emphasis on it 'childrenizes' older people." (Quoted by Jules Willing in *The Reality of Retirement*.)

In America the "childrenizing" has been a life-long conditioning under the label of "recreation" or "relaxation." Work is regarded as a necessary evil between play times. Professional athletes have million-dollar contracts to keep Americans amused. TV sit-coms and game shows soak up hours and hours of otherwise productive time. On weekends, people must go to the mountains or the beach or a ball game or fishing. And then at 65 or before, they "retire" so they can do full-time what has heretofore been their major activity.

I am first a servant. I am to be a producer, not simply a consumer. May it be physical or mental incapacity, not lack of will, that slows or halts my productivity.

Father, I want to bear fruit in old age. Amen.

MARCH 14

Up and At Them!

Warn those who are idle. (1 Thessalonians 5:14)

It is a recurring theme. I need again the admonishment of God's Word regarding idleness. With no demanding schedule, I find it easy to be lazy, hard to discipline myself.

I recall reading what one business person, used to a tightly structured time schedule, said about retirement: "It was a frightening excess of freedom, and it did not sit well until it was fettered and limited by self-imposed restraints, an inner voice that tells me I can't take a walk now because it is time to get ready for dinner."

Discipline is more than rising at six o'clock each morning—or eating dinner at a set hour. It begins with a schedule of worthwhile things to do—things of sufficient importance and interest to make me want to get an early start on the day, things demanding enough energy that I will welcome the dinner break whenever it comes in the household routine.

Idleness seems so innocuous at first. I deserve a break. All my life I've pushed, pushed, pushed. Relax for once! Take it easy! But as Solomon observed,

> A little sleep, a little slumber,
>   a little folding of the hands to rest—
> and poverty will come on you like a bandit
>   and scarcity like an armed man. (Proverbs 6:10–11)

Even if financially I need not work, still I am accountable to actively promote God's kingdom and glorify Him. Now is not the time to be lazy.

Father, hold me to Your purposes for my life. Amen.

MARCH 15

Stoke the Fire

Do not put out the Spirit's fire. (1 Thessalonians 5:19)

Here is another in that series of staccato admonitions God inspired Paul to put near the end of his first letter to the new Christians in Thessalonica. But exactly what is God saying to me in this particular warning? What would I have to do in order to "put out the Spirit's fire"?

Do I put out the fire by loafing instead of filling my days with profitable activity? ("Warn those who are idle," Paul says in First Thessalonians 5:14.) Do I put it out by "pay[ing] back wrong for wrong" (5:15)? by "treat[ing] prophecies with contempt" (5:20)? by failing to "test everything" (5:21)? by embracing some particular "kind of evil" (5:22)?

Rather, is it a mechanical attitude toward worship that discourages the expression of the gifts of God's Spirit in the local gathering of believers? The Thessalonians, as I noted, seem to have been treating prophecies with contempt.

Maybe I should ask the question positively: *How can I ensure that the fire of God's Spirit will blaze in my heart?*

Is the fire burning at all? If not, I must rekindle it at all costs. Jesus commanded the Ephesus church, "Repent and do the things you did at first" (Revelation 2:5). About face!

If the fire is indeed burning, have I possibly blocked the draft by a "bitter root" that "grows up to cause trouble and defile many" (Hebrews 12:15)?

I must fan the flame. By prayer. By reading the Bible. By fasting—"afflicting the soul."

Father, let the heavenly flame blaze within my heart. Amen.

MARCH 16

Proving Ground

Test everything. Hold on to the good. (1 Thessalonians 5:21)

How discriminating am I? Very? Somewhat? Not very?

With the accumulation of years it is easy to adopt an unwarranted tolerance for things I should not tolerate. "Test everything," God says. The Scriptures, in fact, have considerable to say about testing and examination.

In First Corinthians, God advises that "two or three prophets should speak" (14:29). Others present should "weigh carefully" what they say. In First John, God instructs His people to "test the spirits to see whether they are from God" (4:1). The reason? "Many false prophets have gone out into the world."

In Second Corinthians, God warned the believers at Corinth, "Examine yourselves to see whether you are in the faith; test yourselves" (13:5). In First Corinthians He says, "A man ought to examine himself before he eats of the [Communion] bread and drinks of the [Communion] cup" (11:28).

Implied in all this counsel is the strong possibility that something or someone will not stand the test.

It is troubling to think that even from the pulpit I may receive instruction that is inconsistent with God's Word. It is even more frightening to know that *I* may be insincere in my walk with the Lord, that *my* approach to the bread and the cup of Communion may be inappropriate, that *I* may be guilty of error as I seek to instruct others.

The antidote is to test. "Test everything." "Weigh carefully what is said." "Test the spirits." "Examine yourselves."

Father, Your Word is my one sure standard. Amen.

MARCH 17

Mind over Heart

God did not give us a spirit of timidity. (2 Timothy 1:7)

Why do I sense this reluctance when it comes to actually listing our New Cumberland house with the local realtor?

Marge and I have gone through the pros and cons a dozen times. Yes, it is a lovely, comfortable home. Yes, the neighborhood is desirable. Yes, the house is convenient to shopping, church, cultural events, transportation. But, no, we no longer need this much house. It is costly to maintain. The yard is far too large.

And, of course, there are the other persuasive arguments: the house is in Pennsylvania, where winters are inclement; it is not near any of our children; we would be tying up a good share of our assets in a piece of real estate that may not appreciate in the future as it has in the past.

So sell it we will.

Still, it is not easy to abandon a place that holds so many fond memories. Our grown children helped us occupy the house. Over the years a continuous stream of relatives and friends have visited here. There were picnics on the patio and cozy winter nights before a blazing fire and church get-togethers in the spacious living room. Even in just five years, an inanimate house can wrap itself around a person's heart.

Certainly the Lord led us to a good agent in Ben DeFrancesco. I had no person in mind when I walked into the realtor's office. Ben was sitting there at the right moment. Together we went over the preliminary specifications. Ben promised to follow through promptly. I have every reason to believe he will.

Father, mind wins out over emotion. Help me to trust. Amen.

MARCH 18

Esau

See that no one is . . . godless like Esau, who for a single meal sold his inheritance rights. (Hebrews 12:16)

If it were a popularity poll, the older of Isaac and Rebekah's twin sons would have won hands down. Like his father, Esau loved the out-of-doors, loved to hunt. Esau was a man's man with hair on his chest. He was a practical, here-and-now individual. He enjoyed good food, especially wild game.

But Esau was spiritually deficient. He cared little for birthright and patriarchal blessing—those intangible matters so important to the family God had singled out for nationhood.

Esau's brother could not have been more opposite. Yet, despite his faults—and he had them—Jacob had a capacity for God.

Esau took Canaanite wives, raised a large family, did well in all he set his hand to. Jacob went East to seek his fortune. Twenty years later, when Esau met Jacob again, both men were prosperous seniors with flocks and herds and servants.

Despite Esau's on-the-surface cordiality as he met Jacob, there were unresolved conflicts in his heart. The land could not support two such prosperous families. So Esau moved south to Seir—out of Canaan, away from the land God had promised to his fathers Abraham and Isaac. It was Esau's final downward step in a course he had set for himself years before.

Esau ended his days in material comfort but in spiritual impoverishment.

Father, I cannot re-do the past. But I do have today. Amen.

MARCH 19

Jacob

Then the man [who wrestled with Jacob] said, "Your name will no longer be Jacob but Israel, because you have struggled with God and with man and have overcome." (Genesis 32:28)

It is comforting to know that I am never too old for life-transforming encounters with God. Jacob may have been nearly 100 on the fateful night when he wrestled with the angel at Peniel and received his new name.

Jacob had already been through a lifetime of struggle. He was born struggling—his hand grasping his twin brother's heel as though trying to overtake Esau. That was how he got his name. *Jacob* means "heel-grabber."

Some would say Jacob tried too hard in his life-long struggle. Certainly he made himself obnoxious to Esau and probably to his father Isaac by deceptively taking the birthright blessing. He made himself obnoxious to Laban by managing to gain most of Laban's flocks.

As Jacob waited apprehensively for the next-day meeting with his brother, he faced the hardest struggle of his life. All alone on the upper side of Jabbok Ford, he found himself wrestling with a heavenly "man"—probably God himself in human form.

The struggle was more than physical. It was spiritual. It had to do with Jacob's character. The heel grabber who up to that point had achieved success through his self-efforts, was to become Israel—"prince with God"—and depend upon God thereafter to make him victorious.

That night Jacob surrendered. He confessed his name and his grasping character. He let God begin the process of transforming him into a spiritual prince.

Father, You who changed Jacob, change me! Amen.

MARCH 20

Laban

Laban said to Jacob, . . . "You've deceived me." (Genesis 31:26)

Even those whose lives impress me only negatively may convey important lessons I need to learn. Laban was such a person.

Laban must have been well up in years when his sister's son, Jacob, arrived at his remote tent. Life had been relatively good to Laban. He was financially comfortable, thanks to his flocks of sheep, and he still had two daughters, Leah and Rachel, both of marriageable age. In that Eastern culture he could expect a sizeable dowry from their suitors.

Some people of wealth are generous, sharing the bounty God has permitted them to have. Others are selfish and grasping. Laban was selfish and grasping—and deceptive.

The account of how Laban tricked Jacob into marrying Leah rather than the more physically desirable Rachel (Genesis 29:14–25) is one of the Bible's best known stories. But in his nephew Jacob, Laban met his match.

Laban watched approvingly as his flocks increased while Jacob worked out his 14 years of dowry. But in the next six years, the tables turned. In a battle to see who could outwit the other, Laban saw his own flocks decline as Jacob's expanded.

The ultimate irony came as Laban confronted now-wealthy Jacob, secretly fleeing with cattle, flocks, wives, maidservants, children. Laban said to Jacob, "You've deceived me."

We reap what we sow. Laban sowed deception and selfishness. Shorn of flocks, children, grandchildren, Laban in the end had little to show for all his conniving.

Father, free me from all deception and selfishness. Amen.

MARCH 21

Judah

Judah went up to [Joseph] and said: . . . "How can I go back to my father if [Benjamin] is not with me? No! Do not let me see the misery that would come upon my father." (Genesis 44:18, 34)

What a turn-around! Judah, Jacob's fourth-born son, all his life seemed to be a pushy, all-for-Judah type of person. Actually, it was in the interest of having food on the table that he talked Jacob his father into letting Benjamin go with him and his brothers on their return to Egypt.

Now he stands before the prime minister of Egypt pleading eloquently, humbly for Benjamin, whom Joseph feigns to detain.

Judah says to Joseph, "If the boy is not with us when I go back to your servant my father and if my father, whose life is closely bound up with the boy's life, sees that the boy isn't there, he will die. Your servants will bring the gray head of our father down to the grave in sorrow. Your servant guaranteed the boy's safety to my father. . . .

"Now then, please let your servant remain here as my lord's slave in place of the boy, and let the boy return with his brothers" (Genesis 44:30–33).

What an about-face! And at a time in life when men and women supposedly are set in their ways and not inclined to change.

Come to think of it, I have some closet skeletons I am not proud of. Character traits I do not like have hounded me all my life, embarrassing me, marring my relationships with others. Judah is evidence that with God's help I can change. Even now!

Father, continue to conform me to the image of Jesus. Amen.

MARCH 22

Joseph

*"Joseph is a fruitful vine, . . .
the prince among his brothers."
(Genesis 49:22–26)*

Most people lead tame lives compared with Old Testament Joseph.

Joseph started out under the psychological burden of being his father's favorite among 12 sons. That does not endear a boy to his older brothers. Add to that the death of his mother at an early age. Add to that being sold by his brothers into slavery in Egypt before he was out of his teens. In today's jargon, Joseph could be termed "disadvantaged."

Joseph was indentured to Potiphar, captain of the king's guard. He worked so well that his master put him in charge of everything he owned. Then just when life seemed to show promise, Potiphar's scheming wife falsely accused Joseph. And Joseph was jailed.

Resilient as ever, Joseph gained the confidence of the jailer. He interpreted the dreams of two new inmates. And then, at age 30, through a fantastic turn of events, Joseph was elevated from prisoner to prime minister of Egypt. Less than a decade later, he realized the achievement for which all his life until then had been but preparation: the preservation of his Hebrew people from extinction by famine. And there is reason to think he continued to rule until his death at 110.

Joseph accepted life as it came. He made the best of every circumstance. Through adversity and favor, he believed a God of purpose was in control. It was faith well placed. Joseph's life turned out to be exceedingly fruitful.

Father, I accept Your sovereignty over my life. Amen.

MARCH 23

To Be Continued

Continue to work out your salvation with fear and trembling. (Philippians 2:12)

When I see the word continue in an admonition that applies beyond the initial readers, I presume it can refer to me in retirement as well as to those younger in age. When I see the word used in relation to salvation, I have every reason to believe the matter is of utmost importance.

What did Paul mean when he told the believers at Philippi to "work out [their] salvation?" Is salvation, contrary to what the Bible elsewhere affirms, something earned by works?

No. Salvation is unearned. Jesus did it all. It is a gift received from God when people believe the good news that Christ "was delivered over to death for our sins and was raised to life for our justification" (Romans 4:25).

Then why would Paul tell the Philippians to "work out" their salvation? *The JFB Commentary on the Whole Bible* suggests, "Salvation is 'worked in' by the Spirit once for all; it needs to be progressively 'worked out' by obedience, through the help of the same Spirit, unto perfection." To allay confusion, Paul added, "It is God who works in you to will and to act according to his good purpose" (Philippians 2:13).

Why did Paul say they were to work out their salvation "with fear and trembling"? "Not because of doubt," comments Gaffin in the NIV Study Bible, "but with singleness of purpose in response to God's grace." Says JFB again, "Trembling anxiety not to fall short of the goal—as befits servants."

Father, thank You for Your work; help me with mine. Amen.

MARCH 24

The Cross!

May I never boast except in the cross of our Lord Jesus Christ, through which the world has been crucified to me, and I to the world. (Galatians 6:14)

How absurd it all seems. Two rough-hewn pieces of wood ultimately fastened together and planted in the earth. An instrument of diabolical torture, liberally used by the iron-fisted Romans to instill stark fear in those they subjugated.

Yet in the amazing divine prescience, what symbolized man's inhumanity to man became the mark of God's saving grace.

Christ crucified. The very words are anomalous. *Christ* was Israel's cherished hope, the name of her Deliverer, her Savior. *Crucified* had about it a halo of hopelessness and the stench of death. But two words that do not go together God put together to display His greatest sign and His profoundest wisdom.

The sign? God died. God who was life itself died. The miracle was not Jesus' resurrection from the dead. If He was God He had to live. The miracle was that He being God could die and be buried.

The wisdom? God found a way to be merciful and holy.

God's holy righteousness is satisfied whenever a sinner dies. But God is also merciful. He does not want any to perish. How could God be merciful to the sinner and at the same time satisfy His righteousness?

The answer: Christ crucified. Jesus, the infinite holy Sacrifice died in the sinner's stead. At Calvary "love and faithfulness meet together;/ righteousness and peace kiss each other" (Psalm 85:10).

Father, I worship You in awe and wonder. Amen.

MARCH 25

Your Counsel

*I will instruct you and teach you in the
way you should go;
I will counsel you and watch over you.
(Psalm 32:8)*

Moving from Point A to Point B at retirement time is more complex than it might seem.

In our case, as with most retired people, it means selling our present home if we are going to buy or build elsewhere. Since selling and buying or building consume an indefinite quantity of time, there is almost certain to be a gap when we are in limbo—unless we should rent.

Under present tax rules, renting is an option we need at least to consider. Depending on two unknown factors—inflation and interest rates—paid-up ownership of a house may no longer be the best investment of limited resources. Inflation favors ownership. High interest rates may favor renting. Renting might save us a second move. And if Marge or I should find ourselves in need of a retirement home sooner than we expect, it is relatively easy to terminate a rental arrangement.

I am thankful for a God who promises to guide us! My method of operation has been to list on paper the several options, and, under each, as many pros and cons as I can think of. These we discuss—not just Marge and I, but the other family members, too. After a course of action seems relatively clear, we take it. But we remain ready to reconsider if conditions change.

After having our Pennsylvania home on the market just eight days, we now have a buyer. That is Step One in our odyssey from Pennsylvania to North Carolina.

Father, we are depending on Your leadership! Amen.

MARCH 26

How Fleeting Life

*"Let me know how fleeting is my life. . . .
Each man's life is but a breath."*
     (Psalm 39:4–5)

Someone has determined that the average American in a lifetime will spend a total of

*six months sitting at stoplights
*eight months opening junk mail
*one year looking for misplaced objects
*two years unsuccessfully returning telephone calls
*five years simply "killing time."

Trivialities take up much of Americans' time. In addition to waiting at stop lights and looking for misplaced objects, there is television (the largest time waster of all). There are also the telephone calls that *do* get through. (Admittedly *some* of the conversations are non-trivial, and the fact that I cared enough to call may be important.)

How can I account for such an utter waste of irreplaceable minutes? Am I unaware that "life is but a breath," as "fleeting" as the day I now am living in? Am I still under the illusion that life goes on forever? That death may happen to others but not to me? That there will be no time of reckoning when I stand before the judgment seat of Christ?

Each week of retirement brings me closer to the day when I shall give account for the things done while I was "in the body." Each week brings me closer to eternity.

Father, "teach [me] to number [my] days aright,/ that [I] may gain a heart of wisdom" (Psalm 90:12). Amen.

MARCH 27

He Endured

Jesus . . . endured the cross, scorning its shame. (Hebrews 12:2)

Any inquiry into what transpired those hours Jesus hung on the cross must be undertaken with humility and utmost reverence.

Surely for One as sensitive and pure as He, the mockery cast at Him by onlookers and passers-by was as sore a trial as the intense physical agony. It is human to wish to defend one's unsullied name, and Jesus was human.

The passers-by cast their insults: "Come down from the cross, if you are the Son of God!" (Matthew 27:40).

The chief priests, the teachers of the law and the elders added their mockery: "He saved others," they said, "but he can't save himself!"(27:42).

Even the two dying thieves joined in the taunts.

The irony was that Jesus could have saved Himself. He could have descended from the cross. What a dramatic display of divine glory and power it would have been: Jesus physically pulling Himself from the nails that held Him, retrieving His garments from the astonished soldiers and then by superhuman strength bringing instant retribution upon army, priests, rabbis, elders and all the others who were approving His crucifixion.

Instead, Jesus endured the cross, scorning its shame. And in the midst of His unbelievable suffering, physical and mental, He transacted my redemption. On that cross and in His death He paid the penalty of my sins.

Because Jesus endured, I am set free.

Father, do not let the wonder of Calvary ever leave me. Amen.

MARCH 28

"Older Men"

Teach the older men to be temperate,
worthy of respect, self-controlled, and sound in faith,
in love and in endurance. (Titus 2:2)

Paul's short letter to Titus is a blueprint of how God expects the Christian community to function. Included in the letter are God's expectations for "older men." Four words cover the bases: *temperate, worthy, self-controlled, sound*.

Older men are to be temperate. The word applies to every aspect of their lives from food intake to manual labor, from sleep to snow shoveling, from physical exercise to TV viewing. Moderation is the new watchword.

Older men are to be worthy of respect. More so in Bible times than now, old age was honored, gray hair was respected. But there was a flip side: it behooved the older person to be worthy of respect. That onus still rests upon the older man.

Older men are to be self-controlled. Self-control is a sign of strength. Paul writes elsewhere, "I beat my body and make it my slave so that after I have preached to others, I myself will not be disqualified for the prize" (1 Corinthians 9:27).

Finally, older men are to be sound. A board is sound if it is solid and unweakened by knots. Currency is sound if it is backed by tangible assets. Older men are to be sound in faith, in love and in endurance.

Older men displaying these Spirit-actuated virtues are an asset to the Christian community and a powerful witness to the watching world.

Father, help me attain these attainable expectations. Amen.

MARCH 29

"Older Women"

*Teach the older women to be reverent
in the way they live. (Titus 2:3)*

In his letter to Titus, Paul invests the younger minister with instructions first for "older men." Then, in somewhat greater detail, he has instructions for the "older women."

The overarching consideration is reverence—a respect for God and His commands that translates into day-by-day attitude and behavior. Two specific negatives: they are not to slander and they are not to be "addicted to much wine" (Titus 2:3).

Their major assignment is the training of younger women. Paul mentions a seven-point course:

1. "To love their husbands"
2. "To love their children"
3. "To be self-controlled"
4. "To be pure"
5. "To be busy at home"
6. "To be kind"
7. "To be subject to their husbands so that no one will malign the word of God" (2:4–5).

Such instruction needs to be verbalized. After all, this is God's Word, and God's women need to take it seriously. But if God's older women are to communicate adequately to the younger, they must also be models of all they teach. Only when example matches precept will they be taken seriously.

There is, of course, a fringe benefit. As the older women exemplify these biblical instructions, they will discover their own lives crowned with serenity and purpose.

Father, our Christian community needs this lifestyle! Amen.

MARCH 30

Productive Lives

Our people must learn to devote themselves to doing what is good, in order that they may provide for daily necessities and not live unproductive lives. (Titus 3:14)

The "Puritan work ethic," so insidiously maligned today, is in reality the Bible work ethic.

Jesus' admonition to "not worry about . . . what you will eat or . . . wear" (Matthew 6:25) was pronounced in the context of a still higher priority: God's " 'kingdom and his righteousness' " (6:33). Jesus was not denigrating gainful work. Ample other Scriptures underscore the importance of honest work, both to keep people from the temptations accompanying idleness and to provide income for family and the less fortunate.

I note that Paul calls gainful employment "good." It is only good, of course, if it contributes to the well-being of the race. So pervasive has been the infiltration of detrimental products (such as alcoholic beverages in grocery stores) that few jobs can be totally "good" in the biblical sense.

But where does this leave me, a retired person? Is there a cut-off point after which the admonition does not apply? Probably. But probably it is not age 65. Those who *cannot* work are excused. The able-bodied are to work.

If past employment has served to provide for my present necessities, I can still devote myself to doing what is good. If I am paid for what I do, I can find good uses for the money. If I am not, I still have the satisfaction of knowing my work has made a contribution to someone's well-being.

Father, I thank You that I can still be productive. Amen.

MARCH 31

The Real Miracle

Jesus said, "It is finished." With that, he bowed his head and gave up his spirit. (John 19:30)

Christians speak of the "miracle" of Easter. But the real miracle occurred three days earlier—at Calvary.

The real miracle came after the spikes had been pounded and the taunts had been flung and the lonely "Why?" had been asked. It came when Jesus, bearing the sins of humankind, died. In His death, "God was reconciling the world to Himself in Christ" (2 Corinthians 5:19). If Jesus was who He claimed to be—God's coequal—Easter was a foregone conclusion. No grave could possibly have held Him. The miracle that defies human logic is that Jesus, who is Life personified, could die.

Jesus laid down His life. Death was not inadvertent but calculated and voluntary. Situated squarely between the unrepentant and the forgiven, between earth and heaven, the Focus of all humankind at the focal point of all history, died.

The Calvary miracle made possible my salvation. Otherwise, God would have had no reason to even look at me, let alone save me. As Moses lifted up the bronze snake in the desert (Numbers 21:6-9), so Jesus was lifted up, "that everyone who believes in him may have eternal life" (John 3:15). "God so loved the world that he gave his one and only Son, that whoever believes in him shall not perish but have eternal life" (John 3:16). That promise is broad enough to include everyone.

I do not know how God brought about the miracle of Jesus' death. But I thank Him that He did.

Father, let me ever appreciate Your Calvary miracle. Amen.

APRIL 1

Important Census

Only those [will enter the Holy City] whose names are written in the Lamb's book of life. (Revelation 21:27)

The United States Constitution mandates a census every 10 years in order that representation in the lower house of Congress will remain proportional.

Keeping statistical track of people is as old as civilization itself. Bible readers have long been impressed by the remarkably detailed genealogies of Old Testament times, dating all the way back to Adam. Twice God ordered the numbering of the Israelites (Numbers 1 and 26).

It was a "census . . . of the entire Roman world" (Luke 2:1) that sent Joseph and Mary to Bethlehem on the eve of Jesus' birth. And the early church kept careful track of its "population": the 120 gathered in the Upper Room on the day of Pentecost (Acts 1:15), the 3,000 added that day (2:41), the increase of men to 5,000 shortly thereafter (4:4).

But by far the most important listing anyone will ever attain is in what the Bible calls "the Lamb's book of life." Those on that list will have free access to the promised Holy City, the heavenly Jerusalem, and to God Himself. They are promised aesthetic beauty, security, fellowship, provision, light (see Revelation 21:10–22:5).

Any who miss out on that census have a hopeless future—a future of judgment when "earth and sky" flee before the awesome presence of the One seated on the great white throne, and "the dead, great and small," stand there to be judged (Revelation 20:11–15). "If anyone's name was not found written in the book of life, he was thrown into the lake of fire."

Father, I pray for people who need to be included. Amen.

APRIL 2

Hollow, Hollow

The tempter came to [Jesus] and said, "If you are the Son of God, tell these stones to become bread." (Matthew 4:3)

Satan, who tempted Jesus at age 30 in the desert region of the lower Jordan Valley, does not give up on Jesus' followers at age 60, wherever they live. But the fact is, Satan's temptations are as hollow now as they were then.

Satan thought he had a one-two punch for Jesus by suggesting Jesus command the stones to become bread. First, he knew that Jesus was hungry, as Matthew informs us (Matthew 4:2) in the understatement of understatements. Second, Satan pretended to be begging for visible proof of Jesus' deity. In one creative fiat Jesus could have dispelled Satan's doubts, at the same time satisfying His own need for food.

But like all the temptations that Satan flings, this one had no real substance. Satan did not need proof that Jesus was God's own Son. And the bread would have brought Jesus only momentary satisfaction.

The "cravings of sinful man, the lust of his eyes and the boasting of what he has and does" (1 John 2:16) involve transient things. The luxurious new car, that attractive younger woman, my boasts about past accomplishments—the satisfactions are hollow, hollow. God alone provides what I need; in that provision I am to be both content and thankful.

"The world and its desires pass away," the Scriptures advise me, "but the man who does the will of God lives forever" (1 John 2:17). To do God's will must be my ever-present goal.

Father, when Satan knocks, I will just say no. Amen.

APRIL 3

In Writing

The tempter came to him and said ... Jesus answered, "It is written ..." (Matthew 4:3–4)

Lest I should forget, God reminds me of an important fact: His written Word—the Bible—is His intended means of communicating with His children.

I have just finished reading the second of two books, both by Christian authors, that evidence how far some of God's people have strayed from that bedrock principle. In one, the author made much of her nocturnal dreams. She supposed each one had some message of wisdom or guidance for her. The other author, a military chaplain, relied heavily on inner impressions. He even stopped preparing sermons for the troops. When it came time to preach, he depended on God to put words in his mouth.

The Scriptures attest to God's occasional use of dreams to guide His people (though the isolated incidences across more than four millennia are not a strong argument for depending on this means of communication). Likewise, intuitions and impressions come from time to time—to saint and sinner. My own experience has been mixed: sometimes the intuition has been appropriate; as often, it has been a false signal.

When Jesus did battle with Satan, His resort was the written Word. If He—very God of very God—looked to the written Word for guidance and spiritual victory against the enemy, I, who have far less reason to rely on my intuitions, instincts and dreams, had better follow His lead.

Father, I dare not trust the arm of flesh. Nor need I. You have given me Your written Word. Amen.

APRIL 4

Not Over Yet

When the devil had finished all this tempting, he left [Jesus] until an opportune time. (Luke 4:13)

Luke adds an important detail to his account of Jesus' temptation in the desert, on the high mountain and on the temple's pinnacle. Luke says Satan left Jesus "until an opportune time." Otherwise, I might have concluded that Satan, having been rebuffed three times by Jesus, gave up permanently.

A little reflection on the gospel narratives, however, and I should know that Satan did not leave Jesus alone—anymore than he leaves me alone. Temptation is an ever-present fact of spiritual life. No temptation, no spiritual life.

I am guessing that Jesus' most persistent and threatening temptation during His three and a half years of public ministry was the temptation to abort the whole redemption project. It is hard to imagine disciples quite as obtuse as the twelve whom Jesus selected (who may have been the cream of the candidates). And I cannot imagine the pressures on Jesus in Gethsemane as He faced the raw physical and spiritual torture of the 15 hours immediately ahead of Him. I am eternally grateful that He did not yield to temptation.

Satan continued to tempt Jesus. And I can expect Satan to continue to tempt me. It is not over yet. Satan keeps on looking for the "opportune time." But because Jesus himself "suffered when he was tempted, he is able to help those who are being tempted" (Hebrews 2:18). I need not face Satan by myself. Jesus has promised to help me overcome.

Father, when Satan knocks, I will let Jesus answer. Amen.

APRIL 5

Two More Miracles

Jesus called out with a loud voice, "Father, into your hands I commit my spirit." When he had said this, he breathed his last. (Luke 23:46)

As I said earlier, the real miracle of Easter came when God's Son, Jesus Christ, the personification of life, died. That was the supreme miracle. But His death on Calvary's cross made possible two other miracles.

The first of the two was my salvation. Through faith, I who was "dead in [my] transgressions and sins," was "made ... alive with Christ" (Ephesians 2:1, 5). I am a forgiven person. The past is behind me. In Christ I am "a new creation" (2 Corinthians 5:17). "The old has gone, the new has come!"

The second miracle was this: Even as Jesus, God's Son, identified Himself with me and my sin, so I was identified with Him. He died for me; I died with Him.

That is important. The Bible says: "Count yourselves dead to sin but alive to God in Christ Jesus. Therefore, do not let sin reign in your mortal body so that you obey its evil desires. Do not offer the parts of your body to sin, ... but rather offer yourselves to God" (Romans 6:11–13).

The Calvary miracle brought atonement for my sins. But my identification with Jesus in that death also was the satisfactory antidote for my sinful nature. "I know that nothing good lives in me, that is, in my sinful nature" (4:18). For that reason, "there is now no condemnation for those who are in Christ Jesus, because through Christ Jesus the law of the Spirit of life set me free from the law of sin and death" (8:1–2).

Father, I accept Calvary's second miracle, too. I no longer belong to myself, but to Christ who died for me. Amen.

APRIL 6

God's Temple

Do you not know that your body is a temple of the Holy Spirit? (1 Corinthians 6:19)

Holy living at age 60-plus is no easier than holy living at age 20 or age 30. For every fading temptation, a new one comes along to take its place. And some of the temptations I thought would have faded by this time are still around. Give Satan credit: he is persistent!

The above question put by Paul to the Corinthian Christians—doubtless a mix of people young and older—was posed in the context of his discussion of sexual immorality. "Flee from sexual immorality," Paul said (6:18)—a warning, incidentally, no less appropriate to retired than to younger Christians.

Because of that context, people tend to think of holy living negatively, in terms of what they should *not* do. But holy living in essence is the Holy One living within me—God's temple—living out His holy life through me. I am holy not because I refrain from the well-publicized sins. I am holy because Jesus lives in me.

At the dedication of the desert tabernacle, the glory of the Lord filled the tent: "Moses could not enter the Tent of Meeting because the cloud [of God's presence] had settled upon it, and the glory of the Lord filled the tabernacle" (Exodus 40:35). God "took over" His house.

Much later, when Solomon dedicated the temple, again "the priests could not enter . . . because the glory of the Lord filled it" (2 Chronicles 7:2).

When the presence of the Holy One fills me, nothing else has a chance to get in.

Father, let me be continually filled with Yourself. Amen.

APRIL 7

Clearing the Air

Then God said, "Let the land produce vegetation: seed-bearing plants... according to their various kinds." And God saw that it was good. (Genesis 1:11)

The National Arbor Day Foundation is diligent in its message to Americans: the ecological well-being of this country is dependent on its trees. Strip the land of its trees and the result is soil erosion, less rainfall and a plethora of ills in an ecological system tied to adequate vegetation.

House plants perform similar ecological services. Not only do they generate vital oxygen, which can be lacking in today's well-insulated houses, but they absorb many home pollutants. One 10- to 12-inch potted plant per 100 square feet of floor space will clear the air of health-threatening pollutants.

For new houses that may have formaldehyde pollutants, spider plants, philodendrons, golden pothos and snake plants are best. Gerbera daisies, chrysanthemums and other flowering plants are especially useful against benzine pollutants. For general air purification, reed palms, English ivy, peace lilies, mother-in-law's tongue, Chinese evergreens, dracaenas, aloes and banana trees are recommended.

In my retirement years I am discovering a latent love for things growing. At little expense, either in finances or time, I can enjoy a part of God's good creation within the environs of my home. And, as in nature itself, that vegetation, while beautifying its surroundings, is hard at work to make those same surroundings a better, more healthful place.

Father, thank You for Your beautiful provision! Amen.

APRIL 8

Rule of Peace

Let the peace of Christ rule in your hearts, since as members of one body you were called to peace. (Colossians 3:15)

When all is said and done, peace has been one of God's greatest gifts to me. How reassuring it is to know that my times are in His hands. I still remember the couplet Harold M. Freligh, my Bible college professor, used to quote:

> In the center of the circle of the will of God I stand. There can be no second causes; all must come from His dear hand.

God's peace keeps me in equilibrium. It keeps me fit to live with. It spares me huge quantities of worry. Probably it has already added years to my physical life.

To be tranquil is not exactly my nature. I am a clock watcher and a worrier. I do not like to sit still, to be without something to do. Push, push, push! Do not walk if you can run! "Give every fleeting moment something to keep in store./ Work, for the night is coming!"

But along with the activity, God gives me peace. Not automatically, however. The exhortation to "let the peace of Christ rule in your hearts" was addressed to a whole body of Christians in Colosse. Paul adds, "As members of one body, you were called to peace." I must *allow* God's peace to rule in my heart. My fellow believers must allow God's peace to rule in their hearts, too. We are to be a peaceful community.

Peace is one objective God has for His church.

Father, only Your peace can keep me peaceful. Amen.

APRIL 9

Broken Cycle

Since the children have flesh and blood, [Jesus Christ] too shared in their humanity so that by his death he might . . . free those who all their lives were held in slavery by their fear of death. (Hebrews 2:14–15)

The life-death cycle that has been repeated since Adam and Eve must seem cynical to the nonbeliever who stops to think about it. Birth, growth, marriage, children, work, old age, death—*ad infinitum*. Is there a purpose in it?

That winsome little first-born of ours that Marge and I, as young parents, welcomed with such joy on a cold December 5th in Bennington, Vermont, now has her own family. And we her parents are aging. At the outside, we may last another 30 years. More realistically, we will be dead in less than 20. And Rebecca, our daughter, is also aging. In due time we will all be forgotten in our graves as succeeding generations follow.

Most of my contemporaries suppose that is all there is to life. They fight to remain alive because they know of nothing beyond death. They prefer life, however demanding or even cruel, to the anonymity of the grave. They do not know that Jesus "shared in their humanity so that by his death he might . . . free those who all their lives were held in slavery by their fear of death." Death is not the end; for the Christian it is the beginning of an exciting eternal existence for which our present life is merely preparation.

Jesus saved physical life from being, in fact, a meaningless cycle. We were born not to die but to live eternally in heavenly glory. Jesus freed us from the fear of death.

Father, thank You for sending Jesus to break the cycle. Amen.

APRIL 10

Generosity/Fairness

"Are you envious because I am generous?" (Matthew 20:15)

The question comes at the climax of Jesus' parable about the workers in the vineyard. The landowner had contracted with day laborers to work his vineyard. When the time came for settlement, the landowner paid each one the same—those who had worked all day and those who had worked only the final hour. "Unfair!" cried those who were hired earliest. To these grumblers the landowner replied, "Are you envious because I am generous?"

Fairness was not the issue. Envy was. Much of human envy springs from another's generosity and masquerades under protests of "unfairness."

Jesus said His story related to the kingdom of heaven (20:1). I happen to be one who entered in the "morning." Actually, I have always regarded God's service as a privilege, not a hardship or a drudgery. When people enter the kingdom late, my only regret is that they waited so long and missed so much.

But one class of late-comers admittedly violates my sense of fairness: those who have committed flagrant crimes against society. It is unfair that God should offer them His salvation and let them enter heaven. *Or is it?* Am I simply displaying my own spirit of envy?

I need to see myself as I really am and own up to attitudes that are not Christ-like. When I was young and future-oriented, such matters of fairness did not bother me. Now that I am older and past-oriented, I find myself taking the part of those disgruntled day laborers in the vineyard.

Father, help me to face up to un-Christian attitudes. Amen.

APRIL 11

Second Residence

*This is what the high and lofty One says—
he who lives forever, whose name is holy:
"I live in a high and holy place,
but also with him who is contrite and
lowly in spirit,
to revive the spirit of the lowly
and to revive the heart of the contrite."
(Isaiah 57:15)*

It is consistent with God's nature that He should live "in a high and holy place." It is harder to understand why and how He can also elect to reside in the hearts of any of His creation—even those who are "contrite and lowly in spirit." That He does so is a mark of His great love.

But as with all God does, there is purpose in His residence within my fellow believers and me. He wishes to "revive the spirit of the lowly/ and to revive the heart of the contrite." I see two things in healthy tension here: (1) To gain God's presence in my life, I must be contrite and humble in spirit. But contrition and humility, while laudable as attitudes, are not of themselves appealing to the onlooking world I am commissioned to disciple. So (2) God breathes animation—new life—into my spirit and heart. He revives me. And the watching world sees not simply the contrition and humility but the deep-seated, indomitable joy and praise resulting from God's presence within. *That* is attractive. *That* stirs people's interest. *That* impresses them.

In such a context God can make known to the whole earth His holiness, His exaltation, His eternity.

Father, I am unworthy—totally unworthy. Revive my spirit and my heart. May Your presence in me attract people to You. Amen.

APRIL 12

Unfailing Promise

*Surely goodness and love will follow me
all the days of my life,
and I will dwell in the house of the Lord
forever.*
(Psalm 23:6)

The well-known conclusion of Psalm 23 takes on new significance for me as a retired person wondering if Social Security will hold out, concerned by the talk of catastrophic medical costs, made lonely by the passing of friends and relatives. God's promise of "goodness and love" covers "all the days of my life."

There is one caveat, however. The promised goodness and love are not to lead me or even necessarily to accompany me. They are to *follow* me. David himself—the writer of Psalm 23—was not always in the best of circumstances. There were times when his soul had to be "restored." There was the "valley of the shadow of death" (the margin reads "darkest valley"). There were times when he needed the Lord's "comfort."

But through the disciplines of rod and staff, through the bleak places *before* the "green pastures" and the "quiet waters," David was aware of a caring God whose goodness and love followed him day after day. With God present in his life, he need "fear no evil." Inspired by what he knew of God's faithfulness in the past and convinced of God's unchanging character, he could project confidently that God's goodness and love would continue to follow him all the days of his life.

For David it worked out just that way—all the days of his life. Cannot I expect the same?

Father, in retirement more than ever I need You. Amen.

APRIL 13

Momentary Trouble

Our light and momentary troubles are achieving for us an eternal glory that far outweighs them all. (2 Corinthians 4:17)

I am walking as little as possible today. The reason? In the darkness last night I tripped over a misplaced footstool in the family room, spraining a toe. It is no major calamity. I managed to get the injured digit into a work shoe this morning, and I should be back to normal soon.

But the incident was another reminder that physical health—at whatever level it may be today—is not going to be forever. Heart disease, cancer or any number of ailments may strike as unexpectedly as that errant footstool.

Had I turned on a light when I ventured through the family room in the darkness, I would be walking normally this morning. It is a reminder that I should be prudent in matters relating to my physical health: sensible diet, proper rest, enough exercise. Prudent, but not paranoid.

And if, in spite of my prudence, disease or injury comes, I need to accept that intrusion as part of the "all things" in which "God works for the good of those who love him, who have been called according to his purpose" (Romans 8:28). I need to recognize God's providence in every circumstance.

God's first concern for me is not my health but my holiness. He wants me to be "conformed to the likeness of his Son" (Romans 8:29). Being human, I do not relish the means God may use to accomplish His objectives. But, remembering the "eternal glory that far outweighs," I must not complain.

Father, I will try not to complain, whatever You send. Amen.

APRIL 14

Back to Work?

... so that you will not be dependent on anybody.
(1 Thessalonians 4:12)

Somewhere along the line, Marge may decide to get a job. (I consider myself gainfully employed with projects like this devotional book and some continuing editorial work for Christian Publications, Inc., in Camp Hill, Pennsylvania.)

Flexible part-time work would be ideal, leaving Marge free to do some of the discretionary things that interest her. If she gets work, her reasons for doing so are several:

1. It will add to her sense of self-esteem. She will know that she is not sidelined, that she still has valuable talents. Such a tonic cannot be lightly dismissed.

2. It will provide intellectual stimulation. Marge will be using her mind, learning new information, solving problems, achieving goals. That, too, is salutary for someone restricted by the circumstances of retirement.

3. It will be socially stimulating. Rubbing shoulders with people beyond the limited circle of friends Marge has met at church and in the neighborhood will appreciably broaden her horizons. More than I, Marge is a social being. I can stand solitude. She—and many women—cannot.

4. It will give her time away from me. She needs that, as I noted earlier.

5. It will add to our income. Insofar as possible, it will be Marge's income to spend on the things she feels are important but which we cannot otherwise afford.

Father, never let me disparage the advantages of work. Amen.

APRIL 15

Leadership

Besides everything else, I face daily the pressure of my concern for all the churches. (2 Corinthians 11:28)

Spiritual leadership demands a full measure of devotion.

It also demands time with God. Gerald W. Welbourn, a Christian and Missionary Alliance minister, once told me of his first visit in the home of his future father-in-law, the late Tracy Miller, also an Alliance church pastor. As a young seminarian, unschooled in the art of prayer, Mr. Welbourn witnessed the five o'clock arising of that man of God, watched as he opened his Bible to hear from God, observed the uninterrupted hour in intercession. That early morning schedule was habitual with Tracy Miller. It was a part of the discipline of spiritual leadership.

Leadership as well demands initiative. E. H. Carne had the distinction of being in China with the celebrated Robert A. Jaffray. On one occasion the two of them were captured by Chinese bandits. Their captors, believing them to be rich businessmen, demanded an exorbitant ransom.

"As they pressed their point with waving pistols," recalled Mr. Carne, "the peace of God kept us calm. To demonstrate that we were indeed missionaries, Dr. Jaffray requested permission to preach to them in their own language. With some reluctance the chief gave permission.

"Down to the level of those sinful men Jaffray went," Mr. Carne continued, "declaring that 'all have sinned,' going on to affirm that there was salvation for all through Jesus."

That kind of dedication is motivated by love.

Father, intensify my love for You and for people. Amen.

APRIL 16

Open Door

Practice hospitality. (Romans 12:13)

It is interesting to note how many people are making "one more visit" before our contemplated move to North Carolina. It is fun to have them with us—people like my sister, Elizabeth Huck. It is fun for me, for at last I have time to participate in the visit instead of being the working person who rushes home for dinner and a brief evening's conversation. Liz looks upon North Carolina as a formidable drive from Warren, Pennsylvania.

I am thankful for a wife who likes to cook, who enjoys entertaining, who has the ability to make people feel welcome. Especially is this so because God enjoins His people to "practice hospitality." It was to be one of the hallmarks of "overseers" (1 Timothy 3:2). Practical Peter carries hospitality a step further. He tells us, "Offer hospitality to one another without grumbling" (1 Peter 4:9). Marge does not grumble.

I wonder if Peter could have been thinking back to that Sabbath when Jesus and presumably some of the other disciples arrived—probably unannounced—at his house after church (Luke 4:38). Poor Mrs. Simon! Her mother sick in bed with a high fever, housework routine in disarray, and a horde of hungry men in her kitchen looking for something to eat!

But Mrs. Simon rose to the occasion, and somehow it all worked out, just as it always does when Jesus is in it. There was, in fact, a bonus blessing for the Simon household. Jesus brought healing to Peter's mother-in-law, and she pitched in to help get the meal on the table.

Father, let hospitality be a habit at my house. Amen.

APRIL 17

Amram and Jochebed

Amram married his father's sister Jochebed, who bore him Aaron and Moses. Amram lived 137 years. (Exodus 6:20)

It would be interesting to make a study of all the *parents* of outstanding men and women. How many of them may have looked on their own lives as failures—accomplishing seemingly little of lasting significance.

Available biographical data affirm one thing overwhelmingly: Behind almost every successful man or woman are parents—and frequently grandparents—whose character and exemplary lives profoundly influenced their offspring.

The Scriptures offer us but the barest of details concerning a couple known as Amram and Jochebed. If the genealogical records in Exodus 6 are complete, they were third generation descendants of Levi, the priestly son of Jacob. Amram died at age 137.

Those are the facts—except for one other detail. Two of their children are mentioned: Aaron and Moses.

Suddenly Amram and Jochebed, otherwise just obscure historical footnotes, spring to life, animated by the fame of their notable offspring. These are the parents who "by faith . . . hid [Moses] for three months after he was born, because . . . they were not afraid of the king's edict" (Hebrews 11:23).

Without Amram and Jochebed, there would have been no Moses or Aaron. Without their able parenting, Moses and Aaron might never have developed into the spiritual leaders they became.

Am I praying for my children and grandchildren? My influence can yet be incalculable.

Father, I give myself to prayer for my children. Amen.

APRIL 18

Miriam

Then Miriam ... sang to [the women]. (Exodus 15:20–21)
Miriam ... began to talk against Moses. (Numbers 12:1)

It is heady to be a spiritual leader, the focus of others' admiration and esteem. A person does not have to be a church pastor or the president of her district women's group to get the feeling. Teaching Sunday school, playing the piano, handling the finances will do. But beware! "Pride goes before destruction,/ a haughty spirit before a fall" (Proverbs 16:18).

Miriam's life is an illustration.

Miriam was Moses' older sister, probably the person who "stood at a distance" (Exodus 2:4) to discover the fate of her baby brother in the basket among the reeds along the bank of the Nile. If so, it was Miriam's timely initiative, when the princess found Moses, that secured for him the care of his own mother.

Miriam was in her 80s on that joyous day when Israel triumphed over Pharaoh at the Red Sea. It was a day of great celebration. Miriam, with tambourine, led the women—also with tambourines—in the chorus of Moses' song: "Sing to the Lord,/ for he is highly exalted./ The horse and its rider/ he has hurled into the sea" (15:21). Imagine half a million tambourine-waving women praising God in song! Unforgettable!

But this prophetess who could sing God's praises could also talk against God's leader—her brother Moses.

God judged Miriam at once, inflicting leprosy on her. Moses prayed, and God graciously healed Miriam. But the stigma of that one sinful lapse has followed her until now.

Father, deliver me from the sin of pride. Amen.

APRIL 19

Aaron

Then the Lord's anger burned against Moses and he said, "What about your brother, Aaron the Levite? I know he can speak well." (Exodus 4:14)

Why is it that in their commentaries on the important people of the Bible, writers say so little about Aaron? Could it be that Moses, his younger brother, eclipsed him?

Aaron was already 83, squarely in the senior citizen category, when he first appears in the Scriptures. Whatever he did during 60 working years besides making bricks as one of Pharaoh's slaves, God does not tell us. What he did upon his retirement from the brickyard contributed immeasurably to Israel's national and spiritual history.

Aaron was a spokesperson for God to Moses (Exodus 4:16). He and Moses stood side-by-side as they faced off against Pharaoh over their people's fate. Aaron was Israel's first high priest, officiating in Israel's desert tabernacle. In the crucial battle against the Amalekites (Exodus 17:10–13), he figured prominently in the victory. Aaron was one of the select few whom God allowed on Mount Sinai to see God in person (Exodus 24:9–11).

Aaron was not perfect. The infamous golden calf (Exodus 32:4) was his doing. He once rebelled against his brother's leadership (Numbers 12:1–2). He was implicated with Moses in disobediently striking—not speaking to—the rock from which God brought forth water (Numbers 20:9–12). Nevertheless, he goes down in history as an exemplary man worthy of our emulation.

Father, age did not keep Aaron from serving You effectively. May I take encouragement in that knowledge. Amen.

APRIL 20

Moses - I

Moses said to the Lord ... "If you are pleased with me, teach me your ways so I may know you and continue to find favor with you." (Exodus 33:12-13)

If we could stretch a line from Moses in the Old Testament to Paul in the New, only Jesus Christ, the Son of God, would stand taller than those two towering giants.

Moses took his "retirement" early—on the back side of the Sinai desert. As he tended his father-in-law's sheep, he had 40 years to reflect on his failure as a self-appointed deliverer of his enslaved kinspeople. There in the desert he met God at the burning bush and received God's commission to deliver Israel from Egyptian slavery—doing it *God's* way. At age 80, Moses returned to work to begin the real mission of his life.

Moses' conversation with God at the Tent of Meeting outside the desert encampment strikes me as almost impudent: "You have said, 'I know you by name and you have found favor with me.' If you are pleased with me, teach me your ways." Is that any way to talk to Sovereign Deity? But God did not consider the request impudent. He welcomed the words because Moses had an inner desire to know God, to understand His ways, to please Him.

I harbor a similar desire to know God and to understand His ways so that I may please Him. God answered Moses' prayer, and, except for that one lapse, noted yesterday, when he struck the rock with his rod rather than to speak to it, Moses pleased God. I may not achieve such near-perfect obedience, but I sincerely want to know God better.

Father, teach me Your ways so I may know You and continue to find favor with You. Amen.

APRIL 21

Moses - II

By faith Moses . . . persevered because he saw him who is invisible. (Hebrews 11:24–27)

Any person who doubts that there is life after 60 has never considered Moses!

In an epoch of outstanding people—Abraham, Joseph, Joshua, Deborah, David, Daniel—Moses stands head and shoulders above them all. Yet Moses achieved all of his greatness in the last trimester of his life, *after he was 80*.

I can tap into any of Moses' accomplishments, from his successful confrontations with Pharaoh to his last address to the Israelites on the threshold of Canaan, and I am looking at a man who "persevered." Even if I should scale down Moses' longevity to more closely approximate today's experience, what he did was achieved in what would correspond to my age 59 through 84. And he was vigorous to the end.

In his advancing years Diogenes, the Greek philosopher, was advised by a friend to rest. To that suggestion the spunky man replied disdainfully, "If I were running in the stadium, ought I to slacken my pace when approaching the goal? Ought I not rather to put on speed?" Diogenes may have overdrawn the analogy—I need to face the limitations of age sensibly—but I cannot help but admire the man's spirit. Far from giving up, he was still ready to take on the world.

Margaret and Bartlett Hess, in *Never Say Old*, observe that "the idea of age as a time to rest may be self-fulfilling." The more I rest, the more I may have to rest!

Father, keep me persevering to the end as I look to Jesus. Amen.

APRIL 22

Jethro

Jethro, Moses' father-in law, . . . came to him in the desert, where he was camped near the mountain of God. (Exodus 18:5)

His name means "excellence." All that we know about this desert-dwelling priest of Midian is positive.

He befriended Moses when Moses fled from Pharaoh, offering him a home and even one of his daughters as a wife (Exodus 2:21). He provided work for Moses (3:1). He cared for Moses' wife and her two sons while Moses was negotiating with Pharaoh and leading the Israelites from Egypt (18:2).

Despite Jethro's pagan background, he praised God, "who rescued [Israel]," adding, "Now I know that the Lord is greater than all other gods" (18:10–11).

The very senior Jethro had constructive counsel for Moses. He observed Moses' extremely demanding schedule not only as national leader and intermediary with God, but as judge of the people's petty and not-so-petty disputes. He advised Moses to "select capable men . . . who fear God, . . who hate dishonest gain" (18:21), and delegate responsibility to them.

Some argue that Moses was wrong to accept advice from a pagan. But constructive advice not contrary to what God teaches should be welcome whatever the source. Jethro's counsel, as Crichton observes, turned out to be precedent-setting. He distinguished between legislative and judicial functions. He taught the importance of insuring that all law is the expression of the Divine will. He stressed that those who apply it must be people of ability, piety and integrity.

Father, let me accept truth, whatever its source. Amen.

APRIL 23

A Brother Passes On

"Aaron will be gathered to his people." (Numbers 20:26)

Did a moment of cold fear grip Moses as God announced to him that Aaron's time had come? So much is left unsaid in the brief account of Aaron's passing.

Aaron and Moses had grown up together in Egypt. Brothers can become very close in the growing up process. I know, because I have a brother, David. Of course, there also had been long years of separation—while Moses lived in Pharaoh's palace and while Moses was a fugitive in Midian.

Then there was that fateful reunion. The two brothers accepted God's call to deliver their people from bondage. Together they faced an irrational Pharaoh. Together they bore the hard-to-take wrath of their own people. The ten plagues, the Red Sea, the water crises, the food crises, the Amalekite crisis—both men stood shoulder-to-shoulder through them all.

They were together on Sinai. Together they saw the tabernacle become a reality. They were together as they carried out God's instructions for the census. Together they survived the rebellion of Korah and company. They were nearly inseparable—the younger, the acknowledged leader of that massive migration; the older, the nation's first high priest.

Atop Mount Hor, Moses took the priestly garments from Aaron and transferred them to Eleazar, Aaron's son. I wonder if there was time for a tearful embrace and a heart-felt "Good-bye for now!" as those two elderly brothers, knowing the separation would be brief, bowed to Aaron's upward call.

Thank You, Father, for brothers and sisters. Amen.

APRIL 24

God Bears My Burdens

Praise be to the Lord, to God our Savior,
who daily bears our burdens.
(Psalm 68:19)

My burden today was an unscheduled waste of time.

I have always been time-conscious, and in retirement more so, perhaps because I know the days are not limitless. My frustration today was a house guest who overslept, delaying breakfast by nearly two hours. And I had mapped out a full day's schedule of things that needed doing.

My irritation was inappropriate for several reasons.

1. If I cannot do the planned things, I can do other things. Time is only wasted if I choose to waste it. I can read. I can pray. I can reflect and meditate.

2. I must be open to the possibility that *God* engineers the changes of plans for a purpose. Is there a lesson He wants to teach me? Is there an alternate duty He wants me to perform? Am I sensitive to His leadership?

3. I must guard against a selfish perspective. *My* time, *my* schedule may be symptoms of an un-Christian attitude that will only get worse with age.

"God . . . daily bears my burdens." I must "cast all [my] anxiety on him because he cares for [me]" (1 Peter 5:7).

Our guest was rested and refreshed for his long drive home. He left our house encouraged in spirit and with pleasant memories. Even if the two hours had been an utter personal waste (and they were not), my friend profited.

That, after all, is the important point.

Father, help me to put far from me my fretting spirit. Amen.

APRIL 25

To Live Is Christ

To me, to live is Christ and to die is gain. (Philippians 1:21)

Paul wrote the words during what most Bible students now consider the first of two Rome imprisonments. The possibility of death lurked in the background, for Caesar's power was absolute. Yet Paul knew that a sovereign God controlled Caesar Nero. Whether Paul lived or died was God's decision, not the crown's.

In his mind Paul carefully weighed the alternatives. "If I am to go on living in the body, this will be fruitful labor for me. Yet what shall I choose? I do not know! I am torn between the two: I desire to depart and be with Christ, which is better by far; but it is more necessary for you that I remain in the body" (Philippians 1:22–24).

I, at about Paul's age, do not yet share his sanguine view of death. Frankly, I would rather "remain in the body" and find my satisfaction in "fruitful labor." But that is because I am not under Roman house arrest, chained to guards who accompany my every step, dependent on friends for my food. There is nothing like adversity to turn the mind toward heaven.

But back to the text. As far as Paul is concerned, to live is Christ. Some have misread his words and suppose he is saying, "For *me* to live is Christ." Not at all! Paul was already dead, crucified with Christ (Galatians 2:20). He is here affirming the secret of dynamic, satisfying life. It is "Christ in you," as he tells the Colossians (Colossians 1:27). It is letting Christ live His life in me.

When Jesus has His rightful place in my life, living is Christ and dying is gain.

Father, I give Your Spirit right-of-way in my life. Amen.

APRIL 26

Things God Cannot Do

Among the gods there is none like you, O Lord. (Psalm 86:8)

God, as the theologians like to say, is omnipotent, omniscient and omnipresent—all-powerful, all-knowing, always present in all places. Christians jealously defend those attributes of Deity. To deny any one of them is to detract from God's essence.

It may then come as a surprise to learn that there are some things God cannot do.

God cannot lie (Hebrews 6:18). He is absolute Truth. His integrity is Gibraltar-solid. He can be depended on.

God cannot sin. God is the "high and lofty One . . ./ whose name is holy" (Isaiah 57:15). He is absolutely righteous. More easily could light and darkness occupy the same space at the same time than could holiness and sin intermix.

God cannot change. "I the Lord do not change," He declares through His prophet Malachi (3:6). It was said in a context of mercy—"So you, O descendants of Jacob, are not destroyed"—and with the plea "Return to me."

God will not remember my sins. He who formed atoms and molecules as well as planets and galaxies, He who numbers every hair and catalogs every sparrow has deliberately forgotten the sins I have committed. "I will forgive their wickedness/ and will remember their sins no more" (Jeremiah 31:34, repeated in Hebrews 8:12 and 10:17).

God will not sleep. "He who watches over you will not slumber" (Psalm 121:3). God is watching over His chosen ones. Nothing escapes His observation.

Father, I am a child of a great, loving God! Amen.

APRIL 27

Sunday School

Do your best to present yourself to God as one approved, ... who correctly handles the word of truth. (2 Timothy 2:15)

Institutions, like some medicines, tend to have a limited shelf life. Some people think the Sunday school, now more than 200 years old, has reached that point.

For me, Sunday school is a 65-year habit. Some of my earliest memories are of Sunday school. I first became a Sunday school teacher when I was a teen, and I have been either a teacher or a regular class member ever since. But it is more than sentiment that holds me faithful to the Sunday school.

I go to Sunday school because *I need the Word that is taught there*. I find the Spirit-instructed Sunday school teacher, even if he or she lacks the formal Bible education I have had, is able to minister the Word to me.

I go to Sunday school because *I want to set a good example*. I am influencing others for either good or ill. I want to be a good influence on those who look to me.

I go to Sunday school because *the Sunday school needs me*. Rare is the school with enough qualified teachers and assistants. I can make the director's job easier by helping.

The Sunday school is important. It acquaints children with the whole body of Christian truth. It integrates youth into the church at a time when many of them want to throw off restraints. It brings new adult converts as quickly as possible to a level of familiarity with the Bible and its application to life. It is an effective means of evangelism and church growth.

Father, make me ever faithful to the Sunday school. Amen.

APRIL 28

Be Still

"Be still, and know that I am God." (Psalm 46:10)

The hyperactive, fully charged 24-hour-a-day society of my work years was not friendly to my desire to know God. Blaring radios, yakking TVs, ringing telephones, *varooming* autos, putt-putting lawnmowers, buzzing chain saws, noisy carpet vacuums, argumentative children, chatting adults produced a cacophony of distracting sound that frustrated my quest.

Only by sheer power of concentration was it possible to filter out the clamor and meditate.

Now that I am retired, I have a somewhat greater command of my environment. Relative solitude is more easily come by. An uninterrupted hour is actually attainable—sometimes.

God tends to reveal Himself in the silence. Elijah witnessed rock-shattering wind, earthquake and fire, but God was in the "gentle whisper" that followed (1 Kings 19:11–12). Moses climbed to the isolation of Mount Sinai—far above the din of the encampment below him—to meet God. Abraham had the solitude of the Judean hills.

"Be still," God says. It is what He said in effect to Peter, prattling on the Mount of Transfiguration about making three tabernacles. "This is my Son. . . . Listen to him!" (Matthew 17:5). It is what He decreed through His inspired prophet Habakkuk: "The Lord is in his holy temple;/ let all the earth be silent before him" (Habakkuk 2:20).

"Be still." Dare to turn off the noise, to be totally alone. "Be still and know that I am God."

Father, I stand on holy ground. I worship You. Amen.

APRIL 29

Bear with, Forgive

Bear with each other. . . . Forgive as the Lord forgave you. (Colossians 3:13)

God's wonderful peace imparted to individual believers has a twofold purpose. He intended it to keep me, as an individual, serene. He intended it to keep His church harmonious.

It is the nature of human beings to offend others—doubtless a by-product of the Fall. Sometimes the offense is inadvertent; I do not realize I have offended the other person until someone calls it to my attention. More frequently, I am soon aware of my transgression. Although I may repent of it at once, the damage has been done.

Those like me whom God has called into public ministry seem to be endowed with thick skin; otherwise we might not survive the criticism. (Some do not.) As a magazine editor, I tried to be empathetic toward writers whose articles did not "fit" and therefore had to be rejected. May they forgive me for all the inner pain my "I am sorry, but" letters cost them.

Now I am entering the most critical time of my life. In the course of the past decades I have amassed a large amount of experience. I am knowledgeable on a number of subjects, even expert on a few. I will be tempted to cut through needed discussion with a final "This is it. This is the way it has to be." But that course will bring disharmony to the fellowship.

And before long I will find myself on the outside wondering why people will not listen.

Father, I learned by trial-and-error. Help me to be tolerant of others who learn the same way. Amen.

APRIL 30

Work Rushes In

Whatever your hand finds to do, do it with all your might, for in the grave, where you are going, there is neither working nor planning nor knowledge nor wisdom. (Ecclesiastes 9:10)

What everyone tried to tell me is true. For the retired person work rushes in to fill the available time. I seem to have no more discretionary time now than when I was employed.

In one sense, I guess that is good. Life would be tedious indeed if I had nothing to do. But I think of the projects I had planned to do—projects I *want* to do—and I begin to wonder if there will be time for them. Will the tyranny of the urgent keep me from the important?

As a child I learned the first part of Ecclesiastes 9:10: "Whatever your hand finds to do, do it with all your might." In other words, be diligent; give every project your best effort; a job worth doing is worth doing well. Now that I am older, I think I understand why. Somewhere out ahead of me is a grave. Life is a race against time. Only my heavenly Father knows how much time I have left. And the question is not simply how much time until death arrives, but how much time do I have until the aging process incapacitates me and I can work no more?

I must re-learn to use that little word *no*. It is easy to become overcommitted. After all, time is plentiful. If not today, there is always tomorrow.

That is a fallacy. The tomorrows are limited. I must set priorities and put first things first. Only in that way can I be a faithful steward of each of these retirement days.

Father, give me grace to say no when I need to. Amen.

MAY 1

Mercy Triumphs

Mercy triumphs over judgment! (James 2:13)

Judgment is ahead. It is on the agenda for the believer as well as the unbeliever. For the believer, the Scriptures suggest a way he or she can "triumph over judgment."

"Speak and act as those who are going to be judged by the law that gives freedom," wrote Jesus' younger brother, James, "because judgment without mercy will be shown to anyone who has not been merciful" (James 2:12).

The words are a reminder of Jesus' own statements in His Sermon on the Mount: "Blessed are the merciful,/ for they will be shown mercy" (Matthew 5:7), and "In the same way you judge others, you will be judged, and with the measure you use, it will be measured to you" (7:2).

Could Jesus and James have had in view the coming day when "we must all appear before the judgment seat of Christ, that each one may receive what is due him for the things done while in the body, whether good or bad" (2 Corinthians 5:10)? Probably.

Should a church gloss over the sins of its members? Hardly. Those in the church who sin are to be judged by the church (1 Corinthians 5:1–5). But the objective of such judgment is restoration. For the offender in Corinth, judgment brought repentance and contrition. Therefore, the congregation was to "forgive and comfort" (2 Corinthians 2:6–7). Restoration.

To the believers in Galatia Paul wrote: "If someone is caught in a sin, you who are spiritual should restore him gently" (6:1). Again, restoration. "Mercy triumphs over judgment!"

Father, deliver me from my vindictive spirit. Amen.

MAY 2

Planning Ahead

*Since I have been longing for many years to see you,
I plan to do so when I go to Spain. (Romans 16:23-24)*

Albert E. Peterson, a public affairs coordinator for the American Association of Retired Persons, used to say that most people plan more for a two-week vacation than they do for the rest of their lives. His point is well taken.

The Bible cautions against worrying about the future, but it is not against planning for the future. God, however, does expect me to recognize in my planning His right to overrule at any time. I am His servant.

As a retired person, I face three possibilities:

1. I can make no plans, set no goals, and suffer the emptiness of having achieved little or nothing.

2. I can let others set my agenda. There will be no lack of eager programmers who want a chauffeur, a shopper, a baby sitter, a for-free handy man.

3. I can set my own retirement goals (subject to God's will) and make each day enjoyable, satisfying.

Option two may at first look very "spiritual." Did not Jesus go "around doing good" (Acts 10:38)? But on closer analysis, Jesus' life was a planned life, not a series of chance events. Even He spent only part of His time helping people.

My plans, like Jesus' plans, must include acts of kindness and helpfulness. I am to be a good neighbor. Thankfully, retirement allows more latitude for such activities. But if I let these things take all my time, I can end up very frustrated.

Father, I will plan as best I can, but You may overrule. Amen.

MAY 3

What Counts

The only thing that counts is faith expressing itself through love. (Galatians 5:6)

The above statement is Paul's summary to conclude his vehement argument against Jewish circumcision for Christians. Despite the decision of the Jerusalem Church Council (Acts 15:1–20), certain die-hard Christian Jews were attempting to convince the believers in Galatia that they must adopt Judaism's baggage, submitting to circumcision and keeping the entire Mosaic Law.

Paul, himself a Law-keeping Jew, recognized that such a salvation-by-works straitjacket for Gentile Christians would totally negate their gracious freedom in Christ Jesus. It was precisely because Jews had been unable to keep the Mosaic Law that God unveiled His Ultimate Solution, Christ Jesus.

The Law demanded total obedience. Anyone failing at any point was under the Law's curse. "Christ redeemed us from the curse of the law," Paul avowed (Galatians 3:13).

The issue, the apostle concluded, was not circumcision versus uncircumcision. He said, "The only thing that counts is faith expressing itself through love."

Faith, of course, does not stand by itself. It requires an object. Jesus is the object—Jesus who died to atone for sins and who rose again to justify all who believe. Love also requires an object. For the Christian, love has two objects: God, who first loved sinful mankind, and neighbor—both those within the family of believers and those who may enter as a result of fervent prayer and faithful witness.

Father, help me major on faith expressed through love. Amen.

MAY 4

Rules for a Good Day

Whoever would love life and see good days must keep his tongue from evil and his lips from deceitful speech. He must turn from evil and do good; he must seek peace and pursue it. (1 Peter 3:10–11)

"Have a good day!" is now the standard blessing after every conversation, every purchase, every encounter. Except for one crotchety soul who did not want anyone telling *him* what to do with his day, people still are warmed by the other person's solicitude, sincere or not.

But simply being wished a good day is not enough. There are five rules I must follow to make good days happen:

1. I "must keep [my] tongue from evil." Though small, the tongue has far-ranging ability. It can wreak great havoc.

2. I must refrain from "deceitful speech." Psalm 34, from which Peter quotes his counsel, reads, "keep . . . your lips from speaking lies" (34:13). Always speaking the truth is essential.

3. I "must turn from evil." Jesus said that just *thinking* evil is tantamount to doing evil (see Matthew 5:21–22, 27–28).

4. I must "do good." Turning from evil is laudable; turning to good deeds completes the transformation. Both are important.

5. I must "seek peace and pursue it." Peace requires an initiator. And often someone willing to go the second mile.

To the keeper of these five rules comes a special personal blessing: good days.

Father, help me keep the rules for good days. Amen.

MAY 5

Dependent Giving

*"We have given you only what comes
from your hand." (1 Chronicles 29:14)*

On my desk is a light bulb-shaped glass jar filled with colored paper clips—a Christmas gift several years ago from my granddaughter, Sarah. I treasure that container with its paper clips, not because of its monetary value but because Sarah chose it herself for me. If someone needs a paper clip from my desk, he or she must take the plain variety from another repository. The paper clips Sarah gave me are for display only!

The above Scripture text would be better illustrated if I had given Sarah the money for that jar of paper clips. Instead, Rebecca, her mother, did. Rebecca gave Sarah money so she could choose and buy Christmas gifts for family members. Sarah gave from the money she had been given.

King David, in donating materials for the temple his son Solomon would build, admitted to a similar circumstance. "We have given you only what comes from your hand," he publicly told God. I have to confess the same.

The moral of the story is two-fold. First, any kind of self-congratulation for what I give to God and His kingdom work is totally misplaced. The resources were God's to begin with. Second, if it is God's gift to begin with, I as a committed follower of Jesus Christ should be very careful about how much of God's largess I divert to my selfish desires.

In retirement as in the earning years, I am a steward of the resources God has entrusted to me.

Father, by Your help I will be a faithful steward. Amen.

MAY 6

Undeserving

"Who am I, O Lord God, . . . that you have brought me this far?" (1 Chronicles 17:16)

If humility is a sign of greatness, David's exclamation as he "sat before the Lord" further confirms his nobility.

At that point in his life, David could have been excused for a trace of pride. After years as a hunted fugitive, he had achieved the kingdom God promised him. He had conquered fortified Jebus, renaming the city Jerusalem and making it his capital. A long list of skilled warriors had joined his army. He had decisively subdued the Philistines in a victory that caused surrounding kings to fear his power. He had brought the ark of God to Jerusalem. His family had greatly expanded.

David wanted to build a permanent house for the ark of God. But God postponed those plans, promising that David's son would build a temple for the ark. Any petulance David might have felt as God countermanded his temple plans was assuaged by the promise that David's dynasty would continue.

"Who am I, O Lord God, and what is my family, that you have brought me this far? And as if this were not enough in your sight, O God, you have spoken about the future of the house of your servant."

"Who am I?" David was just a shepherd boy willing to let God work through him to accomplish His purposes, whether slaying Goliath or ruling 2 million Israelites.

Who am I? No one. But God delights to inhabit the humble and use them in mighty ways.

Father, who am I that You have brought me this far? I praise and thank You. Amen.

MAY 7

God Still Leads

The Lord is my shepherd...
He leads me... (Psalm 23:1–2)

As Marge and I headed the car toward North Carolina on another scouting trip, loneliness gripped us. The "closing" on our Pennsylvania house was only a month away. In North Carolina we as yet had nothing. We felt like people without a country.

A warm, mid-morning sun bathed the Pennsylvania countryside. The dogwood was in full bloom. Picturesque farms on either side of the four-lane were newly ploughed. Surrounded by such beauty, were we foolish to move south? Had we run ahead of God? Somehow, all the pieces of our transition were not falling neatly into place.

That evening in North Carolina, after dinner with our daughter Rebecca and her family, she and I drove up to the lot in Garner that Marge and I had earlier staked out. Our house plans were still in limbo. Whether or not we ultimately built, we obviously needed a place to live soon.

The next morning, we contacted Sonia Bourne, the realtor who on our earlier visit to the area kindly had spent a good part of two days showing us houses. Mrs. Bourne said she had another place or two she would like to show us. And so it was that we found The House.

The moment we turned in the driveway, we sensed that this was it. There was the front porch Marge wanted. And the energy-efficient, well-laid-out interior that I wanted. Only 13 years old, it had been well kept up.

Before the day ended, we had signed a purchase agreement.

Father, will I ever learn that You are always on time? Amen.

MAY 8

Perfection

Our prayer is for your perfection. . . .
Aim for perfection. (2 Corinthians 13:9, 11)

I am a perfectionist. Between those who are perfectionist-high-strung and those who are perfectionist-impossible-to-please, the term has become considerably tarnished. No matter. When it comes to moon shots and compact audio disks, perfection is still a respected word.

When Paul prayed for the Corinthians' perfection, he probably was not thinking of flawless electro-mechanical function or note-perfect performance. Corinth was notorious. The Corinthians were farther down the moral scale than most of the people whom Paul evangelized. As his letters to them indicate, they still had a long way to go before anyone would pronounce them perfect.

But that is the incredible thing about Paul. He had the ability to accept people as they were and to urge and pray them into what they ought to be. So he said to these yet very imperfect Corinthians, "I am praying for your perfection." And a sentence or two later: "Make perfection your aim."

Being a perfectionist and being morally perfect are two very different matters. There are musicians who can play flawless Bach whose lives are a moral shambles. And there are Christians whose walk with God is close to perfect who fall far short of perfection in other everyday ways.

When it comes to the moral perfection Paul most certainly is speaking of, it can only be achieved as I turn over to the indwelling, perfect Christ total, absolute control of my life.

Father, now is not too late to take action. Amen.

MAY 9

Two Worlds

What is seen is temporary, but what is unseen is eternal. (2 Corinthians 4:18)

Carolyn Jenkins, my faithful secretary at Christian Publications, just called. Her news was a shock: Earl Moore, retired printer at the publishing house, a man my age, had died of a heart attack while mowing his lawn.

Only a day or two before, Earl had stopped by Christian Publications to say hello to his friends. No one could have guessed that his time was about to run out.

Earl was a quiet fellow. Like so many Pennsylvanians, he loved the out-of-doors. He loved to hunt and fish. Earl had a subtle, delightful sense of humor. He was very capable mechanically; he could get our aging press to run after everyone else had given up. I hated to see Earl retire because he was such an asset to the company. But his wife, Shirley, was battling cancer, and he felt the need to be at home to help care for her.

It is not for Earl that I sorrow today. Thanks to Jesus, Earl has made the transition from the temporary to the eternal. My prayers and concern are for Shirley. Dear Shirley—so bravely optimistic amid her devastating illness! Whenever Earl visited the office, I would inquire about Shirley. Each time, the report was less encouraging. Shirley is now housebound. Earl's funeral will be at home so she can attend. Thankfully, she has a son and new daughter-in-law to look after her.

Father, God of all comfort, comfort Shirley. And now that You have again reminded me how temporary the seen is, may I fix my gaze ever more intently on what is eternal. Amen.

MAY 10

Encounter with Death

*"Where, O death, is your victory?
Where, O death, is your sting?"
(1 Corinthians 15:55)*

A young wife whom I think I never met, wrote me some years ago about the passing of her mother.

"Mother and I were always very close," said Alice (not her real name). "Because of our similar interests, we did a lot of sharing." When Alice's mother was found to have cancer, the whole family was devastated.

There followed weeks of cobalt treatments. Supported by the family, Alice's mother recovered and put all further thought of cancer from her mind—until the six-month check-up, when more cancer was discovered. "Again," said Alice, "discouragement and despair went hand-in-hand with the horrible word *cancer*."

But Alice made an important discovery: the struggle was maturing her spiritually. As the months turned into years and her mother's cancer progressed slowly but inexorably, Alice found herself "still growing, still learning."

As the end approached, Alice and one of her sisters, with promised assistance from a county visiting nurse, got permission to care for their mother at home. "I will never regret those two weeks," Alice said. "I received much more than I gave."

How does Alice sum up her encounter with death? "It was one of victory and even joy. I knew Mother was in God's holy presence.

"Defeat? Despair? Discouragement? Not in the least! God's grace *is* sufficient. He does not let us face anything without giving us the strength to endure."

Father, give me the victory when I face death. Amen.

MAY 11

If I Should Die

"You now dismiss your servant in peace." (Luke 2:29)

Must I continue this morbid subject? Now is as good a time as any. Unless Jesus intervenes by His second coming, death will come to me at some point. Perhaps now, before it seems too imminent, I can talk about it in a detached manner.

There may be, of course, unwanted prior suffering, but for the Christian who loves God, death is the instant realization of all he or she has lived and hoped for. For the spouse, death is a devastating experience. If the survivor is the wife—and, statistically, she will be the survivor—the loss may be compounded by a lack of knowledge of her husband's business affairs. I need to let Marge know

- what my burial wishes are
- what burial funds there are
- what and where our financial resources are
- what income she as my widow can expect
- what our recurring financial obligations are (bills paid by automatic bank withdrawal, car insurance, property taxes, federal and state income taxes)
- to whom she should go for financial advice.

My reluctance to face the inevitable, coupled with my natural penchant for procrastination, tempts me to put off these matters. But if I truly care for my wife, I will not. If *I* were the one suddenly bereaved, I would be grateful for an orderly list of directions to guide me.

Father, with Your help I will make such a list today. Amen.

MAY 12

Cremation?

... that ... Christ will be exalted in my body. (Philippians 1:20)

The Bible makes no direct statement about cremation. But I must still reckon with its symbolism.

When in Bible times a person died, there were three major treatments of the body: embalming, cremating, interment. The Egyptians embalmed, believing that the natural body continued in the afterlife. Other nations burned their dead—a symbolic denial of any afterlife. Interment was the practice of the Hebrews.

It was with interment in mind that Paul set forth the truth of the resurrection in terms of seed sown and sprouted. "The body that is sown is perishable, it is raised imperishable; ... it is sown a natural body, it is raised a spiritual body" (1 Corinthians 15:42–44).

The symbolism is clear. Neither elaborate embalming (believing the physical body will continue its usefulness) nor fatalistic cremation (a denial of any life beyond the present) symbolizes the Christian concept of resurrection.

The Romans followed pagan Greek custom and cremated their dead. But cremation stopped with the Romans. Why? *Because the vibrant early Christian church opposed cremation.* Not until the late 1800s, under the influence of secular humanism, did Western civilization begin again to cremate.

Of Abel the Bible says, "By faith he still speaks, even though he is dead" (Hebrews 11:4). In the instructions I leave concerning my body, I too, though dead, will still speak.

Father, by Your help, in death I will express my faith! Amen.

MAY 13

Through Generations

*[The Lord's] faithfulness continues through
all generations. (Psalm 100:5)*

More than 35 years ago today, I debarked in Manila with Marge and two children to begin a missionary career in the Philippines. We were met at the wharf by a youngish Ralph Bressler, the mission director, who escorted us through several days of immigration formalities and accompanied us on a DC-3 flight to Zamboanga City, then our Mission headquarters.

Intrepid H. W. Edmonds was on his way home to retirement after a lifetime of ministry among the tribespeople of Cotabato and Davao provinces. E. F. Gulbranson had yet to pioneer the first church of our denomination in Manila. The William Christies were mainstays at what is now Ebenezer Bible College.

There were other young missionaries who entered the work at about the time Marge and I did. Some have persevered to earn the love and respect of grateful Filipinos. Others, like my wife and me, have found our steps directed into other paths.

The years have moved inexorably on. Most of those whom we as young missionaries looked up to are already with Jesus. Younger people who regard *me* as an elder are now our denomination's leaders. And the founding fathers are two generations farther removed.

I have faced these changes with confidence. As in the past, so among my peers there have been godly men and women. And the Spirit-filled leaders who follow will be equally godly and probably even more effective.

Father, Jesus is unchanged—yesterday, today, forever. Amen.

MAY 14

Mother

"Honor your father and your mother, so that you may live long in the land the Lord your God is giving you." (Exodus 20:12)

This fifth command is called by Paul "the first commandment with a promise" (Ephesians 6:2). As I said earlier, I have tried all my life to follow it.

God never intended this particular command to be limited to minors. All ten commandments were first given to predominantly adult Israel. God's admonition to "honor" father and mother, set forth in His fifth command, applied to adult Israelites as well as to their children. It applies as well to me for as long as my parents live—and beyond.

Marge's mother, still living, is the kind of person that inspired the old gospel songs about Mother's prayers and Mother's Bible. How we have appreciated her and her prayers! After Dad Dailey died in 1963, Mother lived with us for a time. She enriched our lives by her presence. All four of our children still feel very close to her.

During these past five years in Pennsylvania, we have lived near Mother, who herself chose to be at The Alliance Home, a retirement center in Carlisle. Although she is very comfortable there, she welcomes the opportunity to come over to our house for a change of scenery and some of Marge's home cooking (Mother especially relishes fresh-cooked vegetables).

We are thankful that one of Marge's sisters, Evelyn Putnam, and her husband, Wayne, also live at The Alliance Home. With that very special provision, we feel more free to relocate.

Father, I reaffirm my commitment to honor my parents. Amen.

MAY 15

Eleazer

The Lord said to Moses, . . . "Get Aaron and his son Eleazer and take them up Mount Hor. Remove Aaron's garments and put them on . . . Eleazer." (Numbers 20:23–26)

A new order was about to begin. Forty years of desert wanderings had produced essentially a new generation of Israelites. Of the old leadership troika, Miriam, older sister to Aaron and Moses, had already died and was buried at Kadesh (Numbers 20:1). Now the summons was coming for Aaron, father of Eleazer, who had served as Israel's first High Priest.

Up the mountain Eleazer went with his aged father and his nearly-as-old uncle. As the whole assembly watched from the plain below, Eleazer waited as Moses transferred the high priestly garments from father to son.

Did Eleazer, certainly at least in his sixties, question the wisdom of such an assignment so late in life? For more than three decades he had been ministering at his father's side. He could rightly have retired, all responsibility behind him. But then there was his name. It meant "help from God." Surely God's call was God's provision. He could count on God's help.

Eleazer plunged at once into high priestly duties that would continue through the conquest and apportionment of Canaan. Immediately ahead was Israel's second census, which he helped Moses accomplish (Numbers 26:1–4). He also assisted in Joshua's inauguration (27:18–23). The new leadership team was complete. At last Israel was ready for the Promised Land!

Father, You are indeed the Helper. Like Eleazer, my need of You increases as I enter this stage of my life. Amen.

MAY 16

Caleb

Caleb ... said, ... "Here I am today, eighty-five years old! I am still as strong today as the day Moses sent me. ... Now give me this hill country that the Lord promised me that day." (Joshua 14:6, 10–12)

Caleb has to be one of the most inspiring people in the whole Bible. Not always are political leaders physically or morally strong. Caleb was both.

Caleb was sent by Moses with the other 11 tribal princes to explore Canaan. Unlike 10 of his compatriots, he was sure Israel could overcome the "powerful" people and their "fortified and very large" cities (Numbers 13:28). "We should go up and take possession of the land," he urged, adding confidently, "We can certainly do it" (13:30). Caleb had faith in God.

It must have been a bitter disappointment to Caleb when Israel's little faith meant a 38-year wait before he could enter the promised land. That wait stretched another five years before the conquest of Canaan had been achieved.

At age 85, having outlived all his contemporaries except Joshua, his strength undiminished, his courage still strong, Caleb finally realized his ambition. "From Hebron Caleb drove out the three Anakites, ... descendants of Anak" (Joshua 15:14).

God leaves to my imagination everything else about this remarkable prince-soldier. But Caleb must have felt a great sense of personal satisfaction as he lived out his final years, surrounded by children and grandchildren in the mountains of Hebron he personally had conquered.

Father, give me faith to wait and courage to conquer. Amen.

MAY 17

Joshua

"As for me and my household, we will serve the Lord." (Joshua 24:15)

Joshua is another of those remarkable older people God has planted throughout His Holy Book. Joshua was 78 years of age when he took over the leadership of the children of Israel from Moses, and he was 85 by the time he had successfully led the nation in its conquest of Canaan.

Twenty-five years of leadership after *that*, at age 110, this hardy patriot and humble man gathered all of Israel's leaders (Joshua 23). And what was on his mind? He was concerned that Israel follow God fully.

Next, Joshua assembled at Shechem "all the tribes of Israel" (24:1) Again, his concern was that the people follow God fully. Speaking as a prophet, he traced God's unmistakable hand in their 717 years of national history from Abraham's lonely sojourn into Canaan through the 430 years in Egypt and the mighty exodus under Moses to their present occupancy of the Promised Land.

"Now fear the Lord and serve him with all faithfulness," the venerable leader counseled. "Throw away the gods your forefathers worshiped beyond the River and in Egypt, and serve the Lord. But if serving the Lord seems undesirable to you, then choose for yourselves this day whom you will serve" (24:14–15).

And Israel agreed to follow God (24:21).

Joshua's final public act was to "[make] a covenant for the people" and to "[draw] up for them decrees and laws" (24:25) binding Israel to its promise. Joshua did all he could all his life to keep Israel loyal to the Lord God.

Father, give me Joshua's zeal to follow You fully. Amen.

MAY 18

Othniel

When [the Israelites] cried out to the Lord, he raised up for them a deliverer, Othniel. (Judges 3:9)

Othniel was not a "name" in Israel—at least, not at first. But he was related to one: Caleb. Othniel was Caleb's younger brother—younger by at least 20 years. Despite the age disparity, the two men had at least one characteristic in common. Othniel shared Caleb's remarkable courage.

Othniel comes in view as Israel has completed the initial conquest of Canaan. Caleb had been promised Hebron as an inheritance—the very land he had scouted as one of the 12 spies sent out by Moses. Joshua complied and Hebron became Caleb's city. When Caleb challenged someone to capture neighboring Debir, Othniel stepped forward and did so. Othniel was courageous.

Othniel could have been no older than 19 when Israel faced its moral crisis at Kadesh-Barnea. Otherwise, he would have perished in the desert, just as the rest of that disobedient generation did. Thirty-eight years of desert wandering and five subsequent years in Canaan probably brought Othniel to senior status by the time he captured Debir. Yet it was to be another 25 years until God called and empowered this man of courage to lead Israel against the encroaching Aramites.

The terse account in Judges reads: "The Lord gave [the] king of Aram into the hands of Othniel, who overpowered him" (3:10). Victory—in the strength of the Lord! And "the land had peace for forty years, until Othniel son of Kenaz died."

Another senior makes his mark!

Father, let me not think that life is already over! Amen.

MAY 19

Gideon

Gideon, son of Joash, died at a good old age. (Judges 8:32)

Frequently, it seems, a young man or woman may rise to prominence—perhaps as a writer, a musician or a sports figure—only to fade with equal suddenness.

Gideon was such a person. He was not a writer, a musician or an athlete, but a military leader. As a young man, he directed the northern tribes of Israel in a spectacular rout of the Midianites, effecting total deliverance for his people from that oppressive quarter and 40 years of peace.

So highly regarded was Gideon that his countrymen wanted to make him king. He wisely declined (Judges 8:23). God was their Ruler. But the people desperately needed a godly human leader who would rid the land of idolatry and teach the true worship of Yahweh. Gideon was the logical choice. Instead, Gideon elected to withdraw from public life.

Following his signal victory against the Midianites, Gideon "went back home to live" (8:29). He married many wives, produced 70 sons—and coasted to his grave.

Gideon, full of so much potential as Israel's deliverer, took the line of least resistance. He fulfilled his days, but he fell far short of being the godly leader he might have been. In the end, he was as much an object of pity as a hero.

The people quickly forgot God, and just as quickly returned to Baal worship (8:33–34). In a revulsive, posthumous slaughter, Abimelech, Gideon's son by his concubine, killed all but one of Gideon's other 70 sons (9:5).

Father, do not let me stop now—so near my goal. Amen.

MAY 20

Manoah

They ... buried [Samson] ... in the tomb of Manoah his father. (Judges 16:31)

Many come into retirement full of heartache because of a wayward son or daughter. To such, Manoah has a message.

The Bible does not divulge the ages of Manoah and his unnamed wife when Samson was born to them. That Manoah's wife was "sterile and childless" (13:3) implies they were not young.

Not only was Samson a miracle baby, but he was also a child of destiny. He was to "begin the deliverance of Israel from ... the Philistines" (13:5). Imagine Manoah's joy!

But what does a father do when his child of destiny fails to follow the script? when he or she rebels against sound upbringing? when he or she marries unwisely?

"Samson led Israel for twenty years," the Scriptures report (15:20). *Led?* Samson *led?* The record is of a petulant playboy whose riddles get solved by trickery, whose anger turns violent, whose superhuman strength is never quite focused.

Manoah went to his grave with that image of his son. For when Samson died in the collapse of the Philistines' idol temple, he was buried "in the tomb of Manoah his father."

The temple collapse inflicted long-term damage on Israel's adversary, the Philistines. It killed the entire ruling class, leaving the nation at loose ends and leaderless. In the context of that physically violent era, Manoah's wayward, playboy son fulfilled his destiny after all.

Father, be pleased to let all of my children realize Your purpose for their lives. Amen.

MAY 21

The Devotional Life

Grow in the grace and knowledge of our Lord and Savior Jesus Christ. (2 Peter 3:18)

The New Testament carries no specific instruction concerning what is commonly called the devotional life. There is no reference to regular Bible reading and prayer.

I need not regard this silence as a gross oversight. That the New Testament writers prayed there is no doubt. They admit as much in nearly every book. But is prayer the major ingredient of the devotional life? What, exactly, does the term mean?

Several New Testament expressions seem to delineate it. Paul speaks of keeping one's "spiritual fervor" (Romans 12:11). In another letter he crowds three separate images into a single sentence: *Live* in Christ *rooted, built up* in Him (see Colossians 2:6–7). An apt expression used by Jesus is *remain in*. "Remain in me," Jesus said. "I am the vine; you are the branches" (John 15:4–5). Sever the vital connection and the fruit withers and the branch is of no value. The devotional life is an every-moment process of living in Christ.

Does this excuse me from a set time for privately meeting God in worship, praise and prayer around His Word? It did not excuse Jesus; it should not excuse me.

But blocks of time and particular routines of prayer or Bible reading do not constitute the devotional life. Rather, every waking moment I am to live in Christ and draw my strength from Him. The devotional life is not simply a time set apart; it is what the name implies: a way of life.

Father, moment by moment, help me to keep in touch. Amen.

MAY 22

Add-On Years

*"The fear of the Lord is the beginning
of wisdom,
and knowledge of the Holy One is
understanding.
For through me your days will be many,
and years will be added to your life."
(Proverbs 9:10–11)*

I am not sure that added years and long life are what I should be interested in. Being with Jesus in heaven seems a more desirable alternative. But I am reminded of what Paul told the Philippians: "It is more necessary for you that I remain in the body. Convinced of this, I know that I will remain, and I will continue with all of you for your progress and joy in the faith" (Philippians 1:24–25). If Paul was willing to postpone heaven for the sake of believers who continued to need the ministry he could give them, I should be willing, also.

I note that God's promise of "many" days and "added" years is tied to a person's "fear of the Lord" and "knowledge of the Holy One." *God* dispenses the blessing of longevity to those who "know" Him and "fear" Him.

As I observed earlier, I have known some very godly Christians who died far short of my present age. Conversely, I am aware of some very ungodly people who are pushing the century mark. I must let that difficulty rest within God's inscrutability.

Whatever effect such fear and knowledge may have upon my length of days in this life, I do want to know God better. In retirement I have the time to enter such a pursuit. May laziness or the press of other worthwhile activities not keep me from the supreme goal of knowing God.

Father, to know You is my highest possible goal. Amen.

MAY 23

New Attire

Clothe yourselves with compassion, kindness, humility, gentleness and patience. (Colossians 3:12)

I think God is placing a challenge before me today. An objective look at myself confirms the fact that I have all five of these virtues—in a measure. That same objective look also confirms the fact that each of them could use some cultivation.

I confess that my usual recourse, when faced by advice like this from God's Word, is to put the responsibility back upon God. "Please, Father, give me more compassion. Help me to be kinder. You know my need for greater humility, more gentleness, increased patience."

But God says through Paul, "Clothe yourselves" (originally this was addressed to the whole body of Christians at Colosse). *Clothe yourselves*—put on compassion, kindness, humility, gentleness and patience as you would put on shirt and pants or a topcoat. Does God really intend for this to be a do-it-yourself project? Am *I* responsible for the development within me of these virtues? So the Word says.

I am thankful for time in retirement: time to cultivate—or improve—these spiritual graces. I am thankful for time to extend compassion to the sick, time to be kind to the needy, time to exercise gentleness toward the wife of my youth, time to show patience toward drivers who pull out in front of me. And amid all my improvement, I hope God will impart to me a spirit of humility as I realize it is not my doing but His working within me to will and to act according to His good purpose.

Father, with Your help I shall begin this project today. Amen.

MAY 24

A Shut Mouth

*He who covers over an offense
promotes love,
but whoever repeats the matter
separates close friends.
(Proverbs 17:9)*

Here is a fitting Scripture for the retired person who has less work and fewer pressures and thus more opportunity for relaxed conversation with friends. That sort of situation becomes the perfect environment for the spawning of gossip.

I distinguish in this proverb between a *sin*—which the Bible indicates must be dealt with in a forthright way—and the "offense," maybe inadvertent, that is unfortunate but not a sin. It is this latter that I must take pains, in the interest of Christian love, to "cover over" and not relay.

Paul had some counsel for Timothy along this very line. It was his observation that younger widows "get into the habit of being idle and going about from house to house." He went on to say, "Not only do they become idlers, but also gossips and busybodies, saying things they ought not to" (1 Timothy 5:13).

If Paul's warning words concerning younger widows seem inapplicable to me, I can hardly say the same about his counsel to the Philippians: "Whatever is true, whatever is noble, whatever is right, whatever is pure, whatever is lovely, whatever is admirable—if anything is excellent or praiseworthy—think about such things" (Philippians 4:8).

James says anyone who "is never at fault in what he says ... is ... perfect" (James 3:2). I do not expect to be perfect—in this life—but God would have me try.

Father, help me to keep my mouth shut when I should. Amen.

MAY 25

Bible Literate

Let the word of Christ dwell in you richly. (Colossians 3:16)

If my state throughout eternity is more important than my 70 years here, and if my assurance of heaven is linked to the message of the Bible, then an understanding of the Bible becomes more important to me than any other knowledge.

Once I appreciate the Bible's importance—I mean, really—the rest follows naturally. I have friends who know baseball team standings from Los Angeles to Boston. Baseball is important to them. They love the game. Just so, a real love for the Bible is the first step to true Bible literacy. Once that affinity is established, the rest is self-evident:

1. I must *read* the Bible. My pastor's sermons, no matter how thorough and how good, are not enough to make me Bible literate. I must read the Bible regularly—in generous quantities. Reading all of it once a year is the minimum.

2. I must *study* the Bible. I must get to know the content of each individual book. I must see the interrelations, the broad truths developed by the inspired writers. I must apply to my life the evident lessons of the Bible.

3. I must *memorize* the Bible. Memorization can be an adjunct to meditation. The Bible is most effective when it "dwell[s] in [me] richly"—when it becomes a part of me.

4. I must *share* the Bible. The most effective way to assimilate Bible truth is to share it with others.

"Turn my heart toward your statutes," the Psalmist prays, "and not toward selfish gain" (Psalm 119:36).

Father, Your Word shall have priority in my life. Amen.

MAY 26

Why Serve Christ?

God so loved the world that he gave his one and only Son. (John 3:16)

Just what is my motive for serving Jesus Christ?

Group pressures could be a motive. I was brought up in the church. Most of my friends are Christians. I must conform to what is expected of me.

The desire to be on the winning side could be a motive. In the agelong good-evil conflict, Christ shall be victor. Why opt for the loser?

Duty is another possible motive. The ingrained Puritan ethic that calls for work above leisure calls also for duty above pleasure. God expects me to serve Him; I shall do so.

Self-interest could be a motive. The fires of eternal punishment are to be avoided. A heavenly mansion in a crimeless city is an attractive option.

Emotions may be a motive. Serving God gives me a good feeling inside. It is a high privilege.

But any one of those motives, or even a combination of them all, falls short of what should really be my reason for serving Christ Jesus.

The one acceptable motive goes back to Calvary and to the sacrifice rendered by Jesus Christ on the cross. "God so loved the world that he gave his one and only Son." "Having loved his own who were in the world, [Jesus] now showed them the full extent of his love" (John 13:1). "We love because [God] first loved us" (1 John 4:19).

Love—Calvary love—is my supreme reason for serving the Lord Jesus Christ.

Father, I confess my love for You. Amen.

MAY 27

"Plentycost"

When the day of Pentecost came, they were all together in one place. (Acts 2:1)

Pentecost marked the birth of the Christian church. For all its intense excitement, Pentecost was expensive for those caught up in it. "Plentycost," someone has described it.

Pentecost cost Jesus' followers their *independence*. The Christians exchanged their autonomy and their privacy for a communal life-style and a sharing of assets (Acts 2:44–45).

It cost those first Christians their *leisure*. They met daily in the Temple and broke bread in their houses (2:46).

It cost Christians their *reputations*. They had to appear before Temple councils (5:27). They were shamed (5:41). Godly Stephen was falsely accused (6:13).

Pentecost cost them their *physical well-being*. Some of them were beaten (5:40).

It cost Christians their *security*. In the persecution after Stephen's death the Jerusalem Christians were "scattered" throughout Judea and Samaria (8:1).

It cost the Christians their *routine*. Philip had to leave a glowing revival in Samaria to be on a lonely desert road when the Ethiopian treasurer passed that way (8:26–29).

Pentecost cost some Christians their *lives*. Stephen was first (7:59–60). James the brother of John followed (12:1–2). Tradition has it that only John of the apostles died naturally.

Yes, Pentecost carried a price. Those early Christians counted the cost and dared to pay it.

Father, is there no price for me to pay? Amen.

MAY 28

Renewed Identity

[Jesus] died for all, that those who live should no longer live for themselves but for him who died for them and was raised again. (2 Corinthians 5:15)

It is a principle as old as Christianity, and I have heard it most of my life. But it deserves renewed emphasis at this point in my life. I am *not* my own boss now that I am retired. I must continue to take orders from a higher Authority.

The rationale is simple to explain, not so simple to practice. Jesus, in His cross death, identified with the whole human race. He bore the sins of everyone in His body on the cross. But identification is two-way. If Christ Jesus identified with me as a member of the human race, bearing my sins, then in effect I died with Him at Calvary. Repeat: I *died with Him* at Calvary. As Jesus arose from the dead, so I "arose" from my deadness in trespasses and sins to live a new life in tune with Christ Jesus my Savior and my Lord.

Those incontrovertible facts must govern what I do, what I say. They must affect all my interpersonal relationships inside and outside the home. Obviously, this new life in Christ Jesus should avoid any kind of open, outright sin. But just as importantly, it should include all the positive things the New Testament stresses.

How is that to happen? In two ways. First, I need to make sure that is my attitude. Second, I need to read and know the Word of God to determine my practice.

Father, thank You for identifying with me, a sinner, through Jesus Christ. Help me to identify fully with Him. Amen.

MAY 29

"Keep Looking Down!"

*God ... seated us with [Christ]
in the heavenly realms. (Ephesians 2:6)*

It has to be the greatest concept any child of God through faith in Jesus Christ can possibly grasp—that my identification with Jesus puts me where He is: seated in the heavenly realms next to God the Father. *I am there!*

"Keep looking down!" I first heard the expression from Atlanta evangelist Walter G. Sandell. He told me a woman in his church used to say it to him every time he was discouraged. What a thought! If I am seated with Christ in the heavenly realms, there is no other direction to look. I am on top of the heap, king of the mountain, triumphant in Jesus!

In his book, *Coping with Cancer: 12 Creative Choices*, John E. Packo calls it "positional thinking." I am to look at every circumstance from the perspective of my position in Christ Jesus. My strength may be small. His is not. My faith may be little. His is not. My will power may be at low ebb. His is not.

My dependence must not be on myself, my mind, my personal inner resources. My reliance is on my exalted, triumphant Lord and Savior, Jesus Christ. When I was "dead in ... transgressions," God made me alive in Christ. God "seated [me] with him in the heavenly realms" that I might live in victory.

Do I find myself discouraged? overwhelmed? frustrated? disturbed? Jesus is victor! I am in the heavenly realms with Him! I can do all things through Him!

"Keep looking down!"

Father, consciously I take my place in Christ Jesus. Amen.

MAY 30

Being Content

*I have learned to be content whatever the circumstances . . .
I have learned the secret of being content in any
and every situation. (Philippians 4:11–12)*

What a blessing from God is contentment! To be able to look back with no serious regrets, to look around without covetousness and to look ahead with confidence—this is blessing indeed. I praise God for such a benefit!

But Paul's comments to the Philippian Christians catch my attention on at least two counts. First, he said he had "learned" to be content. Evidently contentment is not something that just happens. It is a learned response.

Second, he told the Philippians that he had learned the "secret" of being content. The only secret I see here is Jesus. "I can do everything through him who gives me strength" (Philippians 4:13), Paul went on to say. Can I conclude that Jesus is the secret of contentment? That if my life is lived out in His strength, I can be content whatever happens to me?

Being under house arrest in Rome would not have contented many people. But Paul was content. Being "hungry" and "in want" would not be very conducive to contentment. But Paul was content.

Was Paul saying that contentment is an attitude, not a reaction? Was he saying that contentment is dependent on inward, not outward, circumstances? Was he saying that Jesus and His enabling power in my circumstances of weakness and frustration are the real secret of contentment?

Father, I want contentment that is independent of circumstances. Let me find it, as Paul did, in Jesus, Your Son. Amen.

MAY 31

Holding On too Long

"At the age of fifty, [the Levites] must retire from their regular service." (Numbers 8:25)

Those who push doggedly on in their jobs, determined to die in the harness, evoke within me a certain sense of admiration. While others are playing shuffleboard under the palms, they continue to manufacture widgets or wait on customers or walk the corridors of Congress. I have a certain admiration for them, I say, but I do not let them make me feel guilty.

I have observed the working scene long enough to know that people can and do outstay their usefulness. Organizations—even churches—suffer from those who will not step down.

Am I contradicting all I have said about continuing to serve the Lord, about retirement not being a 15-year frolic? In no way. Retirement is a chance to redirect my energies and interests into channels more suited to my limitations.

I might as well honestly face it. If there has not yet been a perceptible tapering off of physical energy, it is coming. If memory has not yet slowed down, it will. The dying process that began decades ago is accelerating.

Moreover, a new generation is eager to test its mettle. The time has come to defer to them.

There comes a time when even that Sunday school class or the job of church deacon should be in younger hands. Retirement becomes a creative search for appropriate work—and, reciprocally, the sensitivity to know when to step down.

Father, please help me to be extra-sensitive, lest in my zeal I overstay to the detriment of Your work. Amen.

JUNE 1

Practical Atheism

*The fool says in his heart,
"There is no God."
(Psalm 14:1)*

John H. Stek, in his *NIV Study Bible* commentary on Psalm 14, uses the term "practical atheism" to describe those who leave God out of their purview. They do not deny outright His being and power, but they live as though He did not exist.

It is a condition that I, newly retired and with unscheduled time on my hands, must guard against.

An astute observer notes with what uncanny precision David lists the symptoms:

"There is no one who does good" (14:1)—as though God does not see His children.

"All have turned aside" (14:3)—as though God does not care what His children do.

"[They] do not call on the Lord" (14:4)—as though God is unconcerned about His children.

"They are . . . overwhelmed with dread" (14:5)—as though God is powerless to help His children.

"[They] frustrate the plans of the poor" (14:6)—as though God does not defend the helpless or punish the unjust.

Is it possible that *I* am guilty of practical atheism? The temptation to leave God out of my reckoning is no easier to battle now than it ever was. Experience can lead to a false self-confidence. But as one whom God will call to account—possibly soon—I had better be diligent to "make [my] calling and election sure" (2 Peter 1:10). To do otherwise is to play the fool.

Father, help me live as one who shall give account. Amen.

JUNE 2

Wayward

"O Absalom, my son, my son!" (2 Samuel 18:33)

Few expressions in the Scriptures carry the anguish that King David voiced for his wayward son Absalom. Even after Absalom died a traitor's death, his father grieved.

I am deeply grateful to God that my children walk in His ways. Despite my shortcomings as a parent, it happened, and I thank God with all my heart for His mercy to these children of mine—and to their mother and me.

But I have been on the human scene long enough to know that it does not always turn out that way. Godly parents, who from all appearance have done everything right, have adult children who seem to have totally rejected God, whose lifestyles are a bitter disappointment to father and mother. What should be the attitude of these parents toward their children?

"Try diligently to keep yourself from being judge and jury in your adult children's lives" is the advice Peter Mustric, the pastor to 600 seniors in a large, west coast evangelical church, gave to his flock. By then, parents have done all they can do, short of their continued love and their prayers. Wayward children of any age need plenty of both.

Paul's agonizing burden for his nation, Israel (Romans 9:2–3), did not prevent him from being a rejoicing, upbeat Christian (Philippians 1:18). Nothing is gained if I let myself be overcome by a problem. In fact, my triumphant spirit may be a more convincing appeal to those who need God than any amount of handwringing exhortation.

Father, thank You for "household" salvation (Acts 16:31). Amen.

JUNE 3

Children

*If anyone does not provide for his relatives,
and especially for his immediate family, he has denied
the faith and is worse than an unbeliever. (1 Timothy 5:8)*

God makes it clear that believing children and even grandchildren "should learn . . . to put their religion into practice by caring for their own family and so repaying their parents and grandparents" (1 Timothy 5:4). But what if the tables are turned? What if one of my children is overtaken by financial misfortune—a business reverse, disastrous medical expenses? When our son, Dan, went into business with another young partner, the two had to mortgage their properties to handle the start-up costs. Dan did not ask me for money. But what if he had?

My heart wants to extend help. My children are my flesh and blood. My love for them has not abated. Although First Timothy 5:8, like its context, seems directed to adult children rather than their parents, it does not preclude an older person's helping children in financial difficulty. But whatever resources I have in reserve primarily are there so that I will not later be a financial burden on others. If I use them now for something else, will I be imposing a future tax on my family or the public?

Is there alternative assistance for my children—possibly even from public welfare that my taxes over the years helped to provide? Could it be that God is trying to teach my children the lessons of trust and dependence that He taught Marge and me—lessons that cannot be learned if I intervene?

If ever retirees need wisdom, it is for such a situation.

Father, keep my heart and head coordinated. Amen.

JUNE 4

Beyond Sacrifice

"I desire mercy, not sacrifice." (Hosea 6:6)

All human beings tend to get set in their ways. The older I get, the more set I get.

Being set in my ways is not necessarily bad. By retirement time, I have spent most of a lifetime receiving information and counsel from parents, teachers, friends, work associates, society generally. Some of it came through trial and error. Some has come direct from God's Word, the Bible.

I have tested this information in real life, keeping what works, rejecting what does not. The result is what I can appropriately consider "my ways"—as distinguished from the ways of every other person. The older I get, the less open I am to ideas that challenge what I have determined to be both good and workable for me.

But I must ever be alert to the realization that my Heavenly Father has more He wants to teach me. The Jews thought they had it all in place with their system of sacrifices and their observances of holy days. But God said in effect, "There is something beyond your routine religious observances. I regard mercy above sacrifice. You have dutifully come to My temple, you have observed the outward ceremonies. But when have you opened your hearts to a neighbor in need or to the stranger within your gates? *I love mercy, not sacrifice.* Your worship of Me is meaningless if it is not accompanied by mercy."

It is a message God is still sending.

Father, forgive me for letting religious routine hinder me from showing mercy to those outside my circle. Amen.

JUNE 5

Procrastination

When you make a vow to God, do not delay in fulfilling it. (Ecclesiastes 5:4)

How does that old saw go? "The meeting of the Procrastinators Club has been postponed . . ." I can identify; procrastination has plagued me all of my life.

I have a certain admiration for the gung-ho type who do not rest until a problem is solved or an idea is carried out—though I am thankful that I do not have their ulcers. My tendency to defer action is not all bad. It has spared me from pitfalls that have entrapped my more impulsive associates. Problems often look much different after a night's rest and a chance to reflect on them and to pray to God about them.

But put-off repairs to the house or car can quickly lead to bigger troubles. A health problem not checked out can worsen. Misunderstandings allowed to fester can kill friendships. And unfulfilled vows made to God can do eternal damage.

If the lethargy of advancing age plays into the hands of procrastination, retirement provides a new counteroffensive: time. I now have time to do what needs to be done. My best excuse for procrastinating has just been blown out of the water!

Thomas Stebbins, former missionary to Vietnam, keeps a "Honey Do" list and checks off the projects his wife, Donna, wants done around the house as he completes them. The list helps him prioritize both the jobs needing to be done and his time.

God has put me on this planet to do His kingdom work. I must not let procrastination keep me from God's will.

Father, may I not defer what needs doing now. Amen.

JUNE 6

Receive Graciously

"Give, and it will be given to you." (Luke 6:38)

To "give" is my delight. Incongruously, I often have trouble with the "it will be given to you." When I am the recipient of someone else's delight, I find it hard to accept the gift graciously. Probably it is just my pride, but it is hard.

For example, there was the time George Perry wanted to give me his watch. Marge and I, enroute through Cincinnati, were visiting George, a Christian "buddy" from World War II Army days, and his wife, Betty. Somehow the conversation got onto the subject of my malfunctioning wristwatch.

"Just a minute," George said, excusing himself. He reappeared moments later with a beautiful, obviously costly watch.

"Here," he said, offering it to me.

"But, George," I protested. "I can't take your watch!"

George pressed me. "I have two!" But I would not accept his gift. I deprived myself of a needed timepiece and George of a blessing. Though I later apologized to George, I fear I also marked myself as a stubborn ingrate.

Now that I am retired, there may be many occasions when I am on the receiving end of someone's largess—whether material things, time or even possibly cash.

I pray that I will be kept from two besetting sins: *pride*—a reluctance to graciously accept what is freely offered—and *begging*—a hinting for handouts.

Father, the Senior Syndrome—either resenting special attention or expecting it—is a trap I need Your help to avoid. Amen.

JUNE 7

Praise Wins

*"Give thanks to the Lord,
for his love endures forever."
(2 Chronicles 20:21)*

The above lines, which could be right out of the Psalms, were spoken under unusual circumstances. Israel's King Jehoshaphat was faced with a vast army from Edom preparing to attack. Israel's forces were few and ill prepared.

But the king had a resource the pagan hordes knew nothing about: God. First, Jehoshaphat called a fast, and "the people of Judah came together to seek help from the Lord" (20:4). God answered Jehoshaphat through the prophet Jahaziel. "The battle is not yours, but God's" (20:15). The king had first to "march down against [the enemy]" (20:16), then to "stand firm and see the deliverance the Lord will give you" (20:17).

Grateful for such assurance, Jehoshaphat "appointed men to sing to the Lord and to praise him for the splendor of his holiness as they went out at the head of the army" (20:21). It may be the only instance in all history when singers praising God led an army into battle. But "as they began to sing and praise, the Lord sent ambushes against the men . . . who were invading Judah, and they were defeated" (20:22).

My crises, however serious they may seem to me, are small by comparison. But Israel's God is just as ready to intervene. He spells out His three-part formula: (1) fasting, (2) seeking His help, and, in a spirit of genuine praise "for the splendor of his holiness," (3) a frontal attack.

Father, help me to face all my problems in an attitude of praise to You. Yours is the victory! Amen.

JUNE 8

Adventure

"The eyes of the Lord range throughout the earth to strengthen those whose hearts are fully committed to him." (2 Chronicles 16:9)

Marge and I are at last on our way to North Carolina, the car loaded to the roof line with all the last-minute things that did not get into the moving van.

I have lived overseas and in scattered locations here at home, but I am unprepared for the sense of aloneness I feel as I head the car south. Behind us is the evident love of our New Cumberland church family and their sorrow to see us leave. We said good-bye to Marge's soon-to-be-89 mother at The Alliance Home in Carlisle. Christian Publications had arranged a lovely farewell breakfast. Now we are on our own—the sale of our New Cumberland house consummated minutes before—heading to an area where we have never lived, the future uncertain.

But, no, we are not alone. God is with us. We are committed to Him. We have sought His direction. A daughter and her family eagerly await our arrival. A house soon will be in readiness to receive us and shelter us. Church people—part of God's wonderful, universal family—will welcome us into their fellowship. Friendly neighbors will make us feel at home.

The miles tick by. Frederick, Maryland. Washington, D.C. Richmond, Virginia. Rocky Mount, North Carolina. Finally, the farm house near Benson where our daughter, Rebecca, and her family live. Sarah, our 10-year-old granddaughter, sees us and runs to report our arrival.

God has strengthened us. We are here!

Father, we are grateful for Your watchful mercy. Amen.

JUNE 9

My Partner

*She is your partner, the wife of your
marriage covenant. (Malachi 2:14)*

I am blessed. I still have the wife of my youth, the wife of my marriage covenant. Neither death nor divorce has separated us. Not only is Marge outwardly attractive but she is inwardly beautiful.

Marge has a mind of her own, and it is made up on a number of subjects from baseball to Browning. But at the same time she is deferential—attentive to my needs, my preferences. She has at heart my welfare. There is domestic tranquility in our home, and that is a blessing *par excellence*.

And I love my wife. Admittedly, I do not love her to the degree that Christ loved the church and gave Himself up for her. But I want to. I try—not always successfully—to sense her needs, her feelings, her moods.

Marge is a better woman for having married me. I say that objectively, not boastfully. If it were not so after more than 40 years, I would have to admit my failure as a husband. I have tried to be a spiritual leader. Marge has responded with an intensity beyond my own. I have tried to provide. With adequate resources, she has given herself to hospitality. I have encouraged her by example and word to keep those middle-/older age pounds off. By prudent diet and exercise, she is healthier than she would otherwise be.

Retirement has become a second honeymoon—with an added blessing: the abundant fruit of a lifetime of faithful devotion and partnership.

Father, I am grateful to You for a happy marriage. Amen.

JUNE 10

Rewarded

*I have no greater joy than to hear that my
children are walking in the truth. (3 John 4)*

When the time comes for me to depart this life and be with my Heavenly Father forever, I will enter His presence stripped of all the material things I have valued. No one is likely to ask about me, "How much did he leave?" The obvious answer, even if my wealth was great: "All of it!"

But there is one priceless asset that I can and shall take with me to heaven: my four children—Rebecca, Deborah, Daniel, Esther. To Marge and me God entrusted the never-dying souls of four children whom we love above any earthly possession.

In retrospect, it seems that we had them such a short time before they were gone to live their own lives, to make their own marks in the world. I loved them then and I love them yet. I tried to be available to them when they needed me—and I still do. I prayed for them, and that ministry continues, too. Diligently I have tried to place the kind of value on those children of mine that their never-dying souls deserve.

I am inexpressibly thankful that all four of my children love the Lord. Nothing God could give me—health, wealth, status, power—can even remotely equal the great blessing of knowing "my children are walking in the truth."

My heart goes out to parents who, despite their diligence and prayers, have unbelieving children. My message to them: *Keep holding on to God!* God's unwillingness that any should perish is a promise for them as well as me.

Father, keep my children "walking in the truth." Amen.

JUNE 11

Balance I Need

An anxious heart weighs a man down. (Proverbs 12:25)

A "Cathy" comic one of my daughters clipped and sent me describes me better than I want to admit. It is Father's Day, and Cathy is home for the occasion. She is seated on the sofa between her father and mother. On the end table is a small still-wrapped gift to which a "Happy Father's Day" balloon is attached. They are looking at family photos.

Mother says: "Here's a picture of your father gnashing his teeth when he thought about you driving on the freeway by yourself." And the next frame: "Here's a shot of Dad getting an ulcer worrying about you being alone at night." And still another frame: "And here's dad sleeping with the phone next to his face, just in case you called and needed him to rescue you."

Finally Cathy breaks in: "Oh, Dad! I put you through so much! Aren't you relieved those days are all behind you?"

Mother comments: *"These were just taken last week."*

Parents never quite outgrow their concern for their children. At least, this one has not.

Balance is what I need. Although long "out of the nest," my children continue to need—and count on—my prayers. They appreciate my concern and would feel deprived if it were absent. But I dare not be weighed down under an unhealthy anxiety for them. God is totally "able to guard what I have entrusted to him for that day" (2 Timothy 1:12). He will look after my children just as He has looked after me. I must "cast all [my] anxiety on him because he cares for [me]" (1 Peter 5:7).

Father, help me to strike the right balance. Amen.

JUNE 12

Stumbling Blocks

Be careful ... that the exercise of your freedom does not become a stumbling block to the weak. (1 Corinthians 8:9)

When people put a house on the market, they generally do some fix-up work to give it sales appeal. One of the projects cared for by the former owner of this house in Garner, North Carolina, was a new cement driveway from curb to carport. Part of it was, in fact, so new that when we took possession, the wooden forms, carefully staked in place, had not yet been removed.

Those protruding stakes were an accident waiting to happen. Because of polio a number of years ago, I walk precariously at best. I knew I should take time to remove the forms and the stakes lest I trip over them. But I was busy with other priority projects. And—enough said! Thankfully, two bruised knees and my injured pride were the only damage. But I set aside what I had been doing long enough to do what I should have done first. I removed the stumbling blocks.

The Scriptures say my freedom—freedom to say where and what I will eat and drink, freedom to observe or not observe holy days—could cause a weaker Christian to stumble. In deference to those in Christ who might get hurt because of my example, I must be very careful.

I should be sufficiently concerned for fellow Christians, those who are my contemporaries in retirement and the many younger ones who look to me for example, to deny myself legitimate liberties that for them would be sinful. Remove the stumbling blocks, prudence says, before someone gets hurt.

Father, let me not cause anyone to stumble. Amen.

JUNE 13

Modifying

"These hands of mine have supplied my own needs." (Acts 20:34)

Finding things that need to be done is not hard when a person moves into a different house. Even this one, so made-to-order for our early years of retirement, cries out for certain modifications. Thankfully, I have always enjoyed working with my hands. Now I have the time.

Storage space is the most pressing need. Not that the closets and other storage areas are deficient, but we came encumbered with twice the possessions we will need. The only thing about which we were unsure was which half was surplus! We are thankful that John and Rebecca have a barn on their farm to accommodate some of what will not fit in our house!

A storage shed in the back yard—standard equipment in this area of cellar-less homes—will accommodate garden tools and some other items. Plywood shelving in the small but high-ceilinged, enclosed storage area off the carport will care for light-weight large items without infringing on the room's limited floor space. From the same sheet of half-inch stock I can add a small workbench and make space for my three-inch vise.

Commercial metal closet shelving discovered in a Raleigh department store (and a day's time to install it) is doubling the useful capacity of the closet in my office. I prefer it to wooden shelves I might have built because it allows for ventilation. It freed a shelf board to add to Marge's clothes closet.

Little by little, things are taking shape!

Father, how much Americans accumulate! But re-buying things wantonly discarded makes no sense. Amen.

JUNE 14

Patriotism

*Show proper respect to everyone:
... honor the king. (1 Peter 2:17)*

For a while it looked as though my generation of Americans might be the last patriotic generation.

I cannot be completely sure when patriotism began to erode. Maybe it was when a newcomer to American politics, Wendell L. Willkie, wrote his famous *One World*. Or perhaps it was 1945 when the United Nations was born.

Patriotism has not been an unmixed blessing. It has provoked wars that never should have been fought. It is to blame for senseless hardship that could have been avoided. It has excluded people who should have been included.

As a Christian I am to have a supranational world view. God has commissioned me to make disciples of "all nations" (Matthew 28:19). In still a different sense, my "citizenship is in heaven" (Philippians 3:20). This world is not forever.

God commanded the survivors of the Flood to "fill the earth" (Genesis 9:1). When they did not, He nudged them, confusing their language (11:9), insuring the national divisions that continue to be the pattern in the world.

The Scriptures command God's people to pray for "all those in authority" (1 Timothy 2:1–2), to "submit . . . to the governing authorities" (Romans 13:1), to "pay taxes, . . . revenue, . . . respect, . . . honor" (13:7). The immediate context was the Roman Empire, but also its subdivisions. By legitimate extension, it applies to me within my governmental structures.

Father, make me a good, honest citizen of my country. Amen.

JUNE 15

Awaiting a Savior

*We eagerly await a Savior from [heaven],
the Lord Jesus Christ. (Philippians 3:20)*

The Bible declares it. Saints through the ages have anticipated it. I believe it. Jesus is returning to earth. Over the centuries of the Christian era, this assurance of Christ's return has been a stimulating, driving force.

After announcing his eager expectation, Paul outlined the two effects Jesus' return to earth will have. First he says Jesus will "bring everything under his control" (Philippians 3:21). *Everything!* There will be righteous rule over all the earth. Evil will be effectively suppressed. Justice will prevail. This polluted globe, abused by the people who call it home, will be habitable again, its waters clear, its air clean.

Equally exciting, Jesus "will transform our lowly bodies so that they will be like his glorious body" (3:21). As I age, I am increasingly aware of the physical impediments associated with the process. But this "lowly" body of mine will be transformed. And what a transformation it will be!

The aged apostle John, isolated on Patmos Island, saw Jesus, His head and hair radiantly white, His eyes like fire, His feet like glowing brass, His countenance like the full-strength sun. *This is my prospect, too,* for Jesus will transform my lowly body to be like His glorious body!

Immortality. Do I understand what it means? No more death. Life forever. Vigorous, purposeful life, with faculties sharp, memory perfect, heart tuned to the rhythm of eternity.

Father, I eagerly await the return of my Lord Jesus. Amen.

JUNE 16

Patience

But the fruit of the Spirit is . . . patience. (Galatians 5:22)

My wood desk, with its three-by-six-foot top, was the bulkiest, heaviest item of our move. To spare the movers as much weight as possible, I carefully loaded the contents of the drawers into cardboard cartons. And the movers carefully locked both pedestals (by depressing a cylinder on the end of the side boards) so the drawers would not come open during the move. There was just one problem: not for years had the desk been locked; I had no idea where the key might be.

The movers dutifully set up the desk in the room designated as my "office." But except for the huge top and the middle drawer (which had no lock), it was a useless piece of furniture. All my files, my paper supply and the other accumulation that normally goes into desk drawers was stacked in the cartons that seemed always underfoot in the small room.

Marge and I looked in vain for the key. In desperation, I spent a whole evening taking one end of the desk apart, hoping I might manually release the locking mechanism. No success. We called a local locksmith; he could not immediately come. And then, after that flurry of activity, I suddenly discovered in my rotating dispenser of paper clips and rubber bands an overlooked compartment labeled "keys." There was the missing key—right where it had been the past five or more years!

Why could I not have found it sooner, I wondered partly to myself and partly for God's benefit, *before I wasted all that time?* I think I know the answer.

Yes, Father, I still *need to learn patience! Amen.*

JUNE 17

Abandoned

*Though my father and mother forsake me,
the Lord will receive me.
(Psalm 27:10)*

It never occurred to Marge and me that any of our adult children would find our relocating after retirement traumatic. All four of them had been "out of the nest" and on their own for years—two of them in overseas missionary service that normally puts them half a world away from us.

Belatedly I have learned that such a relocation is frequently a major adjustment for grown children, especially if they have not yet established solid roots of their own. I guess it can be attributed to that built-in desire for a place where they belong. Of course, God has promised heaven to the believers, but even most Christians are still too earth-oriented for heaven to be a totally acceptable substitute for a place on earth called home.

As might be expected, Rebecca, our oldest, was overjoyed at the prospect of our move. After nearly a decade of relative isolation, she would have us near her.

Although we involved all four children in our plans to move, we sensed that it was especially hard for Esther, our youngest, to see us leave Pennsylvania. Esther, on furlough from missionary duty in Burkina Faso, West Africa, was completing her seminary studies in Nyack, New York. Our house in central Pennsylvania was the only tangible home she could claim, and suddenly it had been denied her. The fact that there was another in Garner, North Carolina, to take its place did not seem to count. For her, the loss was wrenching, and she grieved.

Father, make us sensitive in all of our decisions. Amen.

JUNE 18

A Good Name

*A good name is more desirable
than great riches;
to be esteemed is better than silver or gold.
(Proverbs 22:1)*

The Bible says it. Not even financial wealth can match the priceless advantage of a good name. Should I be tempted to doubt that widsom, I have only to reflect on the life of my father, Harry Russell Cowles.

My father was a hard-working man all his life. At 80 he could still outdistance me when it came to physical endurance. Dad had his family during the Depression years. Money was scarce then and he and Mother had a hard time making ends meet on a reduced salary. But Dad had steady work. He could be counted on to do an honest day's job—and a little extra.

When Dad died, he had no monetary accumulation for his three children to inherit. But he left us something much more valuable: a good name. Now that I have lived most of my life, I realize just how valuable Dad's good reputation was.

Dad's good name opened doors for me. People did not know me, but they knew I was the son of my father. Because of his reputation, they gave me a chance.

Dad's good character has rubbed off. He was an excellent role model for my sister, my brother and me. We, too, have come to realize the transcending value of a good name.

The world is better because of Dad. He left his imprint on more than one community. Though dead, he still speaks.

Father, may I do nothing to sully Dad's good name. Amen.

JUNE 19

Anything, Everything

Do not be anxious about anything, but in everything, by prayer and petition, with thanksgiving, present your requests to God. (Philippians 4:6)

What a beautiful antidote for those anxious moments—or days, as the case may be—that manage to find me even in the isolation of retirement in North Carolina!

"In everything"—the important and the not-so-important, the "spiritual" and the mundane, the delightful and the obnoxious, my agenda and Marge's agenda.

"By prayer and petition"—the formal prayer times, when I have opportunity to reflect on what I am saying to and asking of God, the impromptu occasions when I only have time for a quick S.O.S. for divine help, the running conversational prayers as God and I walk together through the day.

"With thanksgiving"—thanksgiving for the good and the not-so-good, thanksgiving for the difficult as well as the easy, the dreaded as well as the pleasant, the bitter as well as the sweet; thanksgiving to God who hears and answers prayer.

Can it be that God means *everything* is a fit subject for prayer? that He does not become weary with my frequent coming or the trivia I tend to trouble Him with? Today it is a dental appointment (I dislike dental appointments!). Tomorrow it may be a cut finger or the bills in the mail.

Of course God expects me to bring the important matters before Him. But if I want not to be anxious in *anything*, I had better follow instructions and pray about *everything*.

Father, I intend to be an "in everything" pray-er! Amen.

JUNE 20

By Prayer

In everything, by prayer and petition, with thanksgiving, present your requests to God. (Philippians 4:6)

It was not good news that a replacement thermostat for our kitchen oven would cost us $103.00. At least, there would not be the expense of a service call. My church friend, David Leland, an experienced technician, had volunteered.

He arrived at the prearranged time, the new thermostat under his arm in a cardboard carton. We were not far into the job of extracting the malfunctioning part when David suddenly stopped. "We forgot to pray!" he exclaimed.

I must confess that as long as I have been fixing things (and that goes back a long ways), I have never prayed before I started a job. Sometimes *into* a job I have prayed—usually because things were not going as they should. David must have read my surprise. "I *always* pray before I start a repair job," he said. So right then we paused and prayed.

We got the old thermostat out. A kink in the small tubing could have been the problem. I opened the box containing the new thermostat. It did not look new. Neither did it look like the thermostat we had just removed.

"Maybe we can get the kink out and reuse the old thermostat," David suggested. Carefully we straightened the tubing and reattached it. We recalibrated the thermostat, and—it worked! After lunch with us, David returned the $103.00 part for a full refund.

The lesson: Things go better with prayer.

Father, let me learn the lesson well. Amen.

JUNE 21

Naomi

Naomi took the child, laid him in her lap and cared for him. . . . They named him Obed. He was the father of Jesse, the father of David. (Ruth 4:16–17)

Her name means "pleasant," and Naomi was. But her pleasant nature was in spite of the bitter circumstances of her life.

First it was the famine in Judah that drove Naomi and her husband, Elimelech, and their two sons to Moab in search of a livelihood. While in Moab her husband died. Her sons married Moabite women, and—tragedy upon tragedy—both sons died, leaving Naomi and her two foreign daughters-in-law a trio of widows in what was for Naomi a foreign land.

By then the famine had lifted in Judah, and Naomi decided to return home. Orpah and Ruth, her daughters-in-law, determined to go with her (a clue to Naomi's pleasant personality). Naomi urged them not to—for their sakes. Orpah stayed in Moab. Ruth went with Naomi.

The exquisite love story that unfolds in the grain fields of wealthy Boaz, a leading citizen of Bethlehem and Naomi's near kinsman, is well known.

Dear Naomi! Would wedding bells have rung for Ruth and Boaz without Naomi's behind-the-scenes efforts? But the bells did ring, and in course of time Boaz and Ruth had a baby. Naomi, her bitter past now forgotten in the joy of God's blessing, "took the child, laid him in her lap and cared for him." Naomi's later years could not have been more pleasant.

Father, however bitter the past, You are giving me the present. And the future is bright beyond imagination! Amen.

JUNE 22

Eli - I

"Those who honor me I will honor, but those who despise me will be disdained." (1 Samuel 2:30)

God spoke the words through an unnamed prophet to an older man, Eli, Israel's high priest. It was an angry, foreboding message. Eli had failed to discipline his sons. Not only had he failed to correct his sons' immoral behavior, but he had put them in positions of spiritual leadership in Israel. In their ministry in the tabernacle, they brought such reproach on God's name that people simply stayed away.

God takes pains to inform us that Eli was overweight—likely the result of overindulgence in the sacrifices brought to the tabernacle. It is hard for an overindulgent person to address another's sins. The message lacks authority.

God accused Eli of despising Him—refusing to take to heart His Word, declining to act on His commands. That is serious. Ultimately, it cost Eli his sons he had failed to discipline. They died in battle at the hands of enemy troops. It also cost Eli his own life. When he learned that the Ark of the Covenant had been captured in the same battle, he fell backward off his chair, breaking his neck.

For a highly placed leader with such potential for spiritual good, in an era when strong moral example was desperately needed, it was a disappointing and an ignominious end.

The message is transparent. God expects His people to conform to His Word. Those who honor Him will be honored; those who "despise" Him will be "disdained."

Father, may I never, never despise Your Word. Amen.

JUNE 23
Eli - II

When [the messenger] mentioned the ark of God, Eli fell backward off his chair by the side of the gate. His neck was broken and he died, for he was an old man and heavy. (1 Samuel 4:18)

Eli evokes mixed emotions.

Pity: One tragic battle robbed him of all that was dearest: his two sons and—more importantly—the Ark of God. Death, likely from a stroke, was a merciful ending for the sightless old man who had served Israel as priest and judge.

Anger: Eli's two sons were scoundrels, and Eli made no serious effort to discipline them. "They had no regard for the Lord" (1 Samuel 2:12). They made worship at God's altar odious for Israel, demanding the best cuts of meat before they could be sacrificed, committing adultery with the women who served at the entrance to the Tent of Meeting. Perhaps the advancing years that had taken his eyesight had dulled Eli's mind as well. Not only did he fail to address the deplorable situation, but the layers of fat on his frame came from the animal sacrifices his sons had confiscated (2:29). As I noted yesterday, Eli could hardly discipline his sons while he was the beneficiary of their deeds.

Sadness: Eli failed to be the priest God meant him to be. Eli is presumed to be the first from the Ithamar lineage of Aaron to be a high priest in Israel. Clearly God arranged the shift from the Eleazer lineage (2:30) for a purpose. God had high expectations of Eli. Like Saul, Israel's first king, Eli was a bitter disappointment to God.

That last was Eli's ultimate tragedy.

Father, I do not want to disappoint You! Amen.

JUNE 24

Samuel

Samuel said to all Israel, . . . "Here I stand. . . . Whose ox have I taken? . . . Whom have I cheated?" (1 Samuel 12:1–3)

"You have not cheated or oppressed us," [the people] replied. "You have not taken anything from anyone's hand" (1 Samuel 12:4). It was a remarkable testimonial. But, then, Samuel was a remarkable person. Dedicated to God before birth, he grew up in God's house. He was just a child when God first spoke through him. In the course of his long life he was Israel's prophet, priest and judge. He anointed Israel's first king. Now he was saying good-bye to the people he had shepherded.

Were I to stand before the multitude of my contemporaries—those I grew up with, those I have worked with, those I have served in the course of my years of gainful employment, those who are now associated with me in retirement—if I were to stand before them and ask the same questions Samuel asked of Israel, what would be their reply?

Could Internal Revenue Service probe all of my tax returns and find no incriminating evidence? Could the people I have done business with say unequivocally, "You have not cheated us"?

"Be careful to do what is right in the eyes of everybody," the Scriptures admonish (Romans 12:17). Paul, in accepting custody of the Corinthians' offering, took witnesses with him. He explained, "We want to avoid any criticism of the way we administer this liberal gift. For we are taking pains to do what is right, not only in the eyes of the Lord but also in the eyes of men" (2 Corinthians 8:20–21).

Father, are there past failings I need to rectify? Amen.

JUNE 25

Fasting

"When you fast..." (Matthew 6:16)

Few Christian practices are as obscured by misunderstanding as is fasting. On one extreme is the handful who suppose fasting is a precondition to good health and body tone. At the other are the many who depreciate the whole idea of fasting.

I find no "you-shall-fast" rule in the Bible. But the Scriptures leave me in no doubt that God's people fasted both in the Old Testament (Moses, the Israelites, Elijah, David, Daniel, Ezra, Nehemiah) and the New (Jesus, the "prophets and teachers" at Antioch, Paul, Barnabas). Strongly implied is the message that I should be fasting, too.

In instructing His followers, Jesus tells them to make their fasts private (Matthew 6:17–18). He does not say, *"If you fast,"* but, *"When you fast."* Clearly He expected they would.

An examination of all the Scriptures dealing with fasting leads me to these conclusions:

1. Fasting is a normal response to crisis or severe emergency. It is tacit admission that God must help—or else.

2. When properly carried out, fasting is always a *spiritual* exercise—seeking God's forgiveness, assistance, fellowship.

3. Fasting is to be private. Although not necessarily done in isolation from other believers, it never parades.

Fasting carries solid Old and New Testament endorsement. Although not an explicit New Testament command, fasting puts me in good Bible company. And retirement makes fasting easier than it ever was before.

Father, I need You. I shall seek You by fasting. Amen.

JUNE 26

Imitating God

Be imitators of God . . . as dearly loved children and live a life of love, just as Christ loved us and gave himself up for us as a . . . sacrifice to God. (Ephesians 5:1–2)

Me? Imitate God?

It would be preposterous were it not a biblical command. How does a finite creature imitate his exalted infinite Creator?

First, I need to discover God's essential attributes. I learn from the Bible that God is infinite, eternal, immutable, self-sufficient, perfect, free. He is omnipotent, omnipresent, omniscient, just, truthful, merciful, gracious. He is spirit, he is love, he is holy.

Some of those attributes I cannot possibly imitate. I am, for example, finite and I cannot be infinite. I am restricted to one place at a time and I cannot be omnipresent. Other attributes, such as God's mercy and grace challenge me to compliance.

But when Paul asked the Ephesians to be imitators of God, he had one particular attribute in mind. God is love. I am therefore to imitate God by my love. And how was God's love evidenced? In Christ His Son, God "loved us and gave himself up for us." Calvary remains the supreme example of God's love.

Calvary love is *non-selective*. Christ died for all. No one was excluded.

Calvary love is *selfless*. Jesus relinquished the prerogatives of Deity in order to save humankind.

Calvary love is *gracious*. No person deserved to be saved. Salvation is exclusively of God's grace.

Father, help my love to be like Yours. Amen.

JUNE 27

Sunset Law

Do not let the sun go down while you are still angry. (Ephesians 4:26)

The Bible is very practical. I am instructed to "rid [myself] of . . . anger" (Colossians 3:8). At the same time, as Paul must have realized from his own heated disagreement with Barnabas (Acts 15:36–39), even good Christian people do get angry. And so the inspired apostle sets forth God's "sunset law": "Do not let the sun go down while you are still angry."

This practical rule makes sense. It makes even more sense during the years of retirement when small irritations have more chance of festering into full-blown conflict. In a somewhat different context Jesus said, "Each day has enough trouble of its own" (Matthew 6:34). In other words, do not carry over today's problems into tomorrow; tomorrow does not need them.

Actually resolving whatever the conflict was by day's end (as opposed to calling an overnight truce) is not as easy as it sounds. The reason I do not find it easy usually lies in my pride. Resolution demands capitulation—or, at the least, compromise—and I find it hard to admit I am wrong and to ask forgiveness. I also find it hard to concede a point, to let Marge have the benefit of the doubt.

I need to go on reading Colossians. Paul not only tells me to rid myself of anger, but I am to "clothe [myself] with compassion, kindness, humility, gentleness and patience." Marge and I are to "bear with each other and forgive whatever grievances [we] may have against one another" (3:12–13).

Father, help me to forgive as Jesus Christ forgave me. Amen.

JUNE 28

Serving the Lord

*Never be lacking in zeal, but keep your
spiritual fervor, serving the Lord. (Romans 12:11)*

One thing that I hope will not be denied me as I get older is the privilege of serving God through serving people.

Marge's mother, Alma Fisk, whom I have referred to before, is a model of service. Mother has never had an abundance of money, nor does she today. But she has two things that money cannot buy: access to the throne of God through prayer and an unflagging desire to minister to others of God's children.

How thankful I am for Mother's prayers. She prays for Marge and me. She prays for each of our children. She prays for our daughter Rebecca's daughter Sarah. That same level of concern goes out to each of her children and grandchildren and now great-grandchildren. She literally prays around the world.

I am concerned when Mother's children withhold distressing news from her, thinking it is better not to trouble her. Mother needs to feel involved. Indeed, her prayer ministry is a potent force. Both she herself and those in need are cheated when well-intentioned people do not keep Mother informed.

But in addition to prayer, Mother likes to serve people. Whether it is someone needing a listening ear or someone in the nursing center of The Alliance Home where she lives to whom she can bring a word of cheer, this sense of being needed keeps her going.

God's children are on earth to love Him, to praise Him and to serve Him. Those three assignments should be their chief occupation. Mother sets a good example.

Father, I love You, I praise You, I am Your servant. Amen.

JUNE 29

A Bad Ending

In spite of [God's] wonders, they did not believe.
So he ended their days in futility and their years in terror.
(Psalm 78:32-33)

The reference is to the Israelites on their trek across the Sinai desert after their exodus from Egypt. The implication, expanded in First Corinthians 10, is terrifying. The application is especially to my 60+ generation.

Anyone familiar with the Bible is aware of the Israelites' rebellious, complaining, unbelieving attitude amid what had to be the most remarkable demonstration of divine power since the Flood. They were guilty of idolatry, "indulg[ing] in pagan revelry" (1 Corinthians 10:7). They "commit[ted] sexual immorality" (10:8)—and 23,000 perished in a single day. They "test[ed] the Lord" (10:9), complaining about His provision of food and water—and they died of snakebite.

Kadesh Barnea was the last straw. When the people refused to believe that God could help them overcome the giants and conquer the promised land, His patience ran out. God "ended their days in futility/ and their years in terror."

It is far from the satisfied, tranquil ending to life that the prophets depict, with each man under his own vine and fig tree and children playing happily in the city streets. It was grim and terrifying. And it came about because of unbelief.

What is the lesson for me? It is the same as it was for the Corinthians: "If you think you are standing firm, be careful that you don't fall!" (10:12).

Father, do not let my faith in You falter. Amen.

JUNE 30

Night School

*I will praise the Lord, who counsels me;
even at night my heart instructs me.
(Psalm 16:7)*

The nights can be long when sleep abandons me to a mind full of thoughts and I toss restlessly between the alternatives of too hot and too cold. But those interminable nights can be blessings in disguise. God can use them to instruct His children. He will use them to instruct me if I let Him.

How? Through songs. Songs in the night.

"God my Maker/ . . . gives songs in the night" (Job 35:10). "At night [the Lord's] song is with me" (Psalm 42:8). "I remembered my songs in the night" (Psalm 77:6).

If God is going to instruct me through songs, I had better memorize the hymns and songs that by their comprehensive theology offer such instruction. I think of Luther's "A Mighty Fortress Is Our God," Watts' "O God Our Help in Ages Past," Walter Smith's "Immortal, Invisible, God Only Wise," Grant's "O Worship the King," Cowper's "God Moves in a Mysterious Way," Charles Wesley's "Oh, for a Thousand Tongues," Fanny Crosby's "Blessed Assurance," Bliss's "Hallelujah, What a Savior!" Stennett's "Majestic Sweetness Sits Enthroned." The list is nearly endless.

Then, too, I dare not overlook the Psalms—Israel's own hymnal and the original "songs in the night." This inspired compendium of counsel and guidance can be as close as my memory, and never farther than my open Bible.

Father, when sleep flees, I will hear Your instruction. Amen.

JULY 1

Time

*There is a time for everything,
and a season for every activity.
(Ecclesiastes 3:1)*

Take time to work—
 It is the price of success.

Take time to think—
 It is the source of power.

Take time to play—
 It is the secret of perpetual youth.

Take time to read—
 It is the fountain of wisdom.

Take time to be friendly—
 It is the road to happiness.

Take time to love and be loved—
 It is nourishment for the soul.

Take time to share—
 It is too short a life to be selfish.

Take time to laugh—
 It is the music of the heart.

Take time to dream—
 It is hitching your wagon to a star.
 —Anonymous

Father, thank You for the gift of time. Amen.

JULY 2

Rich Provision

*God ... richly provides us with everything
for our enjoyment. (1 Timothy 6:17)*

Today I am with Marge, our daughter Rebecca and our granddaughter Sarah at Kure Beach, North Carolina. We are occupying John and Marian Holbrook's beach house.

It is delightfully relaxing after the incessant pressures of getting our new place in Garner settled. At Garner every attempt to relax was opposed by cartons yet to open, pictures yet to hang, shelves yet to be built. Down here we are a hundred miles removed from those dictatorial pressures. There is nothing to do but walk the sandy beach, swim, read, eat, relax.

Through the living room windows of this retreat, I can view the panorama of blue ocean, see the huddle of beachside cottages, watch the vacationers as they carry surf boards and beach chairs to the beckoning shoreline.

How generous of my brother- and sister-in-law to share their lovely second home with us! How true to form for God to "richly [provide] us with everything for our enjoyment"! Such a place is beyond my means. Yet I have the pleasure of it without the responsibilities attendant to ownership.

Come to think of it, most of the really pleasurable things of life are free. Sunshine. Invigorating air. Beautiful sunrises. Peaceful evening walks. Stimulating, loving friends. Christian fellowship. Grandchildren. Grandchildren's puppies.

My financial assets may be modest, but I am rich indeed!

Father, thank You for the abundance of things You give me to enjoy. Best of all, thank You for giving me Yourself! Amen.

JULY 3

Time for Revival

"If my people, who are called by my name, will humble themselves and pray and seek my face and turn from their wicked ways, then will I hear from heaven and will forgive their sin and will heal their land." (2 Chronicles 7:14)

Revival is a universal need. *I* need revival. Revival, however, never just happens. God has set certain criteria. God's conditions for revival presuppose an ingredient that even retirees consider to be in short supply: time.

But whatever other inequalities there may be in this world, time is not one of them. Child, adult, rich, poor, brilliant, retarded—everyone has the same number of hours in each day. There may be wide disparity in the way each one uses his or her hours, but there is no disparity in their daily number.

What, then, is the problem? Essentially it is one of priority. God says, "If my people . . . will humble themselves and pray and seek my face and turn from their wicked ways, *then* . . ." Or, as He states it through Jeremiah, "You will seek me and find me when you seek me with all your heart" (Jeremiah 29:13).

Shall revival always elude me? Must those of this current generation—my children and grandchildren included—who have not known revival except in a few localized instances, be doomed to live out their lives without experiencing the gracious outpouring of the Holy Spirit?

God has left the answer with me and my fellow retirees. Could any pursuit during these next years have a higher priority? If revival does not come, who is to blame?

Father, You wait for me to ask, seek, knock. Amen.

JULY 4

Remember Mercy

Lord, . . . in wrath remember mercy. (Habakkuk 3:2)

"The Lord is with you when you are with him," said the prophet Azariah to Asa, one of Judah's reform kings (2 Chronicles 15:2). It was a time of spiritual revival. Almost singlehandedly, King Asa had returned Israel to the worship of Jehovah God.

The message Azariah had for Asa was one that should have been obvious to any serious historian of the Israel monarchy: Acknowledge God, exercise justice and righteousness as He commanded, and national well-being is assured. Reject God, turn from His ways, and disaster follows.

Though the pattern was consistent, it somehow escaped the attention of Israel's sinning kings. Ultimately the issue was national deportation and captivity, first in Assyria for the Northern Kingdom, then in Babylon for the Southern Kingdom. Although God ultimately brought some of His people back to the Land, Israel as a nation never really recovered.

I dislike to be pessimistic about my own nation, perhaps because my father was pessimistic 60 years ago when I was growing up. Somehow America has survived—much longer than my father ever supposed it would. But my nation veers ever farther from a godly course. Barring heaven-sent revival and another Asa to lead it (which are not impossibilities), Dad's dire predictions could very soon be upon us.

Father, I love my nation. I thank You for it. But America has turned from You and strayed far from your precepts. In Your justifiable wrath, please remember mercy. Amen.

JULY 5

The Right Spirit

Do not get drunk on wine, which leads to debauchery. Instead, be filled with the Spirit. (Ephesians 5:18)

It is incongruous. The same New York newspaper that reported record state-wide sales of beer, wine and liquor a few pages later carried a picture of an automobile wrecked beyond recognition in an accident that had proved fatal to one of the passengers. On a fairly clear stretch of pavement the car hit a tractor trailer slowing down for a turn. The top of the car was sheared off in the impact. Beyond the obvious fact of excessive speed is the nagging suspicion that alcohol played a part in the fatality, as it does in so many highway accidents. *But readers too infrequently make the connection.*

I find only limited scriptural support for abstinence, but that was a different era. The pace was slower. Life tended to be more physical, more pastoral. Camels, donkeys and mules presumably could get a man home in one piece, however impaired his reflexes might be. Today abstinence makes sense, especially in cultures that entrust 3,000 pounds of high precision machinery to the skill of licensed drivers.

To be filled with God's Spirit is the best antidote for the desire to be filled with spirits. The Spirit-filled life results in "love, joy, peace, patience, kindness, goodness, faithfulness, gentleness and self-control" (Galatians 5:22–23). Moreover, being filled with the Spirit is much easier on those whose physical lives are in my hands when I get behind the wheel of an automobile or a truck.

Father, for the sake of others and myself, I will stay clear of alcohol's entrapment. Amen.

JULY 6

Seizing Opportunity

Be wise in the way you act toward outsiders; make the most of every opportunity. (Colossians 4:5)

While I was in my backyard clearing some brush, Chuck and Myrtle, my neighbors in the house on the corner, backed their Chevy Carry-All to the rear of their property. Thinking they were preparing to hitch up their pop-up camper and might need an extra hand or a strong back, I strolled over.

Chuck and Myrtle are late middle age. They are Southerners—friendly, non-stop talkers, admittedly irreligious, big-hearted, devoted to each other, interesting, likeable. Chuck is legally blind, but he has a responsible computer job in Raleigh. Myrtle does the family driving.

They had moved the Carry-All not to hitch up their trailer but to off-load a large wooden bird cage for Myrtle's in-the-house aviary (she raises birds as a hobby). In the course of helping them unload it, I learned there was a second, still larger cage in north Raleigh that had to be disassembled and transported. Would I be interested in going along?

I had other things to do, but the opportunity to get better acquainted with these "outsiders" who are my neighbors was too good to pass up. I grabbed my work gloves and a hammer and went along. And I am glad I did. The Langleys got to see me not as a retired "preacher" but as a fellow human being.

Moreover, when the time is ripe to share with them the claims of Christ, can they refuse to listen?

Father, thank You for good-hearted, friendly neighbors. Give me the opportunity—and ability—to introduce them to You. Amen.

JULY 7

"D. V."

You ought to say, "If it is the Lord's will, we will live and do this or that." (James 4:15)

Deo volenti, often shortened to *D. V.*—the Latin for "God being willing"—has fallen out of use. There was a time when I found it in letters written by godly overseers, and in books authored by the same genre of men and women. The admonition that prompted the expression is from James.

James chides his Christian readers for making plans that do not take God into account: "Now listen, you who say, 'Today or tomorrow we will go to this or that city, spend a year there, carry on business and make money.' Why, you do not even know what will happen tomorrow" (James 4:13–14).

James continues: "What is your life? You are a mist that appears for a little while and then vanishes." Written to readers not necessarily in the upper age brackets, the counsel applies even more to those like me who are.

Here in the air-conditioned South, it is not uncommon when I step out of the car into the humid summer atmosphere to have my glasses "steam" up. But it is very temporary. The mist can vanish as quickly as it collected. Just so volatile is my life.

Does that fact call me to morbidity and pessimism? No. It rather calls me to keep God's divine purposes in mind in all my planning. He is Lord. He has the right not only to open and close doors but to extend or cut short my very life.

I who am but a heartbeat from death need to recognize God's sovereign control over all my life and all my plans.

Father, let me daily acknowledge Your Lordship. Amen.

JULY 8

Saul

Samuel said to Saul, "Why have you disturbed me by bringing me up?...Tomorrow you ...will be with me." (1 Samuel 28:15, 19)

It was an eerie scene: King Saul and a handful of his closest advisers crowded clandestinely into the cottage at Endor. An astonished spiritist medium seeing the specter of an old robed prophet. The voice of the departed Samuel communicating freely with the desperate king.

Most of what Samuel said to Saul was not new. As Israel's first king, Saul had chosen a course counter to God's. He had passed the point of no return.

Saul was an anomaly. He could at one moment be under prophetic inspiration; at another, a slave to vengeance and raw envy. At one moment he could plead with Samuel to know God's will; at another, he could walk in his own carnal ways. He could at one moment rid the land of practicing occultists; at another, himself consult a spiritist medium.

Saul is one of the very few Bible characters to know in advance the day of his death. Even that solemn prediction by Samuel seems to have brought no remorse, no repentance, no effort to make peace with the Judge of all the earth.

Saul had committed the unpardonable sin. Not that God was—or is—unwilling to pardon sin. But Saul himself had passed beyond the point of wanting pardon and reconciliation.

Thankfully, those with the spiritual interest to read this meditation are *not* in that category.

Father, keep me open and obedient to Your Word. Amen.

JULY 9

David

David... died at a good old age, having enjoyed long life, wealth and honor. (1 Chronicles 29:26–28)

What can I say that has not been said of David, Israel's great monarch, poet and national "father" as certainly as Abraham was Israel's biological father?

Ewald's summary is worth repeating:

"We find the very foundations of [David's] character to be laid in a peculiarly firm and unshaken trust in Jehovah, and the brightest and most spiritual views of the creation of the world. [David possesses] a constant, tender and sensitive awe of the Holy One in Israel: a simple, pure striving never to be untrue to Him, and the strongest efforts to return to Him all the more loyal after errors and transgressions....

"[David's] mouth continually overflows with heartfelt praise of Jehovah, and his actions are ever scented with the nobility inspired by a real and living fear of Him. The errors by which he is carried away stand out prominently just because of their rarity....

"In the clear daylight of Israel's ancient history, David furnishes the most brilliant example of the noble elevation of character produced by the old religion" (*History of Israel*, Volume III, pages 57–58).

Musician, poet, warrior, ruler, judge, prophet, national hero—David stands exceedingly tall among the Old Testament's outstanding men and women. Into old age God blessed his service, allowing him to *enjoy* long life, wealth and honor.

Father, give me David's love for You and Your ways. Amen.

JULY 10

Joab

Benaiah entered the tent of the Lord and said to Joab, "The king says, 'Come out!'" But he answered, "No, I will die here." (1 Kings 2:30)

A battlefield promotion elevated Joab to commander-in-chief of Israel's army under King David—a position he held with distinction for three decades. Actually, Joab was David's nephew, the son of David's sister, Zeruiah. But the relationship between the two men was built more on mutual fear than kinship.

It was hard for David to admire a military officer—even his nephew—who gained his position by climbing over the murdered bodies of others better than he. It was hard for Joab to admire a king who preferred sleeping with a loyal soldier's wife to going out to battle like other kings. But David needed Joab and Joab needed David, so their uneasy truce held.

At least, it held almost to the end. When Adonijah tried to wrest the throne from the elderly, fast-failing David, Joab—also up in years—unwisely cast his lot with Adonijah.

I can only guess at Joab's rationale for siding with Adonijah. Did he naively suppose that he was able to lead Israel's armies indefinitely?

Whatever the reason, Joab in his advancing years chose unwisely. It is a pitiful scene as I watch this once fearless man cower in front of the bronze altar at the tent of the Lord, clutching the horns of the altar.

And soon, all too soon, he is dispatched by the executioner—a sorry ending for Israel's illustrious general.

Father, protect me from making bad decisions. Amen.

JULY 11

Gad

*The Lord said to Gad, David's seer, "Go and tell David,
... 'I am giving you three options.' "*
(1 Chronicles 21:9–10)

Gad had had a long and useful relationship with David, dating back to the days when David was being hunted by King Saul, who was bent on putting him to death. As a prophet of God, Gad had advised David of Saul's whereabouts, thus enabling David to outmaneuver Saul.

If Gad had a regular prophetic ministry during David's years as king, the Scriptures are silent on the point. But Gad did have two assignments from the king during those years. One was to assist in setting up the music for the house of the Lord—a worship tradition that was still recognized three centuries later by Hezekiah. Gad also was charged with recording the events of King David's reign. In all probability details that Gad recorded have found their way into Second Samuel and First Chronicles of the Old Testament.

Thus, as a senior and trusted member of the king's staff, the prophet Gad was in a favored position when God needed a special messenger to confront the king. For David had sinned; he had taken a census of the people contrary to God's instruction not to do so. Conscience-stricken by his deliberate disobedience, David waited for God's retribution to fall.

It was through Gad, David's long-time associate, that God spoke. Gad had not let the busyness of other worthy duties choke his contact with God. In his senior years, he was still ready to be God's spokesperson.

Speak, Father, for Your servant is listening. Amen.

JULY 12

Shimei

"You have with you Shimei son of Gera, the Benjamite. . . . Bring his gray head down to the grave in blood." (1 Kings 2:8–9)

I feel a certain compassion for Shimei, of the clan of King Saul. Shimei lived just over the Mount of Olives from Jerusalem. He must have been overjoyed when Saul was named king of all Israel. The later overthrow of Saul's dynasty by David obviously left a deep root of bitterness in Shimei.

But how do you protest against a sovereign who has life and death power over his subjects? Shimei did what many do. He bottled up the venomous hatred inside him. When Absalom usurped the throne and David had to flee for his life, the cork popped and Shimei spilled all his pent-up anger on the fleeing king and his entourage.

Shimei had a sudden change of heart when he learned that Absalom was dead and David was returning to the throne. Shimei was the first to greet the king on Jordan's east bank, falling prostrate before him, begging forgiveness, promising unconditional loyalty. David forgave, but he did not forget.

David's final recorded words: "Bring [Shimei's] gray head down to the grave in blood."

The Scriptures warn me, "See to it that . . . no bitter root grows up to cause trouble and defile many" (Hebrews 12:15). Bitterness starts small. But it grows—as Shimei learned. And in the end it not only defiles but it consumes.

I must trust God to redress any wrongs done to me. "It is mine to avenge," the Lord says (Deuteronomy 32:35).

Father, help me to extract every root of bitterness. Amen.

JULY 13

Let Down

Joshua said, "Ah, Sovereign Lord, why? . . ."
The Lord said . . . "Israel has sinned." (Joshua 7:7–11)

It was the first of several embarrassing setbacks Israel was about to suffer.

After the heady victory at Jericho, the town of Ai looked like an easy target. So easy, in fact, that the men who went up to reconnoiter advised that there was no need to "weary all the people" (Joshua 7:3) by sending in the whole army. So about 3,000 men went up to battle against Ai. And—yes—they were roundly defeated by Ai's few inhabitants. Thirty-six Israelites were killed in the encounter.

Joshua, leader of the Israelites, was devastated. He and the elders of Israel "fell facedown to the ground before the ark of the Lord, remaining there till evening" (7:6). "What can I say, now that Israel has been routed by its enemies?" Joshua asked (7:8). In other words, "Lord, You have let us down."

God in effect answered, "You have let yourselves down." An Israelite had taken some of the forbidden spoil from Jericho in direct disobedience to God's command.

God cannot bless disobedience.

Once the culprit Achan and his family were dealt with (when will God's people learn that sin injures family members as well as the perpetrator?) Israel faced off against Ai once more. This time the whole army engaged in the battle. And God gave Israel undisputed victory.

Father, it is a thin line between faith and obedience. Help me to demonstrate my faith by implicit obedience. Amen.

JULY 14

Lasting Mark

*"Establish the work of our hands for us—
yes, establish the work of our hands."
(Psalm 90:17)*

Sometimes I stroll through a cemetery, taking time to note the tombstone tributes to the persons buried there. Innate in most people is the persistent desire to make their mark in the world—to leave something of tangible benefit to those generations that will succeed them.

Few achieve lasting recognition. For every George Washington or Fanny J. Crosby, there are a million John Publics and Mary Smiths whose record, if any, is in the memories of a few descendants who themselves will soon be forgotten.

But the brutal reality that I may not be remembered for long need not prevent me from repeating David's sincere, heartfelt prayer: "Establish the work of our hands for us–/ yes, establish the work of our hands."

And God will. I need not attain political fame or be a public figure in the arts or science or religion to have the satisfaction of knowing that my life has made a positive contribution to someone else. It may simply be the encouragement I have been to a person ready to give up. It may have been the word of testimony that turned a friend from a dead-end future to an eternity with Jesus. It may have been my prevailing prayers that brought God's renewal to a church in some overseas nation or to my own fellowship here at home. It may simply be the cup of cold water given in Jesus' name.

Yes, I *can* make a mark in life. Thankfully, it is not too late to get started!

Father, let my life accomplish some lasting good. Amen.

JULY 15

Broken-down Walls

*Like a city whose walls are broken down
is a man who lacks self-control.
(Proverbs 25:28)*

In the days when the Proverbs were being compiled, broken-down city walls were serious.

1. Broken-down walls left the city open to aggressors in much the way broken skin opens the body to infection.

2. Broken-down walls meant piles of rubble that could impede travel, interfere with defense, weaken adjacent walls and adjoining structures.

3. Broken-down walls rendered the city unregulated. Vendors could bypass the checkpoints at the official gates. Citizens could leave without their departure being noted.

In similar ways, the lack of self-control can have serious consequences.

1. If I permit my emotions and whims to rule me, I shall be as directionless as a sailboat without a tiller. My appetite for food will make me blubbery—or my disdain for food will wizen me. I will find myself sleeping when I should be up and doing, and wakeful when I ought to be asleep.

2. The lack of self-control will prevent me from accepting responsibility in my home, my church, my community. I will not be dependable.

3. The lack of self-control will leave me open to temptation and to sin. I will tolerate the risque humor, the sensual advertisements, the lewd TV shows.

Broken-down walls are a sign of serious trouble. So is the lack of self-control.

Father, help me to discipline body, mind and spirit. Amen.

JULY 16

Sacrifice, Sacrilege?

"Freely you have received, freely give." (Matthew 10:8)

Everyone knows—or thinks he or she knows—the meaning of sacrilege: the desecrating or disrespectful treatment of sacred things, places, persons or ideas. But sacrilege has another, lesser-known meaning: the appropriating for secular or personal use of that which was intended for God.

Each Christian, if his or her experience is genuine, has at some point acknowledged the Lordship of Jesus Christ. But it is not always easy to translate creed into practice. All around me are people who have no such understanding concerning the Lordship of Christ. The material resources that for me are a trust from God are for them possessions to be used as they please. What for me are hours to be redeemed in God's service are for them hours to be spent as they wish.

In the Old Testament era, God was very demanding when it came to Israel's sacrifices. The people were not to come before Him empty-handed (Deuteronomy 16:16). Moreover, the sacrifice had to be flawless (Leviticus 22:20). It was not that God wanted to work a hardship on His people. It was simply that He deserved their best. And He, in turn, was anxious to prosper those who worshiped Him sincerely (Malachi 3:10).

True worship is giving God the costly. It is the two or three hours of time I wonder how I can spare. It is the substantial monetary offering that makes me ask how I can ever get along if I give God *that* much.

Sacrifice or sacrilege. Which will it be?

Father, freely I have received; freely I give! Amen.

JULY 17

Communicating

Always be prepared to give an answer to everyone who asks you to give the reason for the hope that you have. (1 Peter 3:15)

In an era when knowledge is doubling every five years, most people—even in enlightened America—are spiritual illiterates. They have not got through the first primer.

Worse, as one schooled back in the 1930s when the Bible and biblical values were still a part of the curriculum, I may not realize the abysmal spiritual ignorance of those who have come along later. "Are you saved?" I ask. "Jesus paid the penalty for your sins. Repent. Look to Jesus and live."

The words are familiar enough. *Saved. Paid. Penalty. Sins. Repent. Look. Live.* Common, everyday words. Biblical words. But Christians of my generation made them into a religous shorthand. They make sense to me. To most non-Christians they do not communicate. They are obscure concepts.

The resulting confusion has cost the church a double penalty. Some who might have responded have been thwarted by the theological code words they did not understand. And some others who have taken their places in the church are there under false pretense. They never really comprehended what it was to be born into the kingdom of Jesus Christ.

If I am to be an effective communicator of the gospel to those raised in an era of spiritual illiteracy, I must first know precisely the steps to salvation in Christ. Then I must make sure I can explain those steps in language that can be understood by the one to whom I am speaking.

Father, help me to communicate clearly. Amen.

JULY 18

The Gospel

*Christ died for our sins according to the Scriptures,
. . . he was buried, . . . he was raised on the third day
according to the Scriptures, and . . . he appeared.
(1 Corinthians 15:3–5)*

No one can say he or she really understands the process whereby a person one moment dead in sins can the next be alive as a new creation. But the steps are clear, and I need to be able to clearly state them.

The first step is awareness of guilt. I have been Mr. Good Guy. I never murdered. I do not cheat on my wife. But sin is also lying (even for a good cause) and coveting and failing to believe what God says. I am *guilty*! Step one.

So I have told a white lie. So has everyone else. If I do some good deeds to compensate for my bad ones, ought I not to escape God's displeasure? After all, He cannot condemn everybody.

Very reasonable. Except that our only available record of God's attitudes disagrees. The Bible says that everyone *does* stand condemned. And the penalty is death.

Death? Just for telling a lie? That may sound harsh. But will I take a chance on the correctness of my own logic, or will I believe what the Book says that "the wages of sin is death" (Romans 6:23)? As God's Spirit does His convicting, I realize I stand *condemned*. Step two.

Once I understand my jeopardy, I am a candidate for God's good news that Christ at Calvary died for me, the just for the unjust. I am at last prepared to forsake my sins (repentance) and put my *trust in Jesus Christ*. Step three.

Father, help me to make the good news plain to others. Amen.

JULY 19

Why Suffering?

*"Man is born to trouble as surely
as sparks fly upward."*
(Job 5:7)

Eliphaz, who made the above comment in the course of consoling Job, may have been a miserable comforter, but at least on that occasion he spoke the truth.

The "thorns and thistles" of Genesis 3:18 have expanded to include disease and debt and deformity and that ultimate of scourges, death.

And just as Job dared to ask why calamities should be heaped upon so righteous a person as he, so saints today ask why God, to whom they have committed themselves, should permit suffering and adversity to roil their overflowing cup.

If God is omnipotent, if God is love, if God is the believer's refuge, how can a Christian account for the adversity that hounds him or her?

Job, to whom suffering came in overwhelming doses, offers one answer. He discovered in the ordeal of pain and painful debate that his perfection was really only self-righteousness. God used suffering to bring the patriarch to the end of himself. When Job despised himself—note the expression in Job 42:6—and repented in dust and ashes, he was at last where God wanted him. He was in tune with God's purpose and in the proper condition to pray for his three friends.

We know not how Job's three friends fared. But God turned Job's captivity and restored double all that he had once had, including a new family of seven sons and three daughters.

Father, if it takes pain to purify me, send pain. Amen.

JULY 20

Paul's Goal

*I want to know Christ ... and the fellowship
of sharing in his sufferings, becoming like him
in his death. (Philippians 3:10)*

I call it Paul's goal because I shrink from making it mine. Not the first part, of course, about knowing Christ. But "the fellowship of sharing in his sufferings" and "becoming like him in his death"? Why would Paul desire to participate in Jesus' sufferings and to be like Him in His Calvary death?

It is not the only time Paul used similar language. He told the Colossians, "I fill up in my flesh what is still lacking in regard to Christ's afflictions, for the sake of his body, which is the church" (Colossians 1:24).

To the Corinthians he spoke of "the sufferings of Christ flow[ing] over into our lives" (2 Corinthians 1:5). And he said, "We always carry around in our body the death of Jesus" (4:10). He told the believers at Rome that they had a "share in [Christ's] sufferings" (Romans 8:17). He said to the Galatians, "I bear on my body the marks of Jesus" (Galatians 6:17).

Not only Paul, but also Peter speaks of the fellowship of Christ's sufferings. He tells his readers to "rejoice that you participate in the sufferings of Christ" (1 Peter 4:13).

There seems to be some mystical sense in which the afflictions of God's people complete the suffering of Jesus in His Calvary death. Perhaps that is why so many of God's children over the centuries have suffered. I do not know that I should pray to suffer. But if God sends suffering, I have the satisfaction of knowing there must be divine purpose in it.

Father, make me ready to follow Jesus to Calvary. Amen.

JULY 21

Done with Sin

He who has suffered in his body is done with sin. (1 Peter 4:1)

In addition to the mystical "completing" of the Lord's passion, suffering has another important purpose, as applicable to the retired person as to the younger Christian: *Suffering is an expurgator.* "He who has suffered . . . is done with sin."

In April, 1955, I walked normally for the last time. I was then just two years into my missionary service in the Philippines. That month, polio felled me.

Those days—more accurately those *nights*—in Davao City were some of the darkest of my life. The pain was constant; the weakness, terrifying. I could not even turn over in bed without assistance. Evacuated to the United States for concentrated therapy, I gradually recovered functional use of arms, hands and one leg. From wheelchair, I graduated to crutches, then to cane, finally to walking unassisted. But not normally. To this day I have a markedly lurching gait as I balance my weight on my knee-locked "polio" leg.

From this vantage point, I can trace the unmistakable hand of God in what befell me. He used the experience to redirect my service for Him. My family and I returned to the Philippines for another term of fulfilling, fruitful ministry. When circumstances made it inadvisable for us to continue overseas, God opened unbelievable doors here at home.

But God also used my "suffering" to keep me from sins of the flesh. Some of my ministerial contemporaries have fallen victim and are sidelined. God used polio to spare me.

Father, if suffering will keep me from sin, so be it! Amen.

JULY 22

Commit, Continue

Those who suffer according to God's will should commit themselves to their faithful Creator and continue to do good. (1 Peter 4:19)

If an unpleasant subject seems to be getting too much coverage, bear in mind that older people come in for a disproportionate share of suffering. Thus the coverage is justified.

Not all suffering is physical or disease-related. Peter mentions suffering "as a murderer or thief or any other kind of criminal, or even as a meddler" (1 Peter 4:15). Christians, he said, should keep themselves from *that* kind of suffering.

Peter knew what it was to suffer for the sake of the gospel. Twice he had been jailed by Jewish leaders (Acts 4:1; 5:18) and once by King Herod (12:1–3). On each occasion, his crime was preaching the good news about Jesus Christ. For the same offense he and the other apostles had also once been flogged (5:40), a particularly painful punishment.

Thirty years of Christian church development had not changed the situation much. He advised the believers to whom he was writing not to "be surprised at the painful trial you are suffering" (1 Peter 4:12). Rather, he said, "Rejoice that you participate in the sufferings of Christ" (4:13).

The Scriptures hold out an encouraging promise to the believer who is suffering: "God is our refuge and strength,/ an ever-present help in trouble" (Psalm 46:1). If my suffering falls within the will of God, I am to "commit myself to [my] faithful Creator and continue to do good."

Father, I do commit and I shall continue. Amen.

JULY 23

Courage

"Be strong and courageous, because you will lead these people to inherit the land I swore to their forefathers to give them. Be strong and very courageous." (Joshua 1:6–7)

Joshua and Caleb were cut from the same cloth. Courage marked their lives. Whether at Kadesh-Barnea, as Joshua and Caleb urged Israel to invade Canaan at once, or 40 years later as they conquered Canaan at last, they were men of great courage.

Courage may not seem of high priority for the over-60s, but it should be. I think of my friend Marion, who lost her husband unexpectedly to a heart attack. I think of Ray, who faces recurring bouts of depression that medication only partially keeps in check. And Jeanne, once extremely active, who now has difficulty walking and must use a cane. Yes, courage is a central need for the over-60.

Joshua and Caleb's courage was more than the power of positive thinking. It was based firmly on God and His promises. Their eyes were on the Lord, not on the giants who inhabited the land to be possessed. Like Paul, each could say, "I can do everything through [the Lord] who gives me strength" (Philippians 4:13). Everything? Everything God wants me to do. What God wills for me to do God provides the means for me to do.

Courage is sometimes active, like Joshua's as he led the conquest of Canaan, or Caleb's as he took Hebron. Courage can be passive, too, like Marion's as she bravely picks up the pieces of her life, or like Ray's as he faithfully bears up under an affliction God has not seen fit to deliver him from.

Father, I, too, can be courageous through You! Amen.

JULY 24

Transformed

We, who with unveiled faces all reflect the Lord's glory, are being transformed into his likeness with ever-increasing glory, which comes from the Lord. (2 Corinthians 3:18)

Life Magazine, back in the 1930s, published a series of mature husband-wife photos in which the two partners showed a striking resemblance. The magazine was suggesting that people who gaze at each other long enough begin to look alike.

On the spiritual level, it is a fact. As I reflect the Lord's glory, I am "being transformed into His likeness with ever-increasing glory." If it is not happening, something is wrong in my walk with God.

Paul contrasts the Christian in this era of grace with Moses in the era of law. Moses, when he descended from the divine presence, covered his face with a veil. The reason, says Paul: "to keep the Israelites from gazing at [his face] while the radiance was fading away" (3:13).

In Christ the veil has been abolished. Through Him I am in God's very presence. The more time I spend in God's presence, the more glory I shall evidence to others.

The man on the street is unimpressed by my church activities. He may not be impressed by my efforts to assist the less fortunate or to redress local injustices. But if I can reflect God's glory, he will take notice. If I can somehow let him see Jesus, he will be brought up short.

I have to be in the Presence. That is my responsibility. The rest "comes from the Lord."

Father, I have the time. Make me willing to spend it. And may the image of Christ I reflect be undistorted. Amen.

JULY 25
"Submit" - I

Submit to one another out of reverence for Christ. (Ephesians 5:21)

It is a little hard to tell if God, in inspiring Paul to write those words, intended them to go with the preceding admonitions to the church at large or with his words directed to wives and husbands that immediately follow. In fact, they are appropriate to either application. I relate them here to the wife-husband partnership.

I am a husband, happily married to a wife who has faithfully loved me, comforted me, honored and kept me, in sickness and in health. Our missionary service in the Philippines was a shared calling before our marriage. When family circumstances dictated a geographic change, it was *my* work—first at our denominational headquarters and later at its publishing house—that determined where we would live, and Marge deferred to those decisions. In both places she found meaningful, missionary-related work. But the point is that her activity was subservient to mine.

That is why in retirement I have purposely deferred as far as possible to Marge's wishes. I owe that much to her after her lifetime of faithful partnership. Thankfully, her decisions have not been hard to live with—in part because she is unselfish and thoughtful. And, also, by this time our thinking and our desires have approached a point of mutuality.

"Submit to one another." It is advice as apropos to a husband as to a wife. As apropos to a retired parent as to his or her adult children.

Father, submission is Your idea. I will submit. Amen.

JULY 26
"Submit" - II

Submit to one another out of reverence for Christ. (Ephesians 5:21)

If this imperative speaks to marriage partners (yesterday's meditation), it applies more broadly as well. What does it say to me, a senior member of the human community?

First, I need to understand that Paul wrote it to a *church* community. That is its focus.

Like any gathering of human beings from age one and up, Christian church members have opinions—ranging from the color the sanctuary should be to whether Calvin or Arminius was more nearly correct. Church members generally resolve their cultural and theological differences by segregating themselves into congregations holding similar views. They resolve their aesthetic and the other lesser differences by submitting to one another— that is, by a democratic process of consensus that defers to the other person and his or her opinion.

The trouble is, the older I get, the less flexible I am. Instead of opinions, which by connotation are open to influence and compromise, I am opinionated. I have a built-in tendency to insist on what happens to please me.

If my preferences do not coincide with the majority's, the majority may politely but grudgingly defer to my seniority, but I will have created an unhappy and potentially unhealthy climate within the community. Or, the majority may carry the day despite my opinion, leaving me to nurse my bitterness and my wounded pride.

Neither scenario is desirable. Neither fulfills the biblical mandate to submit.

Father, keep me flexible on the non-essentials. Amen.

JULY 27

Ultimate Submission

Submit yourselves ... to God. (James 4:7)

The Scriptures command Christians to "submit to one another" (Ephesians 5:21)—an imperative, as I have noted, that may be specifically aimed at husbands and wives. Christians are to submit to church leaders (1 Corinthians 16:16; Hebrews 13:17). They are to submit to civil authority (1 Peter 2:13–14). Those who are younger are to submit to those who are older (1 Peter 5:5). Wives are to submit to their husbands (Ephesians 5:22).

But there is an ultimate submission for the Christian, and that is to God.

Why? Because God gives grace to the humble (James 4:6, quoting Proverbs 3:34). Submission is a mark of humility.

Why? Because God "envies" intensely. He wants me to put no one and no thing above Him (James 4:5). "Friendship with the world is hatred toward God" (4:4).

Why? Because God wants me to ask in prayer for things He can freely give me. That means I must check my motive whenever I pray (4:3). Am I asking selfishly—to "spend what I get on [my] pleasures"? Or am I asking for those things, those developments, those relationships that will glorify God and draw me closer to Him? My prayers can be embarrassingly selfish.

But does not submission go contrary to everything my American culture has taught me? Exactly. It is not modeled on television. I will not find submission in the corporate office. It is not the advice of the legal profession. Submission is uniquely God's way, and it is only possible by His enabling.

Father, I submit first to You. Amen.

JULY 28

A Mind for Others

Each of you should look not only to your own interests,
but also to the interests of others. (Philippians 2:4)

Admonition like the above needs to be qualified. Nobody grates like a busybody. And with extra time on my hands now that I am retired, the busybody trap would be easy to fall into.

But isolation and withdrawal are probably greater temptations for most retired people than is the temptation to intrude uninvited into others' personal lives. How providential that at the very point in life when I most need outside fellowship, I have the time to cultivate such friendships!

Without forcing myself on people, I discover there are any number of ways I can "look . . . to the interests of others." For example, there is a nursing home up the street filled with lonely people who would welcome a chance to chat with someone from the outside. Also, Garner has a new senior citizens center. The staff is gearing up for a full-blown program, including low-price lunches, for the older residents of this area. There is plenty of opportunity to pitch in. And within the fellowship of my church, the occasions to lend a hand and help out are more than I really have time for.

Like with Chinese checkers, one move leads to another—and often to two others! There is no end to the opportunities once I make up my mind to act.

Attitude and approach make the difference between being obnoxious and being welcome. Help that is humbly, cheerfully rendered is seldom resented.

Father, deliver me from self-centeredness. Amen.

JULY 29

Unknown Influence

"None of us lives to himself alone." (Romans 14:7)

One fringe benefit of living this long is to learn on occasion the unknown, unexpected ways my example or attitude or word has positively affected another person.

There was that time shortly after I was flown home from the Philippines with polio, barely able to walk. After a church service in which I had shared my experiences, I happened to say in conversation with those who had come up front to talk to me, "I have no regrets." I certainly did not consider the remark profound or heroic. But God used it as a positive encouragement to at least one person who heard me say it.

I think of the missionary in Brazil who told me my presence one year, as a furloughing missionary, on the campus at Nyack College had influenced him toward missionary service.

And I recall, too, what my daughter Debbie said as she remembered how I would close the door of my at-home office when the time came each evening for me to pray. I closed the door so that I could pray without interruption. But that innocuous, regular act made a lasting impression on at least one of my children. It was a signal to her that Dad was in God's sacred presence and not to be disturbed.

When I finally assemble with the saints in heaven, I will have opportunity for unlimited conversation with my contemporaries and those who have followed. Then I shall discover to what extent God used my life to bless and influence others.

Father, I am sobered to think that "none of us lives to himself alone." Make me a positive model for others. Amen.

JULY 30

Harvest Coming

Let us not become weary in doing good, for at the proper time we will reap a harvest if we do not give up. (Galatians 6:9)

As I drive the 15 country miles between our house and our daughter's, the fields are a kaleidoscope of colors, from the white, newly plowed North Carolina "sand hills" to the green of soy beans and the gold of ripening wheat.

Most of the fields I pass are relatively small. Bronzed farmers in bibbed overalls are out there in the elements making as sure as they can that there will be a harvest. But beyond the dawn-to-dusk, back-breaking toil, each knows that an essential ingredient in a farmer's life is patience. If spring is late, he has to be patient. If the rains are slow, he must be patient. He can do little to hurry the harvest. But it will come!

The Scriptures carry that analogy to my life in Christ Jesus. Not only am I "to devote [myself] to doing what is good" (Titus 3:8). I must also "not become weary in doing good."

By this point in life, I have already begun to reap some of my harvest, as I reflected earlier. There are grateful people who have thanked me for material assistance and for encouragement. Some have also been introduced to Christ through me.

The surprises are a special delight. Someone thanks me for an act of kindness or a timely word that meant much to him or her, and I cannot even recall the occasion! For sure, the harvest is much more abundant than I suspect.

I must not stop now. I must not become weary in doing good. There is a harvest for me to reap if I do not give up.

Father, let me not become weary in doing good. Amen.

JULY 31

Gotcha!

*A man's ways are in full view of the Lord,
and he examines all his paths.
(Proverbs 5:21)*

This proverb reminds me of the introduction to an article on radar detectors I saw in *Popular Science* magazine. Covering half the title page was a uniformed patrolman, radar gun aimed point-blank at the reader. Above the patrolman, in headline type, was the caption, "GOTCHA!"

Of course, God has never needed radar or a surveillance camera to keep tabs on His children. Ever since Adam and Eve's unsuccessful attempt to hide from God in the Garden of Eden, God has demonstrated His uncanny ability to track His creatures wherever they are, in whatever they are involved. None of my sins is secret to Him. I cannot hide from His presence.

That knowledge has helped me over a good many temptations. I might have succeeded in covering my actions from family members and friends, but God's searchlight was something I had to reckon with. I knew I could not escape His gaze.

Why, though, do I always think of God's surveillance in negative terms? God "examines" my "paths" for a totally positive purpose as well. He is concerned about my ways and my direction of travel. I am important to Him. Left unattended, I would stray from the straight and narrow; I would wander into forbidden or harmful bypaths.

I thank God for guiding me so satisfyingly all my life. His record of performance until now makes me confident concerning the unknown future.

Father, please keep me under Your surveillance. Amen.

AUGUST 1

Marge

May you rejoice in the wife of your youth...
May you ever be captivated by her love.
(Proverbs 5:18–19)

Today is my wedding anniversary. On this special day I want to say a special word about Marge, my wife of more than four decades. I loved her the moment I saw her on a March Sunday morning at the Waverly, New York, Christian and Missionary Alliance church. And our lifetime of experiences together in ministry as well as in the raising of our four children have served to confirm and deepen that love.

I have tested Marge's love for me to the limit. Polio reduced me for a time from a self-sufficient husband to a dependent invalid. Marge not only saw me through that ordeal, but cared as well for Debbie, our daughter, whose concurrent paralysis was in some ways more severe than mine and whose battle with the disability involved much more suffering.

I am deeply thankful to God for Marge's spiritual dimension. She follows after God. She *prays*—not just for family and close friends, but for people the world around. She has a sensitivity of spirit far keener than mine.

Marge is hospitable. Our home has been a peaceful haven for students, for friends of our children, for our own friends and relatives. They appreciate Marge's cooking. So do I. They are impressed by her housekeeping. So am I.

At least half of any success I have had in these past years can be attributed to the good wife God gave me. Marge makes my life contented, and I am thankful.

Father, thank You for the good gift of a loving wife. Amen.

AUGUST 2

Peace and Quiet

*Better a dry crust with peace and quiet
than a house full of feasting, with strife.
(Proverbs 17:1)*

I am grateful for a peaceful house—plus considerably more than the "dry crust." God has given me two decades of marital bliss, and it is my fault that the figure is not double. Not that Marge and I were close to breaking up. But we argued and bickered. The change came almost imperceptibly.

"You've changed," I said to Marge one day. "What happened?"

"You've changed," Marge replied. "Ever since you returned from the Canadian revival." My mind flashed back to that Sunday night in Saskatoon, Saskatchewan, as I sat in the balcony of the city's largest church. The wall-to-wall, floor-to-ceiling congregation was singing Fanny Crosby's "Draw Me Nearer":

> I am Thine, O Lord, I have heard Thy voice,
>   And it told Thy love to me,
> But I long to rise in the arms of faith
>   And be closer drawn to Thee.

Somewhere in the second stanza I quit being a reporter of the revival and became instead a participant.

"Be at peace, first, in yourself," Thomas à Kempis wrote, "and then you will be able to bring others into peace." Thomas à Kempis was right.

Peace and quiet. What a beautiful benediction these have been upon my life and family. More to be desired are they than abundant food and the wealth to buy it.

Father, I am deeply grateful for Your peace. Amen.

AUGUST 3

My Choice

Though outwardly we are wasting away, yet inwardly we are being renewed day by day. (2 Corinthians 4:16)

Being essentially honest, I am only too aware that outwardly I am wasting away. Tasks that once I breezed through now require more effort. I find it harder to pull back names. Even faces do not always look familiar. Numbers that used to lock into my mind now float in and out haphazardly. Although a positive mental attitude toward life will do wonders, I must face the inevitable. The "wasting away" has begun.

But the Scriptures suggest the possibility of a glorious corollary. As my physical life diminishes, my spiritual life can intensify, can grow more robust!

Moreover, this intensification happens by means of the very processes involved in the wasting away of my physical life. Paul continues by speaking of "our light and momentary troubles" and says these troubles "are achieving for us an eternal glory that far outweighs them all" (2 Corinthians 4:17).

But all of this does not happen automatically. It happened for the Apostle Paul because he made it happen. It will happen for me if and as I make it happen. Attitude is the all-important factor. I can let afflictions and circumstances embitter me. I can be self-centered—a miserable old man radiating misery to all who come near me (and the number will quickly diminish). Or I can let those same circumstances leverage me into the heavenlies, with my mind and heart set on Jesus Christ and the absolute joy of our face-to-face meeting. The choice is mine.

Father, I choose to draw closer to You. Amen.

AUGUST 4

Even to Old Age

"Even to your old age . . .
I am he who will sustain you."
(Isaiah 46:4)

As many as a million elderly Americans each year are physically abused by family members caring for them. Christians, for several reasons, have a better chance than others of weathering old age with dignity and serenity.

First, they have inner tranquillity through the abiding Prince of Peace. They have the promise: "In all things God works for the good of those who love him, who have been called according to his purpose" (Romans 8:28).

Second, they have an optimistic long-range outlook. For them the icy fingers of death do not signal the end of all things bright and beautiful. Heaven is ahead, and so is Jesus, and so are loved ones gone on before.

Third, they likely will have the ministration of a caring church community and a concerned pastor. The importance of this support network cannot be overemphasized.

Fourth, they have God's assured provision: "Even to your old age . . ./I am he who will sustain you."

This is not to say that elderly Christians are never objects of abuse and never unhappy. But they have advantages the non-Christian can only wish for. To the righteous God promises:

> They will grow like a cedar of Lebanon; . . .
> They will still bear fruit in old age,
>   they will stay fresh and green.
>   (Psalm 92:12–14)

Father, I am relying on Your promises. Amen.

AUGUST 5

God Cares

[God] cares for you. (1 Peter 5:7)

I am thankful for a God who involves Himself in the minutiae of my life. Still.

I was assembling a wooden gym set for little Karl Isham next door—a project I had approached reluctantly because of the press of other responsibilities just then. John Isham, Karl's dad, did not know about those other important matters when he asked me, and I did not tell him. Neighbors are important, too.

In addition to space for two swings, the gym called for climbing bars at one end, to be set in holes I was to drill in the upright members. As I was spreading the glue to permanently fix the uprights in place, I "happened" to notice that the holes I had drilled were misaligned. I had cut the holes to pattern, but inadvertently I had reversed the assembly process. A few minutes more, and I would have learned my mistake *after* the misaligned uprights had been permanently bonded. I could have corrected the error later, but not very easily.

I have never been one to believe God *has* to be involved in all the little matters of my life. Keeping the planets on course strikes me as more in keeping with His status than helping me properly assemble a wooden gym set for Karl Isham. But that only betrays my human perspective. God who created solar systems also created atoms. Galaxies or atoms—and everything in between—they are all within His purview.

God never sleeps. God is never inattentive. *God cares.* He cares for me and for what concerns me.

Father, I shall bring to You the little matters, too. Amen.

AUGUST 6

Making Friends

"Suppose one of you has a friend...." (Luke 11:5)

"A man that hath friends must show himself friendly" (KJV) may be a poor translation of Proverbs 18:24, but I am finding that the principle applies. Friendship demands of me an aggressive reaching out to others.

This is the friendly South, not suspicious New York City or even conservative south-central Pennsylvania. People greet us on the street. They do not mind striking up a conversation if we are likely to be where they are for more than a minute. Neighbors pause in their outside chores to chat.

But those contacts are superficial. Total strangers speaking the same language can manage that much. We humans need friends whom we can know in depth, friends with whom we can share our burdens and frustrations, friends who will accept us in our work clothes as well as our Sunday best.

A psychologist has estimated that the average person in a lifetime has but three to five friends in whom he or she can truly confide. Such friends do not normally just happen. They are chosen, pursued and cultivated.

I look to my church as the primary reservoir of such potential friends. While I need to offer my friendship to non-believers whom God places within my sphere of influence, I should expect to find my most satisfying friendships among people whose spiritual goals approximate my own. What better place to look than within the church fellowship where God has placed me?

Father, good friends are important. Thank You for those of the past whose friendship continues. Help me seek others. Amen.

AUGUST 7

Finding a Friend

He goes to him at midnight and says,
"Friend, lend me three loaves of bread." (Luke 11:5)

Friendships are important. In retirement I want friends who will be not only a moral but a spiritual encouragement to me. The person who decides to "stay put," has his or her network of friends already in place. When Marge and I elected to relocate, we had to start over. The most logical place for us to seek helpful friendships was in the church where we worship.

We did not expect dozens of strangers to swarm over us, anxious to commit themselves in mutual friendship. It just does not work that way. These members have already established their social networks. We are the outsiders, the "intruders." We must earn acceptance.

I think back to New Cumberland and a spry little widow, Yonka Billingsley. At first, Yonka came to church only Sunday evenings, going into Harrisburg to attend her Orthodox church Sunday mornings. Yonka and we had little in common. But because she lived near us, we offered her a ride to church whenever she wanted to go. It soon became Wednesday evenings as well as Sunday evenings, and sometimes even Sunday mornings.

Yonka in return, invited us to her apartment for meals or sent home with us some of her tasty *baklava* for dessert. Marge and I became Yonka's confidants. Yonka made no pretense about it: we were her friends. She worked to make it so. And, over the years, our friendship has deepened.

The point: *I* need to take the initiative.

Father, help me to aggressively seek new friendships. Amen.

AUGUST 8

Younger Friends

To Timothy, my dear son... (2 Timothy 1:2)

Despite that innate desire for long life, age has some drawbacks. For one thing, it seldom comes unaccompanied by physical maladies that sap the joy of attainment. It is a pyrrhic victory to reach 100 attached to a heart-lung machine.

An equally serious drawback is that many of my contemporaries may lack my endurance. They die. When death overtakes a younger person, it is news. But after the initial shock, other people are available to help fill the void. Life returns more or less to normal. But in retirement when a friend passes away, there are fewer contemporaries to fill the gap. And if life continues long enough, ultimately there are no contemporaries.

This is why I have determined to take Paul's example and seek a mix of friends from various age levels. Paul had his Priscillas and Aquilas—people of his own generation. He also had his Timothys and Tituses—those who were chronologically younger. Our neighbors are mostly younger than Marge and I. At church there is a good mix of people. Some are approximately our age. Many are friendly younger people who seem quite willing to include us oldsters in their social orbit.

Cultivating younger friends will require flexibility and adaptability on the part of Marge and me. Hopefully the experience will serve them as well as us. By precept (when asked) and example, we can help bring them to Christian and social maturity. And if we outlast our contemporaries, these younger friends will cushion us against the loneliness at the top.

Father, thank You for younger friends. Amen.

AUGUST 9

Exclusive Friends

There is a friend who sticks closer than a brother. (Proverbs 18:24)

It is important for Marge to have a network of special friends in addition to those we mutually share. There are some very good reasons for this.

Statistically, the probability that Marge will be widowed is much higher than that I will be a widower. Moreover, women are more dependent on their friends than are men.

If, upon a partner's passing, the couple's mutual friends would reach out in long-term support of the surviving spouse, a special network of friends would be less necessary. Alas! Too many wives have discovered in their devastation that the couples they depended on tend to shut them out. Couples used to going places with couples do not quite know what to do when a part of their social circle is no longer a couple. So they tend to do nothing, and the widow, bereaved of her partner, finds herself bereaved of her friends as well.

Marge has found friends and meaning in a neighborhood Bible study she and a younger mother started. Also, women have almost unlimited opportunities for community service. Beyond the satisfaction of helping others is the gaining of new friends—their *own* friends, unshared by their husbands.

That modicum of independence at a time in life when a couple is suddenly seeing much more of each other, is important for both partners.

Father, how grateful I can be for friends! Amen.

AUGUST 10

Spiritual Leaders

Respect those who work hard among you, who are over you in the Lord and who admonish you. (1 Thessalonians 5:12)

In the New Testament pattern, God arranged for the appointment of elders in each church. These were men who by age, gifts and spiritual maturity (though young in the faith) evidenced the leadership qualities needed by that particular congregation. If I understand it right, it was usually a partnership of oversight—elders (plural) in each church—a team effort rather than a solo performance. This team approach is again gaining favor in our era, and that can be beneficial.

I am to "respect" these "who work hard" within the church. They may be only half my age—some of them hardly one-third—but my seniority does not give me license to denigrate them. In the military, the uniform, not necessarily the person, is saluted. But in the church I am to respect both the office and the officer. Paul says of these leaders, "Hold them in the highest regard in love because of their work" (1 Thessalonians 5:13).

How beautiful it is when those with the maturity of years can advise, encourage, support, complement the church's ministry team. How sad, how disruptive if I should demand my own way, making myself generally obnoxious, hindering growth, stifling fellowship, quenching the Spirit's fire.

I thank God for the high privilege of continued ministry within the spiritual body. Christ loved the church and gave Himself for it. I should do the same.

Father, help me, too, to love the church, to not become crotchety and sour, to accept majority decisions. Amen.

AUGUST 11

The Dillens

*A generous man will prosper;
he who refreshes others will himself
be refreshed. (Proverbs 11:25)*

How thankful Marge and I are for Fred and Eva Dillen. We got to know Fred and Eva at New Cumberland Alliance Church. I hope I may be as useful and as contented in my retirement as they are!

I doubt that the Dillens are wealthy. My visits to their cozy self-built bungalow in the hills a bit south of town left me with an impression of comfortable frugality. Surely it is from more than habit that Fred still cuts and splits his own firewood. And the garden he and Eva take delight in planting and nurturing each year might not need to be as large if they were not dependent upon its produce.

But Fred and Eva have discovered ways of being generous with a money-substitute: their time. Almost everywhere a person turns in and around New Cumberland Alliance Church, there is evidence of Fred's carpentry. Colorful plantings around the church are partly the effort of this dedicated couple. They have been some of the backbone support of the "Fifty Plus" Fellowship and its outreach to retired people in the community.

And as they have refreshed others, God has refreshed them. From the living room windows of their hilltop home they point their visiting friends to where the deer and other wildlife pass. Eva displays her latest needlework project. It is a priceless scene of happy contentment.

What good models they are for us!

Father, please make me as giving as are Fred and Eva. Amen.

AUGUST 12

Wake Up!

"You have a reputation of being alive, but you are dead. Wake up! Strengthen what remains." (Revelation 3:1–2)

I wish I knew more about the church in Sardis that was the focus of Jesus' imperative "Wake up!" He had not found their deeds "complete" (Revelation 3:2). Whatever life yet remained among the body of Christians was about to die (3:2). The people had a good heritage of truth, but they were not obeying it (3:3).

But there were individuals in the Sardis church whose clothes were "not soiled," whom Jesus called "worthy" (3:4). He promised they would walk with Him (3:4) and that their names would remain forever in His book of life (3:5).

In His admonition to the Sardis Christians to wake up, Jesus has a message for me as well. My public reputation, like theirs, is still quite impeccable. But the farther I progress into these early months of retirement, the harder is the battle to stay awake. Without the discipline of a five-day-a-week job and regular working hours, I find it very easy to waste time. I also find it harder and harder to get up in the morning—sometimes because I fail to go to bed on time the night before.

Even my priorities are hard to keep sorted out. I want to put off the spiritual matters in favor of the material, the difficult in favor of the easy, the long-range in favor of the immediate. These are all symptoms of "sleeping sickness." God has sounded for me the "wake up" alarm. It is now up to me to respond to it. By His help I shall. At once!

Father, the struggle against sloth is harder than I had imagined it would be. I need Your help in this battle. Amen.

AUGUST 13

Ahithophel

When Ahithophel saw that his advice had not been followed, he saddled his donkey and set out for his house in his hometown. He put his house in order and then hanged himself. (2 Samuel 17:23)

Ahithophel. The name, incongruous in an era when names were so linked to personalities, means "brother of folly." But in retrospect, perhaps the name *does* fit the man.

Ahithophel was King David's counselor—a man whose reputation for wisdom was "like that of one who inquires of God" (2 Samuel 16:23). Ahithophel also had another claim to fame. He was the grandfather of one Bathsheba. Bathsheba had been honorably, happily married until David eyed her, committed adultery with her, had her husband killed and added her to his harem.

Perhaps it was that long-festering injury which persuaded Ahithophel to go with David's rebel son, Absalom. And when Absalom asked, Ahithophel gave counsel that, if followed, would have put the monarchy solidly in Absalom's hands.

Ahithophel, however, had not reckoned on a second opinion—Hushai's—or on the fact that Absalom would reject Ahithophel's counsel in favor of Hushai's. The reputation he had labored a lifetime to build suddenly was in ruins. David would return to the throne, but without Ahithophel; Ahithophel's loyalty to David had been irrevocably compromised. There was no way out.

In the end, *Ahithophel*—"brother of folly"—became appropriate after all. No matter how desperate the personal problem, suicide is *not* a wise solution. Life is too important for me to take it into my own hands.

Father, whatever comes, my life is in Your hands. Amen.

AUGUST 14

Abiathar

Solomon removed Abiathar from the priesthood of the Lord, fulfilling the word the Lord had spoken at Shiloh about the house of Eli. (1 Kings 2:27)

One bad decision may not only undo a whole lifetime of diligence, but it can have adverse consequences on succeeding generations as well. Abiathar, who was Israel's high priest during David's long reign, is a case in point. And Abiathar's bad decision came in his senior years.

As a young man, Abiathar alone had escaped when King Saul in a demented rage put the high priest Ahimelech and all his house to death. Abiathar fled to David. He served as David's priest during his years of exile. When David gained the throne after Saul's death, he named Abiathar as co-high priest with Zadok, who was Saul's incumbent appointee.

Abiathar remained loyal to his long-time friend when Absalom tried to wrest the throne from his father David. But some years later, when Adonijah made a similar attempt, Abiathar, for reasons known best to him, sided with Adonijah in what turned out to be a failed coup.

It marked more than just the termination of his own high priestly service. It meant that his son and his son's son would also be denied that important position.

Unfortunately, I am not excused upon retirement from decision-making. It behooves me to trust in the Lord with all my heart, to lean not on my own understanding, to acknowledge God in all my ways and let Him make my path straight (Proverbs 3:5–6). God promises me His wisdom (James 1:5–6) if I ask Him in faith.

Father, I look to You for decision-making wisdom. Amen.

AUGUST 15

Barzillai

Barzillai was a very old man, eighty years of age. He had provided for the king during his stay in Mahanaim, for he was a very wealthy man. (2 Samuel 19:32)

"A friend in need is a friend indeed," goes the adage. Barzillai became a true friend to King David as he fled from Absalom, his insurrectionist son. Barzillai is one of only three specifically named people who furnished King David with food, bedding and housewares in that time of crisis.

The coup successfully put down, David wanted to reward his benefactor. The offer would have excited most people. It was a chance to join the palace household—for life.

Barzillai wisely resisted. "How many more years will I live?" the 80-year-old man asked (2 Samuel 19:34). In Rogelim, his home village (17:27), were everything that really mattered to him: family members and the tomb of his father and mother.

Barzillai is a picture of alert contentment. Probably all his life, this Gileadite had lived in Rogelim, as had his parents and maybe his grandparents. Hard work in the fields, his willing sons assisting, had brought prosperity. Suddenly, the tranquility is interrupted. The government has fallen. King David, his household and his troops have fled the insurrection and are actually encamped almost on his doorstep. And Barzillai, voluntarily and at great personal risk, gives aid.

I do not have Barzillai's great wealth. But I can have his great contentment. And if the need arises, I hope I will be as generous with my resources.

Father, thank You for this good model from Your Word. Amen.

AUGUST 16

Bathsheba

[Bathsheba] said to [David], "My Lord, you yourself swore to me: . . . 'Solomon your son shall be king after me, and he will sit on my throne.' But now Adonijah has become king, and you, my lord the king, do not know about it." (1 Kings 1:17–18)

Introduce a new queen—Bathsheba. Introduce an adulterous king—David. Introduce a tangled web of deceit, murder, an illegitimate baby, intrigue, incest, a revenge killing, a military coup, civil war, power struggles. What consequences a single act of sin can generate! The repercussions of that black night when raw lust short-circuited King David's normally spiritual mind hounded the man almost to the day of his death.

Lust may have put Bathsheba in David's arms, but to his credit he stayed with her, even into old age. And it was Bathsheba who kept the kingdom on course when Adonijah tried to wrest the throne from his aged father David.

Bathsheba, now much older and the queen wife of a very elderly king, alone had the power to thwart the ambitious plans of Adonijah. Bathsheba was in the right place at the right time, and she did what needed to be done. Her action preserved the life of Solomon, her son, and her own life. It worked to assure God's sovereign plans for Israel, including the building of the Temple and the genealogical line of Jesus, the Messiah.

The implications for me are transparent. Like David, I too am a forgiven sinner. Like Bathsheba, I am in God's right place at God's right time. God expects me to speak up, to act. My service is not insignificant.

Father, help me to be open always to Your leading. Amen.

AUGUST 17

Solomon

As Solomon grew old, his wives turned his heart after other gods. (1 Kings 11:4)

How could the world's wisest man make the stupid mistake Solomon made? After his auspicious start, after the magnificent Temple, after world acclaim and God's evident blessing upon his reign, Solomon allowed his heathen wives, whom he "held fast to . . . in love" (1 Kings 11:2) to turn his heart to idols.

I never approach this era in my reading of First Kings and Second Chronicles without wishing that somehow the action might have been frozen midway through Solomon's reign, leaving Israel permanently happy, peaceful and righteous. Alas!

I am intrigued that this spiritual declension came "as Solomon grew old." Is there something about aging that makes me more vulnerable to spiritual decline? For Solomon, it was the pressure from his harem of idolatrous wives. But they had not turned his head during his middle years. It happened as he aged. I have one wife and, thankfully, she is a godly woman. But I am concerned that whatever inner immunity kept Solomon on track most of his life failed him as he grew older.

Was it presumption—supposing that such a thing could not happen to him? Was it spiritual carelessness—a little letting down of the bars until the whole demonic horde scaled the barrier and stampeded him? Was it conceit—a feeling that he could manage his own life from here on out? I do not know. One thing I do know. I do not want to end up as Solomon did. As I grow older, may nothing and no one turn my heart from God.

Father, lead me not into temptation. Amen.

AUGUST 18

Hiram

There were peaceful relations between Hiram and Solomon, and the two of them made a treaty. (1 Kings 5:12)

I dislike being taken advantage of. It happens all the time—from drivers who cut me off on the road to unprofessional repairmen to people who, supposing I have nothing to do now that I am retired, want to create agendas for me.

Hiram was "had" by King Solomon. And he was probably in his sixties when it happened. Hiram had been a longtime friend of Solomon's father, David—a friendship that extended to his son. Hiram had the honor of supplying the cedar and pine required for the Temple construction. He also supplied artisans to work on the Temple and its furnishings. (Do not confuse King Hiram with Huram, mentioned in First Kings 7:13–14, a part-Jew from Tyre who was the Temple's chief artisan.)

Hiram as well supplied gold to Solomon. It was this gold that almost ruined a good friendship. In exchange for $135 million in gold, Solomon gave Hiram 20 Galilean "cities." When Hiram took delivery, he was not at all pleased with them, terming them "Cabul"—good-for-nothing. But he made no international waves about the injustice. He seemingly did not let the matter mar his friendship with and continued helpfulness to Solomon.

Of Jesus Peter says, "When he suffered, he made no threats. Instead he entrusted himself to him who judges justly" (1 Peter 2:23). Ancient Hiram, long before the Christian era, also knew how to turn the other cheek in the face of injustice.

Father, when people wrong me, make me willing to entrust the matter entirely to You. Amen.

AUGUST 19

Giving, Receiving

*Sons are a heritage from the Lord,
children a reward from him.
(Psalm 127:3)*

Marge and I have a deep love for the four children God gave us. It is a love that now encompasses spouses and grandchildren as well. They are our heritage. Rebecca, living near us, drops in often and invites us to her house for activities and meals. The telephone and letters keep us in touch with the others.

As time goes on, Marge and I need to insure that the relationship does not deteriorate. Obviously it is not reasonable that those living at some distance should visit frequently. But if the intervals between visits get too long, and we pine for our children, we should not hesitate to let them know. They are immersed in responsibilities of their own. Time may pass more quickly for them than for us. They may even suppose that we are too busy with our own activities to want their visit.

Marge and I need also to put ourselves in our children's place when it comes to gift giving. Right now we have no needs that our own funds cannot supply. We may even be in more favorable circumstances financially than our children with their mortgages and orthodontal expenses.

But our children need to feel that they are helping. They live under the scriptural command to honor father and mother. We must allow them that opportunity. No matter how sacrificial the gifts, we must accept them with grace and appreciation. They are more than gifts. They are tokens of our children's love for us and their obedience to God.

Father, keep me sensitive to my children. Amen.

AUGUST 20

Truthful People

The Lord detests lying lips,
but he delights in men who are truthful.
(Proverbs 12:22)

If God "detests lying lips," there are plenty of Bible people who disappointed Him profoundly.

Jacob lied to obtain his father's birthright blessing (Genesis 27:19). Rahab, the Jericho prostitute, lied to protect Israel's spies and bring them military victory (Joshua 2:4–6). The Gibeonites lied to Joshua (Joshua 9:7–9). The people of Israel lied to Joshua (and God) when they covenanted to serve the Lord (Joshua 24:16–18). Samson lied to Delilah (Judges 16:10). David, fleeing from Saul, saved his skin by deceiving the Philistines into thinking he was crazy (1 Samuel 21:12–13).

God commanded Israel, "You shall not give false testimony against your neighbor" (Exodus 20:16)—in effect, "You shall not lie." Much later He said to Israel through Zechariah, "Speak the truth to each other" (Zechariah 8:16).

When Jesus lived on earth, He declared Himself to be the embodiment of truth. He told His disciples, "I am . . . the truth" (John 14:6). He called His Holy Spirit "the Spirit of truth" (John 14:16–17).

The Apostle Paul speaks out against those who have exchanged God's truth for a lie, worshiping created things rather than the Creator (Romans 1:25). John had "great joy" when he was informed that Gaius was continuing to "walk in the truth" (3 John 2).

"The Lord . . . delights in men who are truthful." I want to be transparently honest. I want to bring God delight.

Father, help me to be honest—before men, before You. Amen.

AUGUST 21

New House

*If the earthly tent we live in is destroyed, we have . . .
an eternal house in heaven. (2 Corinthians 5:1)*

Death is something that happens to the other person—or to me when I am really old. I do not want to think about it. But Paul, probably only in his 50s at the time, thought about it. So I will follow his example.

Paul sets forth four contrasts in comparing what was then his life on earth with his future life in heaven.

1. The first of them is just that: one is earthly, the other is heavenly. And Paul assumes I am aware that the heavenly life is better.

2. The second has to do with the quality of the house I live in. The earthly "tent" and the heavenly "house" again leave no doubt as to which is superior.

3. Next he speaks of the builders. Our present bodies are of human construction—put together gene by gene, cell by cell in a cooperative parental project. The heavenly body I shall receive is being fashioned by Jehovah God Himself.

4. Finally, Paul contrasts the duration of the two. This body I now occupy is temporary. At the maximum, it will last 30 more years. It is destined for the grave—spent like a rocket. But my heavenly body will last forever.

On all four counts, the Scriptures make it abundantly clear as to which is the preferred state. There may be altruistic reasons for me to remain on earth somewhat longer—as there were for Paul. But clearly heaven is the place of choice.

Father, help me to shift gears, to anticipate *heaven. Amen.*

AUGUST 22

Down Payment

*God ... has given us the Spirit as a deposit,
guaranteeing what is to come. (2 Corinthians 5:5)*

Having contrasted believers' earthly and heavenly bodies (see yesterday's meditation), Paul moves on to express his personal preference to be in heaven. He longs to be "clothed" in his made-by-God eternal body. This, he declares, was God's very purpose in creating me—"so that what is mortal may be swallowed up by life" (2 Corinthians 5:4–5).

But although God may want me to remain on earth somewhat longer, He has given me His Spirit as a down payment on what is to come. Exactly what is the role of the Spirit?

The Spirit makes me "confident" (5:6, 8). I am not yet in the presence of my Heavenly Father, but the Holy Spirit living within me is a foretaste of that anticipated experience. I have contact with the Father now in prayer and worship through the ministry of the Spirit in my life.

Moreover, the Spirit brings assurance to me that it will all happen just as the Bible says. Death will be swallowed up by Life—eternal life. He who declared Himself to be Life conquered death at Calvary. I go into the next world not as into the unknown but with confidence. "To be away from the body"—this physical body—is to be "at home with the Lord" (5:8).

It is natural for me, after 60 or 65 years, to feel "at home" in this present body regardless of its shortcomings and malfunctions. But five minutes in my heavenly body and I will wonder why I ever clung so tightly to life on earth.

Father, prepare me for the transition! Amen.

AUGUST 23

Judgment Day

We must all appear before the judgment seat of Christ, that each one may receive what is due him for the things done while in the body, whether good or bad. (2 Corinthians 5:10)

Before leaving this subject of my physical, earthly body—the meditation of the past two days—Paul has some sobering words about judgment. Unfortunately, we do not hear much teaching about the Christian's rewards and punishment. The pulpits of our land may be silent on the subject, but the Word of God is not. Note:

1. It is a judgment from which no Christian is excused. "We must all appear."

2. Jesus Christ, the one to whom the Father has "entrusted all judgment" (John 5:22), will preside.

3. Up for review will be "the things done while in the body, whether good or bad." Presumably the good things constitute no problem. I will welcome whatever reward my Lord sees fit to give me. But what about the "bad" things? Will *all* my bad deeds be a matter of record and review? What about the sins I committed in my pre-salvation days? What about more recent sins I have confessed to God and been forgiven of?

On these points the Scriptures are not crystal clear—which probably explains the lack of teaching on the subject of rewards and punishment for the Christian.

It seems only reasonable, however, to suggest that if I want to be on the safe side, I will maintain always the cleanest possible record.

Father, my record even as a Christian is far from perfect. Will You please help me from here on to do better? Amen.

AUGUST 24

Reward Time - I

"The time has come for... rewarding... your saints and those who reverence your name, both small and great." (Revelation 11:18)

Few Christians seem to realize that there are going to be rewards in the life hereafter—rewards that will be based on their job performance in the here and now.

It is not as though the Scriptures were silent on the subject. In His Sermon on the Mount, Jesus promised a "great ... reward in heaven" to those who were the objects of persecution and false accusations (Matthew 5:11–12).

Paul declares that the "man who plants and the man who waters ... each will be rewarded according to his own labor" (1 Corinthians 3:8). Switching metaphors, he likens the believer's efforts to that of a builder whose work will be tested by fire. "If what he has built survives, he will receive his reward" (3:14).

To the believers in Colosse, Paul wrote, "Whatever you do, work at it with all your heart, as working for the Lord, not for men, since you know that you will receive an inheritance from the Lord as a reward" (Colossians 3:23–24). And John cautions: "Watch out that you do not lose what you have worked for, but that you may be rewarded fully" (2 John 8).

Jesus Himself concludes the New Testament with the promise, "Behold, I am coming soon! My reward is with me, and I will give to everyone according to what he has done" (Revelation 22:12).

This is a subject deserving further thought. Tune in again tomorrow.

Father, the time is short. May I acquit myself well! Amen.

AUGUST 25

Reward Time - II

Watch out that you do not lose what you have worked for, but that you may be rewarded fully. (2 John 8)

Why the silence about rewards? Are not the Scriptures explicit that there will be such? And that the believer's good works in this life will determine his or her reward in the next? Why is there so little teaching about rewards?

There are several possible explanations. Ever since Luther and his bold emphasis on justification solely by faith, works have been downplayed. Luther's stress on faith alone was a necessary corrective to the prevailing salvation-by-works notion of the established church of that day. But the concept of rewards for the works I do *after* I am saved by faith does not conflict with what Luther was advocating.

There is also the biblical account of at least one believer who got into paradise without the possibility of good works *after* he was saved. The dying thief—and everyone subsequently who achieves a death-bed repentance—was probably so glad to escape the alternative that, reward or no reward, he was satisfied just to be in paradise. Indeed, heaven sounds extremely desirable quite apart from additional incentives.

The fact is, God does not give detailed information concerning either the rewards He promises for good works or the relationship between the rewarded and the unrewarded. But I must conclude that the rewards are worth working for. And with time running down, I had better be diligent.

Father, I want to be among the rewarded believers in that eternal day ahead—by Your grace and help. Amen.

AUGUST 26

Why I Give Thanks

Give thanks to the Lord, for he is good. (Psalm 136:1)

Giving thanks to God is a biblical command, often repeated. Giving thanks serves several purposes:

First, my thanks is an acknowledgement that God is sovereign. Had *I* been arranging Paul's mission in Philippi, there would have been no jail episode. But then neither would there have been a converted jailer and his household!

Second, my thanks is an admission that God is good. Much may happen to me of questionable long-term value. Worse, I am subject to things that I tend to call misfortunes or even tragedies. Not so! *God is good*. He will bring good out of every circumstance. He wants to conform me to the image of His Son.

Third, giving thanks is a declaration of my submission to the will of God. I have presented my body to God as a living sacrifice (Romans 12:1). I have been crucified with Christ (Galatians 2:20). I am not my own (1 Corinthians 6:19).

Fourth, giving thanks may be the only route to victory. It was true for Jehoshaphat (2 Chronicles 20). And for Paul and Silas (Acts 16). Is it not worth some experiment today?

Fifth, giving thanks is the best way to avoid tension and irritability—those two occupational hazards of this era. Giving thanks takes the onus off me and puts the responsibility on God. It is admission that I have turned the problem over to Him.

Giving thanks will be my chief occupation in heaven. Praise is heaven's language. If I do not wish to feel out of place in that fair land, I had better learn how to speak it now.

Father, I will praise you with all my heart. Amen.

AUGUST 27

Throne Room Help

Let us ... approach the throne of grace with confidence, so that we may ... find grace to help us in our time of need. (Hebrews 4:16)

Almost 500 years after Martin Luther proclaimed the priesthood of every believer, his heirs are forfeiting their inalienable right. Instead of looking to God for grace to help, they are looking to professional counselors.

What has occasioned this unwillingness—or inability—of Christians to be their own priests?

Certainly the current milieu of interdependence is partly to blame. The rugged do-it-yourself individualism that long characterized Americans has given way within the past generation to a deeper sense of community and interdependence. Students do not study alone; they study together. Young people do not make independent decisions; they consult with their peers.

But the problem is deeper. It springs from a lack of serious Bible study and prayer. The Bible is still a reliable guidebook. But it cannot help the person who does not read it, study it, meditate upon it. God is still on His throne, His ear tuned to the call of His people. But prayer cannot change things for the person who does not pray seriously.

The abdication of the believer's priesthood is not exclusively a problem of the next generation. It is as well a problem of my generation, retired and soon to be. Interdependence and community are good. But I must not let them isolate me personally from access to God's throne of grace.

Father, I want Your fellowship; I need Your grace. Thank you for access through the Bible and prayer. Amen.

AUGUST 28

A Closed Mind

I know whom I have believed, and am convinced that he is able to guard what I have entrusted to him. (2 Timothy 1:12)

By the time of retirement, "set in his ways" is likely how people regard me. To counteract that natural tendency, I consciously try to be open to new ideas, new information. Rigidity is great for steel; it is not necessarily great in people.

But on some things I have a closed mind.

Do not suggest to me that there is no God. Or that there is some alternate way to heaven apart from the merits of Jesus Christ's death on the cross.

Do not try to tell me that the Bible is less than God's absolute Word. Or that salvation is part faith, part works.

Do not suggest to me that religion is all a colossal hoax, that someday death will overtake me and I will be snuffed out into nothingness like an extinguished candle flame. Or met at the end of the tunnel by a "being of light" who will inform me with benign amusement that hell was just a joke, that everybody really ends up in paradise and that I might as well have been selfish and sinful like the others back on earth.

Do not attempt to convince me that private meditation and maybe an electronic church service is just as good as assembling on the Lord's Day with fellow Christians for worship, instruction and mutual encouragement.

I have faced all of those issues. I have come to conclusions about them. To reconsider them now is profitless.

On those points my mind is made up.

Father, You will guard what I have entrusted to You. Amen.

AUGUST 29

Money Enough

... having all that you need. ...   (2 Corinthians 9:8)

I am sure I am not atypical in having less "take home" income now than before my retirement. Thankfully, I can add that my expenses are also scaled down.

Housing expenses are the largest single reduction in our budget. Being able to pay cash for this much smaller house in North Carolina has freed us from mortgage payments. Of course, I must continue to budget for property taxes and for house upkeep, including a cushion against major repairs or improvements.

The smaller house has appreciably cut our utility bills—even with central air conditioning. Another savings.

Being out from under some (but not all) federal, state and local income taxes, including the assessment for Social Security (FICA), is another significant budget cut.

With less income, what we formerly budgeted under "Tithe and Missions" and "Donations and Gifts" has of necessity shrunk. But I have discovered that I can supplement my reduced monetary offerings by contributions of time to God's work.

Medical insurance has become the largest budget increase. I failed to realize what a help employer-provided medical coverage was. Without it, Marge must now be on costly individual health insurance until she qualifies for Medicare. Social Security assesses me outright for Part B of my Medicare, and if I decide to sign up for Medicare supplement through a commercial insurer, that will be a further additional cost.

God does provide. He meets our needs.

Father, You are the God who provides. Amen.

AUGUST 30

Cutting Back

I have learned to be content. (Philippians 4:11)

Another budgeted expense that I can cut back on in retirement is clothing. The need to be dressed in a business suit four seasons of the year, six days a week (including church on Sundays), meant an extensive wardrobe. Even though my suits were not designer models, they represented a considerable dollar outlay. Add dress shirts, neckties, shoes and outerwear, double it so that Marge could also be appropriately dressed, and clothing was a significant item in our personal budget.

In retirement, dress is decidedly more casual. Even at church this is so. Thus we can cut our clothing budget significantly.

We have never taken expensive vacations, an exception being an anniversary trip to West Africa to see our missionary daughter, Esther. Now that we are a little farther removed from family and likely will be making more trips to see our children and other relatives, that budget item should not be reduced.

Christmas has always been our budgetary Waterloo. It was partly that we overspent, and it was partly that I underbudgeted. This is an appropriate time to revamp our whole process of gift-giving. Other family members, likewise hard pressed to keep up with the tradition, favor a scaling back. Instead of exchanging gifts this year with each family member, we will draw one name and buy a gift of predetermined monetary value for that person. Of course, there will be a few exceptions!

Father, contentment is not easily learned in our materialistic society. Help me to be content. Amen.

AUGUST 31

God Will Supply

"[God] ... will ... supply and increase your store of seed." (2 Corinthians 9:10)

Because I have been on a monthly salary nearly all of my working years, I have had no jarring adjustment to monthly pension and Social Security payments. I suspect that a number of retirees find it hard to stretch a pension check a whole month.

Having a realistic annual budget has long helped me keep income and outgo in balance. If the budget is realistic, outgo should remain somewhat behind income. Most bills are monthly, the same as income. Food expense is the exception. Marge and I budget food expense for the year; we withdraw a fixed amount weekly for food and personal incidentals.

We are grateful for our two cars, both fairly up-to-date. If we continue to drive—and at some point we must be sensible and stop—at least one of these cars must be replaced. I have budgeted an amount that hopefully will let us do that.

A realistic budget for us, including tithe and gifts to the Lord's work, is considerably above my anticipated pension income. Here I have two options: (1) I can tap my reserves, hoping that they will not run out before Marge and I end our course; (2) I can find part-time employment (or Marge and I both can find part-time employment). The latter option, as I have noted before, seems the more prudent while health remains. And our reserves can then have a little longer to build against the day when we will be more dependent on them.

Father, we have tried to be generous toward You, and You have been very generous toward us. We praise You! Amen.

SEPTEMBER 1

Wealth

*The Lord your God ... is he who gives you
the ability to produce wealth. (Deuteronomy 8:18)*

Some very godly people of the Bible were wealthy. Job, Abraham, David, Solomon, Joseph of Arimathea, Lydia—to name a few.

The Scriptures set forth seven principles regarding wealth, which when taken together offer guidelines to me.

1. *Wealth is God's gift.* "It is he who gives you the ability to produce wealth." A gracious God has favored His creation with strength, wisdom and a productive earth.

2. *Wealth is an uncertain thing.* Paul said so to Timothy and urged him to "command those who are rich in this present world not . . . to put their hope in wealth" (1 Timothy 6:17).

3. *The desire for wealth is a trap.* "People who want to get rich fall into . . . many foolish and harmful desires that plunge men into ruin and destruction" (1 Timothy 6:9).

4. *I am not to be overly concerned about material things.* "Keep your lives free from the love of money and be content with what you have" (Hebrews 13:5).

5. *There is more to life than possessions.* "Be on your guard against . . . greed," Jesus warned; "a man's life does not consist in the abundance of his possessions" (Luke 12:15).

6. *My love for God is evidenced by my compassion for my brother in economic need.* (See 1 John 3:17).

7. *The more I give to God and His concerns on earth, the more I have left over.* "Give," Jesus said, "and it will be given to you" (Luke 6:38).

Father, help me hold lightly to money and possessions. Amen.

SEPTEMBER 2

Gambling

I have not coveted anyone's silver or gold. (Acts 20:33)

Gambling is an insidious, immoral practice—even when sponsored by the state or the church for a worthy cause.

"Unlike manufacturing and construction," points out William J. Petersen, long-time editor of *Eternity* magazine, "gambling does not produce wealth. It merely redistributes cash, usually away from those who need it the most."

Gambling runs counter to the Bible's instruction to the individual Christian to "work, doing something useful with his own hands, that he may have something to share with those in need" (Ephesians 4:28). The Protestant work ethic is Bible-based. The Christian is to pursue useful work not only to provide for his or her own necessities but to be able to share with the person in genuine need.

"Gambling," said William Temple, a former archbishop of Canterbury, "challenges that view of life which the Christian church exists to uphold and extend. Its glorification of mere chance is a denial of the divine order of nature. To risk money haphazardly is to disregard the insistence of the church in every age of living faith that possessions are a trust and that men must account to God for their use.

"[Gambling's] persistent appeal to covetousness is fundamentally opposed to the unselfishness which was taught by Christ. . . . The attempt to make profit out of the inevitable loss of others is the antithesis of that love of one's neighbor on which our Lord insisted."

Father, I shall not covet. I shall not even gamble a postage stamp! Amen.

SEPTEMBER 3

Misplaced Affection

Set your minds on things above, not on earthly things. For you died [with Christ]. (Colossians 3:2–3)

If I needed proof that earthly things are impermanent, it came with the late night telephone call from our daughter Rebecca. It was not three hours after Marge and I had returned home from a delightful dinner and evening with her and her family.

"Daddy, I have an urgent prayer request. Jim and Brenda's house is in flames! Pray for us all."

It was hard to believe. Jim and Brenda, from whom John and Rebecca had bought their 150-year-old farm house, lived on adjacent property in a large new log home beautifully furnished with heirloom antiques.

I prayed. I also dressed quickly and headed the car the 16 country miles toward Benson. Flames, competing with the revolving red lights of the fire apparatus, still reddened the night sky. The acrid smell of wood smoke was everywhere. Firemen were playing water through naked roof timbers into the burning hulk of what had once been Jim and Brenda's showplace home.

We were helpless as the flames and water did their devastating work. We could only watch—and pray and reflect.

By morning, the charred hulk of that once proud house was a grim reminder that earthly things are impermanent.

"Set your minds on things above." Hold lightly to all else. "You died"—with Christ. Things of this world ought not to matter to someone who is dead.

Father, while I pray for Jim and Brenda, I pray also for myself. Let my mind be set on heavenly, not earthly, things. Amen.

SEPTEMBER 4

Assets

*[The Lord] guards the course of the just
and protects the way of his faithful ones.
(Proverbs 2:8)*

God has been good to Marge and me. He has not only provided Social Security and a small pension for my retirement, but He has permitted us to build some other back-up assets, chiefly through the appreciation of our last two residences in Nyack, New York, and New Cumberland, Pennsylvania.

I am cautioned against turning these assets over to any of my children to manage—unless I have implicit faith in their altruism and integrity. Thankfully, I do. And both Rebecca and Daniel have had considerable financial and business experience. Either will be a responsible, honest conservator of our financial assets should the time come when I no longer want, or am able, to manage them.

Even as I write those words, I realize that my desire to manage my own financial affairs could outlast my ability to do so. This is that precarious aspect of old age that entraps so many of the unsuspecting.

I shall talk to Rebecca this week—in fact, I will put it in writing to both her and Dan. "I intend for one of you to be the manager of my assets, if you are willing, when I come to the place when I am unable, mentally, to do the job myself. If either of you feels before I do that I am at that point, I want you to insist. I pray that I will respond graciously; but even if I am stubborn, please be firm!"

Father, thank you for capable, empathetic children who desire only the highest good for their mother and father. Amen.

SEPTEMBER 5

Living for Jesus

If we live, we live to the Lord. (Romans 14:8)

I am alive physically—still. And since I am a believer, I am alive spiritually through my relationship with Christ Jesus, who died for my sins and rose from the dead. Therefore I should be living my physical life "to the Lord." It is a logical enough conclusion. And it is a conclusion no less incumbent upon me now that I am retired.

I have heard the statement as an older person stepped down from a position he or she has held for a long time in the church: "I've done my share of work. Now it's time for those who are younger to take over."

Younger Christians need to find their place in the Lord's work, and older members may rightly relinquish long-held responsibilities to the next generation. But they should not "sign off," abdicating all responsibility. Rare is the church without work enough for *every* willing person, young and old.

An older person's maturity and experience can be distinct assets to the church. He or she has the time to pray, to prepare thoroughly, to practice, to follow up with personal counsel. In the small church, there likely are hands-on projects waiting to be done, ranging from painting and minor repairs to lawn mowing. In the larger church, there may be elderly and shut-ins for whom regular visits would be a highlight in their week.

Not only does the church need the older person, but the older person needs to be a working, active member of the church. Living for Jesus carries no time limitations.

Father, Jesus gave me my life. I offer it back to Him. Amen.

SEPTEMBER 6

Persevering Prayer

Be... faithful in prayer. (Romans 12:12)

Revisiting Simpson Memorial Church in Nyack, New York, where my family and I worshiped for many years, was encouraging on several counts. But none more so than Gayle Purvis' report that our mutual friend, John Mercurio, is now an enthusiastic Christian. That is good news indeed!

I cannot help but reflect back the 15 or more years to when Dan and Esther, my two youngest children, were actively involved in the church's high school youth group. First God saved Mike Mercurio, John's older son, after the high schoolers witnessed to him. And then Mike won his mother, Jean, and then his younger brother, Andy. John was a holdout. Occasionally he would attend church. Infrequently he might go to one of the men's outreach breakfasts. But these activities seemed to make no impact on him. Now, after 15 years of praying for John, I learn that he, too, is a believer! God answered prayer.

Not that I deserve credit. John's wife and his two sons, both now in active Christian ministry, have prayed much more earnestly than I. But that does not deny me the joy of knowing that John is at last a Christian brother. Or that my faithfulness in remembering him daily in prayer was in some small, mysterious way contributory to his salvation.

What was it Paul said in urging the Corinthians to be generous in monetary gifts to needy saints? "Your generosity will result in thanksgiving to God" (2 Corinthians 9:11). So God's act of saving John Mercurio deserves my thanks.

Father, great You are and greatly to be praised! Amen.

SEPTEMBER 7

A Promise

*He who dwells in the shelter of the Most High
will rest in the shadow of the Almighty. . . .
"With long life will I satisfy him
and show him my salvation."
(Psalm 91:1, 16)*

Here is another conditional promise from the Bible. In fact, three of them. The great 91st Psalm is introduced and wrapped up in three conditional promises: (1) the promise of rest in the shadow of the Almighty, (2) the promise of satisfying long life, and (3) the promise of the revelation of God's salvation.

All three promises may be claimed by—and only by—the person who "dwells in the shelter of the Most High."

As I observed earlier, I know of people—godly people—who died young. And I know of ungodly people who live long. I shall not question my Maker's sovereign ways. But a promise is a promise. And God promises that if I live within His sheltering presence He will satisfy me with long life.

I must not overlook that word *satisfy*. I know a few people who have lived long (only a few) who are miserable. They find nothing for which to give thanks. They hate life and do not mind sharing their viewpoint with others. But God offers me a "satisfaction guaranteed" promise for this life and salvation for the next—if I am willing to meet His condition.

What is that condition? I must live in the shelter of the Most High. Only in God's presence, at God's right hand, can I expect eternal pleasures (Psalm 16:11).

Father, I claim Your conditional promise; by Your grace I shall live out my life in Your sheltering presence. Amen.

SEPTEMBER 8

Antiques

How deserted lies the city,
once so full of people! . . .
The enemy laid hands
on all her treasures.
(Lamentations 1:1, 10)

The words above were Jeremiah's sigh as he beheld the desolation that once was proud Jerusalem.

When Israel deliberately turned its back on God to pursue idolatry and the occult, to welcome practicing homosexuals and witches, God was unpitying. He allowed Nebuchadnezzar, the king of Babylon, to level the city and carry off its treasures.

Why would God do such a thing? Why would He permit those priceless artifacts of antiquity to be destroyed? *Because God is a God of judgment.* "A man reaps what he sows" (Galatians 6:7). I am not told how Israel and Judah reasoned as extinction threatened. I only know that their prophets of God went unheeded, the signs of the times unread.

Thirty-five years before the Babylon invasion, Judah under Manasseh was enjoying a brief national renaissance and economic prosperity. Sixteen years before the Babylon invasion, Judah under King Josiah was experiencing revival, with a celebration of the Passover unlike any since the times of the judges.

But the revival was short-lived. Spiritual decline returned. And God's wrath fell. Swiftly. Irrevocably. All the antiques got trampled or carried away.

Those who supposed it could not happen to them found that it could. And it did.

Father, be merciful to my sinful, heedless land. Amen.

SEPTEMBER 9

To the Work!

"Let us start rebuilding." (Nehemiah 2:18)

A new set of back steps can hardly be equated with the walls of Jerusalem, either in importance or challenge. But my project, like that one, seems necessary. Not that the preformed-concrete original steps are falling apart. They are Gibraltar-solid. But they are railingless, and they leave us poised on the top step to wrestle with an outward-swinging screen door and a sometimes-locked entrance door just beyond. As a post-polio handicapped person I need something less precarious. And so will my daughter Debbie when she visits us. So, to the designing board to see what I can come up with!

Those two-by-fours that Chuck Langley, my neighbor on the south, gave me, will spare me some cash. And I am grateful to my son-in-law, John Swanson, for offering to transport in his pick-up truck the lumber I must buy. My local hardware has a good selection of bolts and lag screws at a fair price. I already have both primer and white paint.

The trick will be to fashion an adequate landing in front of the door without infringing on carport space. Obviously, the steps will have to come off one or the other end of the landing—or perhaps I should have two sets: one leading to the screened porch, one toward the driveway. The railing should be square-spoked, like the railing around the front porch.

With the plan carefully detailed to scale on paper and the cost counted, I am ready to go to work!

Father, I find it invigorating to be creating something like this with mind and hands. Thank You for the pleasure! Amen.

SEPTEMBER 10

Daniel Dreamed

*In the first year of Belshazzar king
of Babylon, Daniel had a dream. (Daniel 7:1)*

I have noticed how reluctant newly-retired people are to admit they are retired—as if it was somehow a shameful admission. They qualify the word by saying "semi-retired," or they immediately add, "But I'm still doing some work for my company." Perhaps it is that ingrained work ethic. Or their unwillingness to admit that they are getting along in years.

Daniel was indeed getting along in years. The Bible does not say exactly when he was phased out of Babylonian government service. Clearly, by the time of the final king, Belshazzar, Daniel was no longer in government employ.

But retirement for Daniel was opportunity for God to open Daniel's eyes to new vistas. In the more leisurely days of Daniel's mandated retirement, God revealed to him His plan for world dominion right up to and including the final triumphant kingdom of our Lord Jesus Christ. Those visions, recorded in Daniel 7 and 8 are the clearest, most comprehensive picture of the future in all the Scriptures.

And they were revealed to a man in his 80s. Clearly in His revelations God is no respecter of age. "Your old men shall dream dreams," wrote the prophet Joel concerning the outpouring of God's Spirit "on all people" (Joel 2:28).

I dare to open my life to the Spirit of God, to keep myself oriented to God's Word, the Bible. Who knows? "Gray power," coupled with God's power, could revolutionize our world.

Father, I am available. Amen.

SEPTEMBER 11

It Is in Your Head!

A cheerful heart is good medicine. (Proverbs 17:22)

Psychoneuroimmunology (PNI for short) is a new field of research that studies the known links between the brain and the body's immune system. It came about because psychologists and medical doctors discovered something Bible readers have known all along: "A cheerful heart is good medicine."

According to an article, "Your Mind's Healing Powers," in the September, 1989, *Reader's Digest*, these doctors discovered that socially active, married people live longer than less active, divorced, separated or single people; that married women had stronger immune systems than the unmarried, and happily married women had the strongest immune systems of all.

In a long-term survey of 99 Harvard graduates, they learned that those most pessimistic at age 25 had more severe illnesses in their 40s, 50s and 60s. In a seven-year follow-up of 36 women with advanced breast cancer, the 12 still alive were those who had the highest level of happiness and joy as measured by a questionnaire.

In a program conducted at the Univerity of Pittsburgh's Cancer Institute, 18 people whose cancer was in remission were helped to cope optimistically with their disease. All 18 generated more active natural "killer" cells to protect the body against tumor growth than patients receiving standard care.

Can a "cheerful heart" help protect me against ravishing diseases such as cancer? Both the Bible and science suggest the answer to that question is positive.

Father, You give me so much to be cheerful about! Amen.

SEPTEMBER 12

Perpetual Joy

Be joyful always; pray continually. (1 Thessalonians 5:16–17)

Statistics give me odds of 55/45 that I will undergo surgery during this first year of retirement. Why such a high incidence? Probably because people in fulltime employment have put off elective surgery until they were less busy.

If Paul's admonition to "be joyful always" indeed wards off disease (see yesterday's meditation), I shall certainly not complain! And if it does not, at least it should expand my circle of friends and make me easier to live with.

But I must keep in mind that this joy cannot be artificial; it has to be genuine. And that is where prayer enters the picture. Only a few people are perpetually joyful by disposition. I and the others find it is only possible by "pray[ing] continually." When the channel between God and me is in order, life is in order. Even if life seems somehow in disorder, I have the relaxing assurance that God who has me in His control is safekeeping what I have committed to Him (2 Timothy 1:12).

The Old Testament prophet Habakkuk had found the secret of joy in the midst of disheartening outward circumstances. He says, Though the "fig tree does not bud," though the vines are without grapes, though the olive crop fails, though the fields produce no food, though there are no sheep in the pen and no cattle in the stalls, "yet I will rejoice in the Lord."

Why? How? God had assured him of His sovereignty. Habakkuk knew that God was in control.

Father, please make me prayerful continually so that I may be joyful always. Amen.

SEPTEMBER 13

Jehu

Jehu was not careful to keep the law of the Lord, the God of Israel, with all his heart. (2 Kings 10:31)

We know Jehu best for the way he drove his chariot—"like a mad man" (2 Kings 9:20). That same reckless abandon characterized much of the life of this 11th king of Israel.

God appointed Jehu to be king. He was to avenge the house of Ahab, his one-time master, for the blood of God's prophets spilled by Ahab's notoriously wicked queen, Jezebel (9:6–7). With almost fanatical zeal, Jehu set out to do all that God commanded. He put to death all of Ahab's remaining family (10:17). He killed the prophets of Baal (10:18–27), completely exterminating Baal worship in Israel.

But Jehu's zeal for reform was selective. He "was not careful to keep the law of the Lord with all his heart." He continued the worship of the two gold calves instituted in Israel almost a century earlier by Jeroboam, first leader of the divided kingdom. As a result, God permitted neighboring nations to chip away at Israel's borders (10:32–33).

By the final years of his 28-year reign, Jehu must have been a man in his 60s.

Assyrian records tell the story of those humiliating final years. On Shalmaneser's Black Obelisk is a pictorial report of "the tribute of Jehu, son of Omni." An ambassador bows before the Assyrian conqueror and presents his nation's tribute: silver, gold and gold vessels. Jehu, who began well, ended in shame—because he failed to follow through with God.

Father, I have promised to serve You to the end. Amen.

SEPTEMBER 14

Jehoiada

Jehoiada... was buried with the kings in the City of David because of the good he had done in Israel for God and his temple. (2 Chronicles 24:15–16)

Jehoiada has gone down in Hebrew history as one of Judah's most remarkable high priests. He was in his 90s when he masterminded the dramatic overthrow of Athaliah, the usurper queen.

The story is in Second Kings 11 and Second Chronicles 23. Very briefly, Jehoiada organized a coup that put seven-year-old Joash, the legal successor to King Ahaziah, on Judah's throne. Equally important, Jehoiada was spiritual mentor to the young king, guiding him in the path of godliness, assisting in the repair of the temple. When Jehoiada died, a grateful people paid him honor by burying him with the kings in Jerusalem.

Several qualities mark this venerable high priest:

1. He was a person of deep convictions. He was thoroughly committed to God and to righteousness.

2. He was a person of action. He was not afraid to take risks if the cause was right. Although elderly even by Old Testament standards, he refused to sit back and do nothing.

3. He had a good sense of timing. He waited until Judah was weary of Athaliah's wickedness. Then he acted.

4. He was a faithful teacher. Carefully he steered Joash, the child king, in the paths of righteousness. "Joash did what was right in the eyes of the Lord all the years of Jehoiada the priest" (2 Chronicles 24:2).

Father, prompt me, too, to be discerning, willing to stand up for my convictions and an apt example/teacher. Amen.

SEPTEMBER 15

Elisha

"The Lord's arrow of victory . . . over Aram!"
Elisha declared. (2 Kings 13:17)

From the time he was called to be a prophet, Elisha was immersed in a frenzy of activity. In the space of 15 years he did twice the miracles of Elijah. He had not only a significant prophetic role in the Northern Kingdom during the reigns of Ahab, Ahaziah and Jehoram/Joram, but his influence was felt in Damascus, citadel of Aramean power.

But Elisha also had time for a ministry of encouragement. He assisted impoverished widows (2 Kings 4:1–7). He restored to life the Shunammite woman's child (4:32–37). He rendered harmless the virulent poison in a pot of stew (4:40–41). He multiplied bread to feed the hungry (4:42–44).

And then Elisha vanishes from the pages of Holy Writ. For upward of 43 years, there is no mention of him. Finally, a new king of Israel—Jehoash—visits Elisha on his deathbed. The king's greeting indicates how highly the old prophet is revered: " 'My father! My father!' he cried. 'The chariots and horsemen of Israel' " (2 Kings 13:14). Jehoash was saying, in effect, "You are more important to my nation than our chariots and horsemen!"

Elisha ignored the tribute. "Get a bow and some arrows," he demanded (13:15). "Open the east window."

With the king's assistance, Elisha shot an arrow in the direction of Aram. "The Lord's arrow of victory over Aram!" the prophet declared.

On his deathbed, Elisha was still encouraging people.

Father, I too want to be an encourager—even to old age. Amen.

SEPTEMBER 16

Hosea

The word of the Lord ... came to Hosea son of Buri during the reigns of Uzziah, Jotham, Ahaz and Hezekiah. (Hosea 1:1)

With a prophetic ministry that stretched possibly 50 or more years, there is no question as to Hosea's eligibility to be included among this survey of Bible seniors.

In his younger years, God had put a heavy assignment on Hosea. He was to marry "an adulterous wife" (Hosea 1:2). His marriage was to be a prophecy acted out, for the adulterous woman represented idolatrous Israel, and the names of the three children produced by the union—"God Scatters," "Not Loved" and "Not My People"—were predictions of God's impending judgment.

But underneath the scattering and the rejection, God continued to love Israel, and He promised restoration: "Yet the Israelites will be like the sand on the seashore, which cannot be measured or counted. In the place where it was said to them, 'You are not my people,' they will be called 'sons of the living God.' ... Judah and ... Israel will be reunited" (1:10–11).

Hosea's prophecy drew to a close as the era of the Northern Kingdom drew to a close. Now elderly, the prophet's message was essentially unchanged: God *does* love you and *I* love you, too:

> How can I give you up, Ephraim?
> How can I hand you over, Israel? (11:8)

> Return, O Israel, to the Lord your God.
> Your sins have been your downfall! (14:1)

Father, let me love people consistently, as You do. Amen.

SEPTEMBER 17

Isaiah

*Then I heard the voice of the Lord saying,
"Whom shall I send? And who will go for us?"
And I said, "Here am I. Send me!" (Isaiah 6:8)*

I struggle over the fact that associates, neighbors and even some of my extended family have turned a deaf ear to my Christian testimony and the God I serve. It breaks my heart to know that these are en route to eternal ruin.

But I do not give up! God has worked some amazing eleventh-hour miracles in response to prevailing prayer. I also find consolation in the example of Isaiah, the undisputed king of Israel's writing prophets.

Isaiah probably was born and bred in Jerusalem among royalty. He received his prophetic commission through a direct revelation of God (see Isaiah 6:1–8).

But right up front, God warned Isaiah that Israel would not heed his message. God painted for Isaiah a gloomy picture of national judgment and desolation (6:11–12).

Although Isaiah's writings are some of the profoundest in all literature, his message went unheeded. In a marathon stretch spanning possibly 60 years, through eras of good kings and bad, Isaiah faithfully proclaimed God's word to unlistening people.

As the years mounted, was Isaiah tempted to give in to disappointment and to think his life had been a failure? I only know that Isaiah continued faithful to the end—and left for the Jewish nation and the Christian church some of its most sublime inspired writings.

Father, Isaiah continued to be Your messenger. Help me not to lose faith now. Amen.

SEPTEMBER 18

Micah

"Micah... prophesied in the days of Hezekiah king of Judah.... Did not Hezekiah fear the Lord and seek his favor? And did not the Lord relent?" (Jeremiah 26:18–19)

Micah is further evidence that age does not necessarily limit a person's usefulness to God. Micah must have been far into his seventh decade when he proclaimed to King Hezekiah one of his most significant prophecies:

"Zion will be plowed like a field,/ Jerusalem will become a heap of rubble,/ the temple hill a mound overgrown with thickets" (Micah 3:12, quoted, too, in Jeremiah 26:18).

By that time, Assyrian forces were threatening and may already have overrun the Northern Kingdom of Israel. There seemed little to keep Judah from the same fate at the hands of the new Assyrian emperor, Shalmaneser. Micah's prophecy seemed not only plausible, but imminent.

Happily, however, Micah's prediction did *not* take place—then. For that, we can thank King Hezekiah's godly leadership. The king called Judah to earnest prayer. God heard the cry of His people and postponed His intended judgment for more than a century. Assyria never did overrun Judah.

It is not easy to bear bad news. Few of Israel's prophets died natural deaths. Many were executed by petulant kings or died at the hands of angry citizens. I do not know Micah's fate. Likely, however, devout Hezekiah saw to his protection.

I do know that Micah's message—and the national repentance it evoked—spared Judah from Assyrian capture.

Father, give me personal boldness to speak for You. Amen.

SEPTEMBER 19

Manasseh

[Manasseh] restored the altar of the Lord and sacrificed fellowship offerings and peace offerings on it, and told Judah to serve the Lord. (2 Chronicles 33:16)

I suppose no Christian comes to retirement without wishing he or she could undo the spiritual failings of the past. Manasseh, 14th king of Judah, had a sordid past to try to rectify. Mercifully, God allowed him that privilege—in part.

Manasseh's father was the great and godly Hezekiah, but Manasseh chose a different course. He desecrated the Temple with idols. He encouraged sorcery, divination, mediums. He burned his own son as an idol sacrifice. So evil was Manasseh that he pushed God beyond the point of no return.

Then an amazing thing happened. Assyria attacked, and Manasseh, a hook in his nose and fettered with bronze shackles, was taken prisoner to Babylon. In Babylon he and other captive kings became slave laborers for Esarhaddon, the Assyrian king, who dismantled a small palace and built in its place a larger one. In those desperate circumstances the young, repentant Manasseh cried out to God. And God heard. Although God would not forego judgment on Judah, He would delay it. God even restored Manasseh to his throne in Jerusalem.

Manasseh spent the next 42 years of his long reign trying to undo the folly of his early years. The innocent victims he had put to death could not be brought back. Those who died in idolatry had no second chance to repent. But Manasseh, to his credit, did what he could.

Father, are there sins in my past that I can rectify? Amen.

SEPTEMBER 20

All My Sins

[Christ] forgave us all our sins, having canceled the written code . . . that stood opposed to us; he took it away, nailing it to the cross. (Colossians 2:13–14)

The gospel song with the profoundest theology? My vote goes to Horatio G. Spafford's "It Is Well with My Soul."

Written in 1873, the song was born out of personal tragedy. En route to Europe, where Spafford intended to join them, his wife and four daughters were on the ill-fated *Ville du Havre*, which sank after colliding with another vessel.

In Chicago, Spafford waited apprehensively for word. Finally a cable from his wife announced the tragic news: "Saved alone." His four daughters, in whom he delighted, had perished.

Wasting no time, Spafford set out for France. As his ship neared the site of the earlier accident and the watery grave of his four little "lambs," Horatio Spafford penned the words to "It Is Well with My Soul." Triumphant though the first two stanzas are, the third makes the song great:

> My sin—oh, the bliss of this glorious thought—
> My sin—not in part but the whole—
> Is nailed to His cross and I bear it no more!
> Praise the Lord, praise the Lord, O my soul!

Exactly how many of my sins did Jesus bear when He died on the cross? The answer introduces me to the most liberating thought in all theology. Jesus bore *all* of my sins—past, present, future—in His body on the cross.

Father, I claim it, I claim it! I am set free! Amen.

SEPTEMBER 21

"I Pray for You"

We have not stopped praying for you. (Colossians 1:9)

A score of years ago, Marge and I made a protracted visit to Warren, Pennsylvania, my hometown, and to the Church of the Nazarene that so profoundly influenced my life.

Over dinner one evening I reminisced with Preston Taylor, one of the elderly saints. Outwardly austere and authoritarian, Mr. Taylor was a man of tenderness and spiritual sensitivity. In old age the same graces had mellowed him even more.

As we talked, Mr. Taylor recalled the names of young people, many of them my contemporaries, who had figured in the life of that Nazarene church. His interest in them was obvious. He had been Sunday school teacher to many of them. Their concerns were his, and he shared their victories.

"I want you to know," Mr. Taylor confided to Marge and me as we were leaving, "I pray for you two every day."

Every day! For 30 years I had been away from that church, more than 20 of them in another denomination. Yet the prayers and personal interest of that saint of God had followed me and my family all that time.

First Church of the Nazarene in Warren has had marked success in retaining its youth. Suddenly I knew why so many of them had continued in the church as adults or gone out into Christian service. It was the interaction of the generations. Adult members had refused to isolate and insulate themselves from the youth. And in that fellowship of mutual concern and interest the youth had felt important—needed and wanted.

Father, I pray for my church's youth. Amen.

SEPTEMBER 22

Project Finished!

So the wall was completed...
in fifty-two days. (Nehemiah 6:15)

Can it be that my back steps have taken me this long? Of course, our trip to Pennsylvania took some time from the project. And I had a few other concurrent responsibilities.

If I do say so, the steps look good. The green "grass" carpeting is a nice finishing touch. It matches what is in the carport and screened room. It should both save wear on the wood and spare the kitchen from tracked-in dirt. The white posts and railing stand out against the green. They match the front porch exactly. If we need to move bulky things through the kitchen door, eight screws detach a section of railing to offer easy access. And there is sufficient clearance to park our car under the carport if we should have snow or sleet.

I am pleased that the landing and steps came in not much above the $100 I had estimated. Not always is that true of my projects! Best of all, I can now go up and down, in and out, without fear of losing my footing and falling. And so can others.

This project has established my reputation among my neighbors. John Isham is sure I must have been a carpenter before retiring. Chuck Langley, my fellow woodworker, who has been monitoring the construction regularly, gave the steps his unqualified approval. Of course, it is not approval per se that I want; I want to be accepted so that I can represent God to these neighbors.

Thankfully, that acceptance seems to be coming.

Father, let those four new steps to our back door put me that much closer to my new neighbors! Amen.

SEPTEMBER 23

All My Needs

My God will meet all your needs according to his glorious riches in Christ Jesus. (Philippians 4:19)

Here I am again with that recurring Bible theme of generosity and its rewards. This assurance by Paul as he wrote under the Spirit's inspiration to the church in Philippi, was given in the context of Paul's gratitude for a congregation of people who had been generous in their financial support.

Little is known about the actual composition of that first century Philippian congregation. But Philippi, a Roman colony, was a favorite retirement community for Roman army personnel and other government officials. If the church represented a cross section of the community, it may very well have had some of these retirees within its ranks.

I wonder if the retirees in the Philippi church (if indeed there were some) contributed to the apostle's sustenance as he bore the tedium and the uncertainty of Roman house arrest. For sure any retirees were included in the apostle's assurances, for he indicates no exceptions. Just as Jesus said, "Give and it will be given to you" (Luke 6:38), so Paul assures those who have given generously, "My God will meet all your needs according to his glorious riches in Christ Jesus."

If repetition counts for anything, then certainly God rewards the generous giver with the ability to give even more. Financial liberality should be my trademark as one of Christ's followers. I must not let the adversary, Satan, rob me of the blessing of being generous.

Father, thank you for the ability to give. Amen.

SEPTEMBER 24

The Uplook Is Good

My times are in your hands. (Psalm 31:15)

Why should—how can—the Christian be optimistic in a world that is totally askew? The answers are several:

1. *The God the Christian serves is sovereign.* The present state of world and national affairs did not take God by surprise. It has come as no shock to the Creator of the galaxies and the Sustainer of all things.

2. The tumultuous times may indeed *presage the great consummation the Christian has been waiting for.* Jesus foretold that the end would be preceded by international warfare and "great earthquakes, famines and pestilences in various places" (Luke 21:10-11). "When these things begin to take place," Jesus said, "stand up and lift up your heads, because your redemption is drawing near" (21:28).

3. Adversity offers the Christian his or her *best opportunity to bring others to faith in Jesus Christ.* When all is well, people feel very adequate and self-assured. Reverses change those attitudes, open people to spiritual considerations.

4. *This world is not the Christian's home.* Says the writer of Hebrews, "You . . . joyfully accepted the confiscation of your property, because you knew that you yourselves had better and lasting possessions" (Hebrews 10:34).

5. *The Christian has the reality of Christ within.* God promises, "Never will I leave you" (Hebrews 13:5). The Christian can say with confidence, "The Lord is my helper; I will not be afraid" (13:6).

Father, help me translate those promises into assurance. Amen.

SEPTEMBER 25

Prayer

Epaphras ... is always wrestling in prayer for you. (Colossians 4:12)

In his highly readable biography, *Rees Howells, Intercessor*, Norman Grubb relates how that Spirit-taught former Welsh coal miner led the students of his Bible college in nightly prayer during the dark days of World War II. Without fail, from 7:00 p.m. until midnight, the whole 100-member student body was in prayer with only a brief interval for supper.

One particular evening, Howells stood before the students.

"The Lord has burdened me with the invasion at Salerno," he told them. "I believe our men are in great difficulties. The Lord has told me that unless we can pray through, they are in danger of losing their hold."

"Before long," recalls one who was in the prayer meeting, "we were on our knees crying to God for Him to intervene. The Spirit suddenly broke right through in the prayers. We found ourselves praising and rejoicing, believing that God had heard and answered. The victory was so outstanding that I looked at the clock as we rose to sing. It was exactly 11:00 p.m."

On Thursday morning, one of the daily newspapers displayed bold headlines: "The Miracle of Salerno." An eyewitness reporter told of the intense hammering by advancing Nazi artillery as the Allies tried desperately to establish a beachhead. Suddenly, for no reason, the firing ceased. "We waited," said the reporter. "Nothing happened. I looked at my watch—*it was eleven o'clock at night*." By morning, the beachhead was secure.

Father, make me an intercessor. Amen.

SEPTEMBER 26

In Favor of Old Age

We do not lose heart. (2 Corinthians 4:1)

Who live longest? In the United States, the answer is midwestern farmers. Farmers living in Nebraska, Kansas, North Dakota, South Dakota, Minnesota and Iowa stand the best chance.

White collar workers survive factory workers; skilled workers, unskilled; college graduates, high school graduates. People doing work they enjoy live longer than people who do not. Clergymen, teachers, lawyers outlive business executives. Married people survive the single and the widowed (the death rate among single men is almost double that of married men).

But as Raymond J. Jeffries observes, "Old age in itself is a curse unless we take advantage of it and use its experience, wisdom and ability to improve the world."

If I can continue a useful, productive life, I am in good company. Benjamin Franklin, at age 81, helped create the United States Constitution. Clara Barton, founder of the American Red Cross, was still working 14-hour days at age 90. Fanny J. Crosby continued her amazing output of hymns and gospel songs into her 94th year. Michelangelo, at 82, became the architect of St. Peter's. Connie Mack still actively directed the Philadelphia Athletics at 85. At the same age Bernard M. Baruch was yet advising United States presidents. Frank Lloyd Wright in his 80s was still producing revolutionary architecture. Winston Churchill, Douglas MacArthur, Thomas A. Edison, Herbert Hoover reached their peak late in life.

Perhaps there is room for me!

Father, if age is no barrier, I want to continue on. Amen.

SEPTEMBER 27

How Long?

"Man's days are determined." (Job 14:5)

Average life expectancy in the United States has now climbed to 78 years. But as everyone knows, few people actually conform to the average. My summons may come at age 67 (I now know it will not be earlier than age 67!). Or I could live beyond the century mark. When it comes to predicting how long I will live, averages are not very dependable.

Doctors continue to say that the best assurance of long physical life is to be born to parents who have a family history of long life. It would be gratifying if clean-living, born-again Christians exceeded the average. Although they may not have some of the vices common to their fast-living, worldly counterparts, they are inclined to other vices (notably gluttony) that cancel out their advantage.

But back to the averages. When I read that life expectancy in the United States is now 78 years, it does not mean that the person arriving at age 65 can expect to live 13 more years. Actually, *on average*, Americans who manage to reach 65 can expect to live another 20 years. Those who reach 75 can expect to live another 12 years. And those who reach 85 can expect to live another 7–8 years. In other words, the longer a person lives, the longer, on average, he or she can expect to live.

But those are simply statistics, and I have no way of knowing if they fit me. Certainly I should be prudent in exercise and diet, for I am God's temple (1 Corinthians 6:19). But, in the final analysis, a sovereign God has determined my days.

Father, do with me what is best. Amen.

SEPTEMBER 28

Old Age? Me?

*Do not cast me away when I am old;
do not forsake me when my strength is
gone.
(Psalm 71:9)*

I find myself lapsing into the too-customary habit of equating retirement and old age. They are not the same. To be sure, there is a relation between the two, but retirement and old age are certainly not synonymous.

When I retired, I was only one day older than when I was working. The widely held concept that all retired people have one foot dangling over an open grave has little validity. If I had strength and mental acumen to put in an honest day's work the day I retired, there is every reason to anticipate that I can expect a similar level of physical and mental energy for an indefinite time. Short of debilitating disease (which can and may occur), old age creeps up, not leaps up.

But whether creeping or leaping, it comes, and there is no use my trying to deny it. King David (assuming he wrote Psalm 71) faced the inevitable the same way he faced every other exigency of life—with prayer. He prayed that God would spare him from being a cast-off and forsaken when that time came.

And the Scriptures say that God heard and answered his prayer. "[David] died at a good old age, having enjoyed long life, wealth and honor" (1 Chronicles 29:28).

My stature is far, far below David's, but I serve and pray to the same God he served and prayed to. May He show mercy on me, also, when retirement turns to old age.

Father God, I will pray it, too: "Do not cast me away when I am old;/ do not forsake me when my strength is gone." Amen.

SEPTEMBER 29

Being Realistic

David went down . . . to fight against the Philistines, and he became exhausted. . . . Then David's men swore to him, saying, "Never again will you go out with us to battle, so that the lamp of Israel will not be extinguished." (2 Samuel 21:15–17)

Probably not this year, and maybe not next, but in some future year I am going to find myself, like David, "exhausted." What I still take in stride now I will do with greater effort then. At some point the task will be beyond me.

I have seen elderly people driving cars who should have quit driving years ago. They are a threat to themselves and to all others on the highway. I have watched men play ball who should bow out of such activity before they are carried out.

What are they trying to prove? That they, contrary to all other people, are not aging? That they have discovered the fountain of youth? A glance in the mirror or a look at their waistline should disabuse them of such nonsense.

If I am totally honest, I must admit that I do not look forward to growing old and decrepit. The mental slowness, the deliberateness, the tremor commonly associated with old age are things I wish I could avoid. I would rather that my years of experience and knowledge (which I cherish) were clothed in a body still young and responsive.

But that is not how God planned it. So I must ask Him for the grace to move over, to slack off, to admit I am no longer 49—or even 59. He is able to make my relationship with old age peaceful, not adversarial.

Father, give me grace to accept what I cannot change. Amen.

SEPTEMBER 30

Fruitful to the End

*The righteous will flourish like a palm tree ...
They will still bear fruit in old age,
they will stay fresh and green.
(Psalm 92:12–14)*

Not yet am I old, but I might as well face it. I am moving in that direction. Unless death intervenes (a distinct possibility!), I will ultimately be old. I mean, really old.

For the righteous person, the palm tree referred to in Psalm 92 is an encouraging simile. I lived part of my life among coconut palms. Tropical rains, tropical dry spells, tropical winds—those coconut palms took them all in stride.

And with seasonal regularity those palms bore their nourishing fruit—*right into old age*. Filipinos used the outer husks for floor scrubbers, the inner shells for charcoal. The palm fronds became thatch for the roofs of their houses.

As frequently as I can, I visit The Alliance Home in Carlisle, Pennsylvania. The Alliance Home is a Christian retirement community for pastors, missionaries and lay Christians. The average age of the residents is more than 80. Most are well aware of the physical limitations imposed by accumulated years.

A few of the residents, due to mental deterioration, are no longer interested in life. But the amazing thing is the number who in spirit continue to be "fresh and green," who "still bear fruit in old age." They encourage each other. They take an active interest in their church. And when it comes to prayer—there is no group on earth I would rather have praying for me.

Father, Your promise of fruitfulness is to the righteous. I want to be sure I am in that company. Amen.

OCTOBER 1

Doing Good

Do not withhold good from those who deserve it,
when it is in your power to act.
(Proverbs 3:27)

Here is another proverb having special application to me now that I am retired. Not that I was excused from doing good to people during my working years, but now I have more time to observe needs and to do something about them.

If I were a woman, I might prepare a tasty casserole for a sick neighbor. Or baby sit some children to give an overworked mother a two-hour break.

Doing good to those who deserve it can cost nothing more than time. I have helped Ray McGarvey house paint. I have helped David Leland put a window in his tool shed. I have done such simple things as pick up nails from the church's parking lot that might puncture tires, or litter that might detract from a person's first impressions of the church.

In a few minutes I will be going out to find an activity book for little Kim Carpenter, who had the misfortune yesterday to break her leg in two places. Dear little first-grader! In church Kim invariably seeks Marge and me out to tell us about her latest activity. She will have plenty to talk about when we deliver the book to her later today.

God seems to put but two conditions to this proverb: the activity must be "within [my] power" and the action must be intended for "those who deserve it." With no shortage of deserving individuals and an ample list of things within my power, I have no excuse for ignoring this command.

Father, Jesus went around doing good. May I follow Him. Amen.

OCTOBER 2

Not the White House

He ... must work, doing something useful with his own hands. (Ephesians 4:28)

God had a message for me today as I helped my friend, David Leland, put plywood siding on his "shop."

"Shop" may be too elegant a word for the termite-eaten storage building that David has been fixing up, little by little, into a combination storeroom and workshop. At least he has stopped the termites dead in their tracks. And the two sides he has resurfaced with deep-stained, rough-cut plywood look almost attractive. Still, the out-of-plumb walls and the inconsistent foundation jar my perfectionist nature.

I was fretting with the fit of a siding panel that had to wrap around our newly placed window when David first said it. "That's good enough," he decreed. "This isn't the White House, you know." The contrast between David's nondescript back-yard shop and America's presidential mansion was ludicrous. But his comment, which we laughingly repeated at intervals as we worked through the afternoon, was insightful. I find it easy to get absorbed in details that end up taking a disproportionate amount of available time. Even in retirement—or perhaps especially in retirement, when time is no longer limitless—some jobs worth doing may not be worth doing to perfection.

God gives special approval to working with one's hands. Jesus was a carpenter who worked with His hands before He was a preacher. (And even then His hands were busy.) I only ask that, like Jesus, I may know how to keep my priorities straight.

Father, keep my hands useful. Keep me useful. Amen.

OCTOBER 3

Nebuchadnezzar

I, Nebuchadnezzar, praise and exalt and glorify the King of heaven, because everything he does is right and all his ways are just. (Daniel 4:37)

That is a remarkable statement from the renowned, probably over-60 head of the first world-class empire, Babylon. The experience that prompted his words was even more remarkable.

Nebuchadnezzar, a formidable military figure, had transformed sleepy Babylon into an impregnable city of grandeur and beauty. His famous "hanging gardens" were one of the seven wonders of the ancient world.

Nebuchadnezzar was not without a witness to the true God. Daniel and his three Hebrew friends had seen to that. And each crisis had brought the king a little closer to Jehovah God. But his pride was a barrier Nebuchadnezzar could not surmount. And it was his raw pride that finally brought God's severe judgment upon this Chaldean emperor.

For seven years, by his own testimony, Nebuchadnezzar lived "away from people and ate grass like cattle." His body was "drenched with the dew of heaven." His nails grew "like the claws of a bird" (Daniel 4:33). At the end of the seven years, Nebuchadnezzar said, "I . . . raised my eyes toward heaven" (4:34), and God restored the king's sanity. Nebuchadnezzar returned to his throne, acknowledging the "King of Heaven" and His "eternal dominion" (4:37).

All Nebuchadnezzar's previous great achievements could not match this important insight gained in his later years.

Father, what about Yourself do You want me to know? Amen.

OCTOBER 4

Daniel - I

So Daniel prospered during the reign of Darius and the reign of Cyrus the Persian. (Daniel 6:28)

Of all the Old Testament seniors, few are as remarkable as Daniel. His civil service under two foreign powers spanned an era of more than 70 years from Nebuchadnezzar's first years as the emperor of Babylonia into the reign of Cyrus the Great, whose Medo-Persian empire conquered Babylon in 539 B.C.

There are people today in government who are honest, fair and ethical, but TV and the newspapers report so frequently on those of an opposite bent that *all* politicians tend to get categorized as self-seeking and unscrupulous. In a long career of public service, Daniel was impeccably honest. Not even his enemies could recall a single instance when he had compromised.

That is an astonishing record.

As a senior, I can look back over the past 60 years and be reminded of a number of lapses in my life—even after I met Christ Jesus at age 17. There is no better time than now to begin being precisely the person God wants me to be.

Daniel kept two things firmly in mind:

1. He never forgot his homeland. In a foreign land, he nevertheless remained oriented to Jerusalem.

2. He never lost sight of his fathers' God. Amid idolatry he lived in the divine presence. Punctually, three times a day, he "got down on his knees and prayed" (6:10).

It is a formula guaranteed to work!

Father, let Your dwelling place be my orientation and Your presence my delight. Amen.

OCTOBER 5

Daniel - II

The king gave the order, and they brought Daniel and threw him into the lions' den. (Daniel 6:16)

Not all of life's great crises occur during the physical vigor of youth or even in middle age.

If the children's artists who picture a young Daniel among the lions would do a bit of calculating, they would discover that Daniel was not in his mid-30s but *above 80 years of age* when King Darius, entrapped by his jealous deputies, consigned Daniel to the hungry beasts.

I cannot say how Daniel's brittle bones survived the drop to the floor of the den. Did the blood-thirsty lions, bent on his destruction, actually cushion his fall? How was the unharmed Daniel "lifted from the den" (6:23) the next morning? Rescue had never before been an option. I only know what the Bible states: Daniel was thrown to the lions; the next morning he was lifted from the den unscathed.

Daniel must have questioned the purpose of the whole ordeal. Well past the age of active duty, he had been brought out of retirement, pressed into service by the new ruler, Darius. Daniel really did not need an overnight among lions to prove his godly lifestyle or his probity as a government official. Is there no chronological cut-off point beyond which God excuses His people from physical duress and even possible violence?

But God knows best. God had His purpose. Daniel's supernatural deliverance from the lions is one of the Bible's most often-told stories, an encouragement to a hundred generations.

Father, not my will but Yours be done. Amen.

OCTOBER 6

Cyrus the Great

*"[I am the Lord,] who says of Cyrus, 'He is my shepherd
and will accomplish all that I please.'"*
(Isaiah 44:28)

I do not know Cyrus's age as he marches somewhat briefly across the pages of Scripture in the 539 B.C. conquest of Babylon and in his celebrated decree that permitted God's people to return to their homeland from Babylonian exile. At that point Cyrus had already for 20 years been king of the Persia-Mede-Elam coalition. I, a fellow senior, will give Cyrus the benefit of the doubt and include him among the "sixty plus."

Cyrus is a person I am honored to claim. *God* claimed him: "He is my shepherd." Although apparently a lifelong pagan, this enlightened ruler reversed the prevailing policy of resettling conquered people outside their homelands. He did it, he said, so that "all the gods whom I brought into their cities [might] pray daily before Bel and Nabu for long life for me."

Cyrus's desire for long life was not to be. He died in battle in 530 B.C. His tomb, long since rifled, is still extant at Pasargadae, Iran. First century Plutarch is quoted as saying the inner sarcophagus of solid gold bore this inscription:

> O man, whoever you are and whenever you come (for I know that you will come), I am Cyrus, and I won for the Persians their empire. Do not, therefore, begrudge me this little earth that covers my body.

Alas! Those who came chose not to care.

Father, help me to work for what is eternal. Amen.

OCTOBER 7

Darius the Mede

Darius the Mede took over the kingdom, at the age of sixty-two. (Daniel 5:31)

Darius falls precisely within the senior citien age category as he rises to his great moment in world history. King Cyrus, victorious over Babylonia, named Darius to rule the newly conquered Babylonian empire.

(This man the Scriptures call Darius the Mede was the Gabryas, or Gubaru, of secular Persian history. The supposition that he was Cyrus's short-term predecessor on the Medo-Persian throne—a gesture to the respected Median portion of the empire—neither coincides with the facts nor is demanded by the reading of the Daniel text. Cyrus deputized Darius/Gubaru to govern Babylon and the by-then collapsed Babylonian empire.)

It was Darius who brought the aged Daniel out of retirement, appointing him as one of three regional administrators. And when he saw the outstanding job Daniel did, he intended to make him prime minister. Those plans aroused the jealousy of both Daniel's peers and some of his subordinates, who plotted a "final solution" for Daniel by way of the lions' den.

Darius may have allowed himself to be entrapped once by his scheming underlings, but he made sure it would not happen twice. The lions had a belated meal, Darius had Daniel and the new government survived its administrative crisis.

Daniel served both Darius and Cyrus, adding another ten years to his previous six decades of government service—a remarkable record possibly never matched.

Father, is there a job you want me yet to do? Amen.

OCTOBER 8

On Wisdom

Better a poor but wise youth than an old but foolish king who no longer knows how to take warning. (Ecclesiastes 4:13)

The preacher of Ecclesiastes was speaking in superlatives. He was contrasting an inexperienced youth with a seasoned elder, an anonymous, rank-and-file boy with a top-of-the-order leader.

And he was contrasting wisdom and foolishness.

There are foolish youth (a superabundance of them, some would say, excluding their grandchildren, of course), and thankfully there are wise kings. There are also wise young people and imprudent kings—as the preacher points out.

My own opportunity to be a "poor but wise youth" passed some 50 years ago. I qualified on the poverty part; whether I was wise is for others to say. The challenge left to me at this point in life is to make sure I do not end up foolish, no longer knowing how to take warning.

I observe that poor judgment in old age is more of a problem than I would like to suppose. It is almost as though some sort of automatic switch in the brain is triggered, and a person who up until then displayed good logic, prudence and mental skill loses the ability to take warning, to act forthrightly, to call the right signals.

Blessed is the man in such a state who has a loving, non-covetous, understanding family to support him in his time of need. Sadly, not even all who have that kind of a support system are willing to divest control.

Father, help me in my later years to find the happy balance between total capitulation and total control. Amen.

OCTOBER 9

Halfway Christians

You must be born again. (John 3:7)

Early New England settlers were for the most part pious men and women who lived close to nature and walked close to God. Church-going was more than a Sunday duty; it was outward evidence of inner regeneration.

Congregationalists of that era saw themselves as heirs of the covenant that God instituted with Abraham. Even as God's covenant was with Abraham *and his offspring* (Genesis 13:15–16), so these Pilgrims reckoned that the divine relationship they enjoyed extended to their children. Accordingly, they baptized the infant children of church members. But the system was flawed.

Many of those children, despite their careful upbringing by godly parents, came into their adult years unregenerate. Most of them remained in association with the church, attended the church services and lived moral lives. But they could cite no personal encounter with God. The church was satisfied to let them remain associated, but in the absence of any witness to regeneration, it could hardly baptize *their* children.

The Halfway Covenant (dubbed that by its detractors) was a compromise measure to give standing to these in-betweens. By "owning the covenant," those not in "full communion" could qualify their children for baptism.

The Halfway Covenant continued, to some extent, for more than a century. The "Great Awakening" that brought men and women to the new birth brought the Halfway Covenant to its end. Congregationalists discovered that God has no grandchildren.

Father, let my children be Your children. Amen.

OCTOBER 10

Another Transition

Abraham was now old and well advanced in years. (Genesis 24:1)

It is inevitable. I need to expect it. At some point down the line—probably much sooner than I think it should happen—my children, after numerous advance hints, are going to gather around me, solemn and a bit nervous.

"Dad," one of them will begin somewhat hesitantly, "we think it's too much for you and Mother to keep up this house. We worry about your living here alone. What if you should fall in the shower? Or down the back steps when the neighbors are at work? And Mother is at the point where it is hard for her to keep up with the cooking and laundering and cleaning..."

And another will pipe in: "You know you are getting sort of forgetful, Dad. Like when you paid the water bill twice. It's a good thing the company was honest..."

My first reaction as a freedom-loving American, will be to bristle a bit (inwardly) at the thought that I am becoming incompetent. Why, who do they think it was who put a roof over their heads and fixed their toys and rescued their hamster from extinction when he wandered down the closet partition? *Outwardly*, I hope I will have the good sense to swallow my pride and trust the corporate judgement of my four children, each of whom loves me dearly and has only my best interests at heart.

I have seen the latter days of some who stubbornly refused to listen. I do not want to go through what they went through. May Marge and I be willing to listen to reason.

Father, thank You for responsible children and other relatives who feel a concern for my well-being. Amen.

OCTOBER 11

The Next Transition

*The eyes of the Lord are on those who fear
him,
on those whose hope is in his unfailing love.
(Psalm 33:18)*

Upheaval has never been easy for me. And the older I get, the harder it will get.

I was reflecting yesterday on that imaginary scenario when my children conclude that Dad and Mom are no longer capable of independent living. That strained conversation may never take place, of course. Death may intervene. Or unanticipated disease or injury may make the whole question moot.

Rebecca, our oldest, who abhors institutional living, has already let it be known that we will come to live with her and John when we can no longer manage independently. At the present time she is the only one of our four children in a situation where she could accommodate us.

I cannot gainsay the benefit we might be to Sarah, who is now pushing toward teenage status. I remember the positive influence Marge's mother was on our four children those years she lived with us after Dad's passing. But I've seen other situations where the care of an aged parent, graciously taken in, became almost a death sentence to the children who extended assistance. I do not want that to happen to my children.

In my thinking, a Christian retirement center offering life-time care is the best possible alternative. It frees our children to pursue their own lives and responsibilities. We will be adequately provided for in a caring atmosphere among people who share our love for God, His Word and His church.

Father, we propose, but You dispose. Do what is best. Amen.

OCTOBER 12

To Go or to Stay

*This God is our God for ever and ever;
he will be our guide even to the end.
(Psalm 48:14)*

I am thankful to God for four loving children, any one of whom would be glad to provide a home for Marge and me in our old age. But for the reasons stated yesterday, we prefer not to impose on their generosity.

We could do what most Christian retirees do: plan to stay put in our own home and hope that God's heavenward call will come before incapacitating illness strikes. If it does not—

In the midst of crisis is not the best of times to figure out alternatives. At that point, we might bow to family pressure and go to live with one of our children, despite our misgivings. The alternatives would be a local nursing home or hospice. And, when money ran out, public assistance. Indeed, many retirees do not have financial resources for any other plan.

The alternative that appeals to us is one of our church's retirement centers: a place with independent living arrangements as long as we can manage, followed by assisted living, followed, if necessary, by full-time nursing care. I say a denominational retirement center because (1) the Christian atmosphere promotes inner renewal and (2) the care is generally better than in for-profit or government-run facilities.

By the time our names get to the top of the lengthy waiting list at one of our denominational retirement centers, we should be ready to move in!

Thank You, Father, for church-sponsored, caring retirement centers where Your people can be provided for. Amen.

OCTOBER 13

A Retirement Center?

"He will renew your life and sustain you in your old age." (Ruth 4:15)

The words were spoken to Naomi about Obed, her newborn grandson, the child of Ruth and Boaz. For Naomi, who had known so much bitter disappointment in life, the turn of events must have seemed like an unbelievable dream.

My life has been very different from Naomi's, but she had and I have the same normal concerns about old age.

A church-related retirement center offering lifetime care has one drawback for people of modest means: likely it will cost me whatever savings or financial investments I may have. That is psychologically hard. Although I trust in God and His promises to meet my needs, I like the thought of a little money to fall back on when and if an emergency arises.

And there are the children. The Bible says I should lay up for my children, not my children for me (2 Corinthians 12:14). Not only do I not want to be a burden to any of them, but it would be a joy to leave them at least something. Marge and I were grateful for the unexpected beneficence we received from my step-mother upon her death a few years back.

But as a son, I know that the well-being of my father in his old age meant much more to us than any possible inheritance could mean. He gave us love and a good Christian example, and they are worth more than money. I have reason to believe my children share that same viewpoint.

Father, thank You for Christian retirement centers. With their lengthy waiting lists, it is time to sign up. Amen.

OCTOBER 14

Contentment

We brought nothing into the world, and we can take nothing out of it. But if we have food and clothing, we will be content with that. (1 Timothy 6:7–8)

"One of the great things about growing old," said Richard S. Emerich, "is the simplicity it can give to life."

As I add years, I find life getting simpler. The gadgetry and fast-track lifestyle that was so appealing three decades ago no longer beckons. I find delight in the simple pleasures of life: a well-kept lawn, the crisp freshness of autumn air, dinner with family or friends. The neighbor down the street with his large house and his fleet of expensive cars evokes no jealousy within me. Our smaller house is plenty large and the four-year-old Pontiac still runs just fine.

My challenge as time goes on, may be to stir up the old *dis*content that kept me thinking creatively, kept me pushing tirelessly, kept me praying earnestly. Paul's contentment with his material circumstances did not blind him to the needs of Christians who were struggling or of a godless Roman society still in need of a Savior. Even in prison he participated in the struggles of his fellow Christians. He made sure that "Caesar's household" had a Christian witness.

For contentment I am thankful. At the same time, I must not let that contentment turn me inward. I must not let it bring my God-ordained servanthood to a halt. As long as I have breath and soundness of mind, God has work for me to do. It is His work. I must be faithful to it and to Him.

Father, You have made me content for a purpose. Amen.

OCTOBER 15

False Economies

"The peoples exhaust themselves for nothing." (Jeremiah 51:58)

Frugality can do strange things to people. Like washing throw-away plastic picnic spoons for reuse or driving three miles to save 20 cents on an advertised head of lettuce. To keep a sense of perspective, I need to remember certain premises:

1. Although I am retired, my time is worth *something*. To spend a morning clipping used postage stamps that may net 25 cents for world missions is not very efficient.

2. The real cost of operating my car is at least 25 cents a mile. Driving endlessly to take advantage of double coupons may not be cost effective. Grouping errands to save mileage is.

3. That chromium-plated, calico-clad turfenfoil is only a bargain if I need it. Garage sales can be a fun way to spend a couple of Saturday morning hours. But unless I have learned to say no, the only gainer is the householder who sold me her stuff. (The same applies to auctions, with the added caution that prices at auctions can be bid up unreasonably.)

4. Doing my own repairs is only economical if I know what I am doing. If I do not, a professional repairman will make the fix in a fraction of the time and probably at less cost.

Not everything can be measured in dollars and cents, of course. The drive to the bargain store may be a relaxing diversion from other duties. Getting to know the neighbor with the discards may be a good contact. My bungling fix-it attempt can be a learning experience. But I need to be sure I am realistic and not just rationalizing.

Father, help me to stay balanced in what I do. Amen.

OCTOBER 16

In the Name of Jesus

*Whatever you do, whether in word or deed,
do it all in the name of the Lord Jesus, giving thanks
to God the Father through him. (Colossians 3:17)*

This has been a good day for me. I enjoy manual work, and when I can do something useful in the place where we gather to worship God, the pleasure is doubled.

Installing a drop ceiling in the one of the two yet unfinished Sunday school classrooms of our temporary church building seemed a useful improvement. That was the project that Marvin McGhee and I set for ourselves today. I am discovering that Marvin McGhee and I have much in common, including our retired status and our enjoyment of manual projects like this one. Pat Roseland, who happened to have the day off from his work at Wake Medical Center in Raleigh, made the perfect third man for our do-it-yourself church improvement job.

I am thankful to God for sparing us from serious accident when the rickety ladder, propped against the wall, on which Marvin was standing slipped. It was only God's mercy that kept my ladder—and me—upright as Marvin made his unexpected descent. Instead of bruised knuckles or broken bones, the only casualty was a wall switch plate. We must not assume that because it is a church job we do not need to be prudent.

It was good exercise and good fellowship. We left with a sense of accomplishment. And Ken Kovarik's Sunday school class will appreciate the aesthetic improvement when the young people gather to meet in the room this next Sunday.

Father, thank you for the joy of manual work. Amen.

OCTOBER 17

Truth on Trial

*When they heard [Stephen's accusations],
they were furious. (Acts 7:54)*

What causes otherwise composed, rational, intelligent people to turn against truth?

Senior men—chief priests, elders, teachers of the law—comprising the Sanhedrin were gathered to hear Stephen's defense. Stephen had been hailed before them on trumped up charges by men who could not tolerate his Spirit-inspired witness. Before it was over, they had murdered Stephen and initiated an intense persecution of the new church of Jesus Christ.

How easy it is to resent the ideas of younger men and women. These men of the Sanhedrin were confronted by inarguable logic. Rather than reexamine their religious tenets, they rejected the truth and did away with its messenger.

Those insanely raging men did not help their own cause and viewpoint. On the contrary, they only succeeded in spreading the hated new "cult." And the system they so jealously defended against Roman domination collapsed totally in the Roman-led holocaust of A.D. 70.

By comparison, my issues and prejudices are minor. But they have the potential to consume me, just as the Sanhedrin's prejudices consumed them. May God grant me the ability to be open to new truth, to think clearly, to not answer with mindless emotion when the forms I cherish are challenged by sincere, Spirit-led younger people.

I *could* be wrong. They *could* be right.

Father, I need the ability to discern truth from error. Amen.

OCTOBER 18

Depression

My soul is downcast within me. (Psalm 42:6)

Fifty-one percent of retired people live with a spouse. Twenty-two percent live with someone else, often other family members. Twenty-seven percent, mostly women, live alone. What relation those statistics bear to this next one, I do not know, but researchers inform me that as high as 20 percent of people over 65 suffer from depression.

Depression has many causes. Sometimes it is due to a chemical imbalance within the body. I have a friend who struggles with this kind of depression. A godly, buoyant Christian when he is on top, he doubts his own salvation when he is down. But a small correction in his medication restores the balance and he is again a very normal, outgoing, joyful person.

Alcohol and other drugs are the source of much depression. Regrettably, Christians are not as immune as they should be to these man-made menaces.

Beyond such causes, there is self-induced depression. Believers who should know better allow themselves to be dragged down by circumstances.

Lloyd John Ogilvie says, "Worry is thinking turned toxic, concern degenerated into inner conflict." God has given me His "very great and precious promises" (1 Peter 1:4) to help me overcome such pitfalls. I am admonished to "be joyful always" (1 Thessalonians 5:16), to "give thanks in all circumstances" (5:18). Obedience to such injunctions is my best immunization against this kind of self-induced depression.

Father, praise must still be my heart-beat. Amen.

OCTOBER 19

Night Ministers

*Praise the Lord, all you servants of the Lord
who minister by night in the house
of the Lord.
(Psalm 134:1)*

More than half of Americans over age 65 complain that they have sleep problems. For those in nursing homes, the figure is more than two-thirds.

Contrary to popular belief, the need for sleep does not abate with age. But sleep patterns change. Older people spend less time in deep sleep. They are more likely to take daytime naps. They tend to go to bed earlier and to rise earlier.

Peggy Eastman, writing in the AARP *Bulletin*, notes that of the sleep disorders plaguing older people, insomnia is by far the most common. To thwart it, she suggests a fixed routine (going to bed at the same time, rising at the same time), using the bedroom only for sleeping, two to four hours of before-bedtime exercise, avoidance of alcohol and caffeine, and a restricted intake of fluids in the evening.

But what if it happens? What of those nights when sleep eludes me and I restlessly suffer through hours of wakefulness?

That is my opportunity to "minister by night." Why should I not redeem the time? Perhaps God has made me wakeful so He can bring relatives, friends, missionaries and churches to my attention. If I will not disturb others, I may want to switch on a light so God can talk to me as I read His Word, the Bible. With no distractions, I have an unparalleled opportunity to minister before God in worship and praise and then to intercede for those He puts upon my heart.

Father, day or night, I am on call. Amen.

OCTOBER 20

Zerubbabel

"The hands of Zerubbabel have laid the foundation of this temple; his hands will also complete it." (Zechariah 4:9)

Zerubbabel was titular head of the tribe of Judah during at least the latter part of the Babylonian captivity. Thus it was that he had the honor of leading the first contingent of Jews back to their own land.

Three other honors awaited him once he was back in Palestine: He participated in the rebuilding of the temple altar and the reinstituting of the morning and evening sacrifices (Ezra 3:2–3). He laid the foundations of what would be the second temple (3:8). And some 16 years later, after surmounting intense opposition, Zerubbabel supervised the temple construction, completing the work in four years.

Zerubbabel organized the courses of ministering priests. He registered returning captives. He arranged for the celebration of the Passover in the seventh year of Darius Hystaspes. There was one other very significant honor granted this senior statesman: He figured in the human genealogy of Jesus Christ (see Matthew 1:12; Luke 3:27).

It was specifically to Zerubbabel that Zechariah prophesied, "This is the word of the Lord: . . . 'Not by might nor by power, but by my Spirit,' says the Lord Almighty" (Zechariah 4:6). Zerubbabel does not come across as a dynamic leader. Everything he did was part of a team effort. But Zerubbabel was in the right place at the right time—and he was willing to be God's channel. God by His Spirit worked through Zerubbabel to achieve His purposes for Israel and the world.

Father, I too want to be available to You. Amen.

OCTOBER 21

Haggai

The word of the Lord came through the prophet Haggai: "Is it a time for you yourselves to be living in your paneled houses, while this house remains a ruin?" (Haggai 1:3–4)

The year was 520 B.C. the Israelites had been back in their land for 18 years when a senior prophet by the name of Haggai asked his penetrating question.

Haggai reminded the people that their crops were not prospering, their money seemed never sufficient, their food never enough. (Does it sound like retirement? Always more month than money? Never quite enough to go around?)

Haggai said there was a reason for the shortages. The people had neglected God's house. The shortages would continue as long as the temple lay in ruins. He challenged them to provide for its rebuilding. If they did so, God would wipe out the shortages.

Spurred by the prophetic preaching of Haggai and Zechariah, the settlers went to work. And as rebuilding began, God encouraged the workers through Haggai: "Who of you is left who saw this house in its former glory?" he asked. "How does it look to you now? Does it not seem to you like nothing? . . . This is what the Lord Almighty says, . . . 'The desired of all nations will come, and I will fill this house with glory'" (Haggai 2:3–7). In four years, the temple was finished.

Is the house of God where I worship in need of rebuilding or repair? Has the project languished for want of money? I should not fear to invest. God has His ways of increasing my store of seed and enlarging the harvest of my righteousness.

Father, I am ready to prove You now. Amen.

OCTOBER 22

Nehemiah

Some time later I . . . came back to Jerusalem. (Nehemiah 13:6–7)

There are men and women who have made significant achievements in life who come to retirement unwilling to be "shelved." They still sense a drive to be doing.

Nehemiah's name will always be associated with the rebuilding of Jerusalem's wall following Judah's 70-year captivity. It was an incredible achievement. Nehemiah mobilized and organized a rag-tag assemblage of returning Jews, many of them doubtless elderly. In 52 days, against recurrent opposition, they rebuilt the city's walls and rehung the gates. Jerusalem was again defensible. The story is a familiar one.

Not so familiar is the fact that Nehemiah was an able reformer, addressing current social and spiritual abuses.

Still less familiar is the fact that Nehemiah was governor of Jerusalem into his old age. After a somewhat brief visit to the Persian capital and the emperor, Nehemiah returned to Jerusalem, probably remaining on as governor until "the reign of Darius the Persian," mentioned in chapter 12, verse 22.

What is known of Nehemiah is confined to the book that bears his name. He may have had other notable achievements. More probably Nehemiah simply "kept on keeping on," insuring by his good influence the spiritual stability and social well-being of those who had returned from captivity to rebuild the nation their fathers' sins had brought to ruin.

Father, sometimes You expect great achievements. Sometimes You simply expect good example and a believable witness. Amen.

OCTOBER 23

Mordecai

When Esther's words were reported to Mordecai, he sent back this answer:... "Who knows but that you have come to royal position for such a time as this?" (Esther 4:12–14)

Most communities are festering because of injustices waiting to be righted, sins needing to be exposed. Without moral leadership, any community retrogresses. But moral leaders need behind-the-scenes enablers. These enablers are not necessarily young. Many are already in their retirement years.

Mordecai became an enabler. Up to then his main achievement in life may have been providing a home for his young cousin Esther after the death of her parents. Certainly Mordecai could not have guessed the sudden turn of events that took Esther from his household, ultimately to become the queen of Persia. Neither could he have guessed that newly-promoted Haman, piqued by Mordecai's refusal to bow to him, would threaten all Jews residing in Persia with extinction.

Faced by this holocaust, Mordecai mounted no demonstrations, mobilized no rebel forces. But he seems to have talked to God a lot. And he talked to Esther.

When Esther tried to beg off from helping, Mordecai appealed first to her fears: " 'If you remain silent at this time, ... you and your father's family will perish.' " He also appealed to her sense of destiny: " 'Who knows but that you have come to royal position for such a time as this?' " (Esther 4:14).

The familiar outcome could not have happened if not for Mordecai and his personal diplomacy.

Father, do You want me to be a Mordecai where I live? Amen.

OCTOBER 24

Preserving the Past

*Remember the former things,
those of long ago. (Isaiah 46:9)*

Martin A. Janis in *The Joys of Aging* has a good suggestion for older people. Commenting on their heightened ability to recall the distant past, he dismisses those who would have seniors "forget the past."

Janis, himself a senior, writes, "As we get older, due to some phenomenon of the brain cells, I suppose, the days we spent in grade school become more vivid than what we had for breakfast this morning. My solution is not to attempt to banish the past, but to retain it in some way."

Janis suggests "a series of letters to your children or grandchildren." These letters can recall the "memories, deep feelings or important ideas" associated with the distant past. "The letters can then be bound into a notebook, which can be handed down from generation to generation."

As alternatives in our technological age, especially for the person who feels incapable of writing, Janis suggests tape-recording the memories. "This has the bonus of preserving your voice for your posterity," he adds. "Now that VCRs are common, consider doing a videotaped interview in which you reminisce about your childhood [and] family memories."

For the non-writing, inarticulate types, Janis has a related suggestion: "Your assignment can be to find all the family pictures, date them and identify the individuals in them. You can't imagine how important this can be to an heir left with a pile of pictures he or she can't identify."

Father, my record shall also tell of Your mercy to me. Amen.

OCTOBER 25

Needed Then?

"Go, sell everything you have and give to the poor, and you will have treasure in heaven." (Mark 10:21)

Ernest Digweed, a Portsmouth, England, schoolmaster turned recluse, died a few years back at age 81, leaving his estate of $44,000 to "the Lord Jesus Christ."

In his will Mr. Digweed imposed two conditions: Jesus must arrive within 80 years, and He must be recognized as the Messiah by the Public Trustee, an official of the state. Otherwise the money is to go to the Crown.

"Clearly," commented a spokesman for the Public Trustee, "Mr. Digweed was a man of religious conviction. The will is certainly valid." But a Portsmouth solicitor saw problems.

"The main stumbling block," said the solicitor, "is the difficulty of proving who is the Lord Jesus Christ. Different people think different things."

Even if the two conditions should be met, there is serious question as to whether Jesus Christ will need the cash when He returns in majesty to establish His rule on earth.

Mr. Digweed may have intended well, but he needed to read his New Testament more carefully. He might then have been impressed by Jesus' words to the rich young ruler: "Go, sell everything you have and give to the poor, and you will have treasure in heaven. Then come, follow me."

Far better that I help bring back the King by ministering now to His needy "brothers" (Matthew 25:40) than that I try to enrich the King later upon His return.

Father, keep me in balance; keep me biblical. Amen.

OCTOBER 26

Wills

*Make it your ambition to ... mind
your own business. (1 Thessalonians 4:11)*

"Mind your own business" has come to mean "Stay out of *my* business!" But God intended the admonition found in First Thessalonians in a positive sense. And a very important part of minding my own business is making sure Marge's and my assets at death, no matter how few they may seem to be now, are distributed as we wish, not as the state wishes.

That vital matter is again cared for. Here in our possession are two newly drawn up wills—one for Marge and one for me. Now I must remember to let our previous attorney know that the old wills in his file are invalid.

Two considerations prompted Marge and me to update our wills now. First, of course, was our move to North Carolina. We wanted to take no chances that our out-of-state wills would be invalidated. Second, retirement has brought about some changes in our financial picture. It was only appropriate for our wills to reflect those changes.

I am thankful for "Gene" Hudson, the capable young Christian attorney who helped us through the process. Very carefully he probed to ascertain exactly our desires. Then he translated those intentions into the "legalese" that can stand up in probate court. As a Christian, Gene was sympathetic with our desire to see that our church denomination shared in any remaining assets. He made suggestions as to how this could best be accomplished—suggestions neither Marge nor I had thought of ourselves.

Father, even in death we want to glorify You. Amen.

OCTOBER 27

God's Will and Mine

*What I want is not your possessions
but you. (2 Corinthians 12:14)*

Death is not a pleasant subject. Couple that fact with the human penchant to procrastinate, and it is not hard to see why seven out of 10 Americans have made no arrangements for the "estate" they cannot take with them.

Benign government has done all that law can do to make the disposition of my material assets fair. The state recognizes a legal document called a will. A will permits me wide latitude in saying to whom my possessions shall go, and when.

If I have no will, the state has attempted to anticipate my wishes. A certain percent goes to my spouse, if I have one, and a certain percent to any living children. But there are flaws in these state-imposed arrangements.

For one, they come at a price. There are court expenses and there is legal red tape. There is the cost of a state-appointed executor. By the time these legal expenses are deducted and the extra taxes imposed, there may be little or nothing left.

For another, the state does not know my particular situation. One of my children may need lifetime medical attention, or I may want the old homestead to stay in the family.

Most serious for me as a Christian, the state is studiously areligious. If I have no will of my own, any hope I may have that my property will be used to further God's work is dashed.

Even if I think I have little to leave, I need to provide a will for its disposition.

Father, my will shall reflect Your will. Amen.

OCTOBER 28

My Will and God's

*With all my resources I have provided
for the temple of my God. (1 Chronicles 29:2)*

Few people consider themselves wealthy. One paycheck barely stretches to the next. They maintain no large bank accounts. Their house is mortgaged and they are making car payments. Taxes absorb more than a third of their income.

But meanwhile that house is appreciating in value and the car gets paid for finally and they have an insurance policy or two and some pension equity. Add up the assets, subtract the liabilities, and the net can be surprising.

Who made that gain possible? Who blessed the work of their hands and minds? Who gave them the health to work productively? Who kept disaster from their door? Whose will do they pray shall be done? Whose kingdom do they pray shall come?

Although I cannot enrich God by a direct gift, I can give to His work on earth. The church that has nurtured me and provided me with Christian fellowship and avenues of Christian service should be high on my priority list, as should its training program for Christian workers and its missionary program to the neglected peoples of earth.

Most church denominations have stewardship representatives who will be glad to help people plan the disposition of their assets according to their wishes and in a way that best benefits them and their interests.

Someday death will come. What peace of mind to know that what I cannot take with me will nevertheless further God's work.

Father, my will shall help Your will to be done on earth. Amen.

OCTOBER 29

What Quality Life?

*The length of our days is seventy years—
or eighty, if we have the strength;
yet their span is but trouble and sorrow.
   (Psalm 90:10)*

Demographers predict that the 50,000 centenarians in the United States today by the year 2020 will swell in number to 350,000! Not only are more and more people entering retirement, but they are living longer and longer.

That poses a double-barreled problem for retirees like me. It is one thing to enter retirement with financial reserves adequate for 10 or 15 years (as a supplement to pension and Social Security). It is quite another to have sufficient reserves for 35 years. If things continue as they are, the number of aging Americans needing welfare will be staggering.

The other part of the problem has to do with the quality of life during those added years. Medical science may keep me alive physically—but in what state of health? And in what mental frame? Reaching the century mark is a hollow achievement if I am comatose when it happens.

The inability of either government or the insurance industry to contain runaway health care costs may make such considerations moot. Health care may become so expensive that only a select few can afford it. The rest of us, like it or not, may have to die without benefit of life-stretching gadgetry and drugs.

Nevertheless, just to be on the safe side, I have made a living will. Doctors are not to hasten my death, but neither are they to delay it beyond reason.

Father, I accept whatever span of life You measure out. Amen.

OCTOBER 30

Making Ends Meet

I was young and now I am old,
yet I have never seen the righteous forsaken
or their children begging bread.
(Psalm 37:25)

The psalmist's observation is one I have reminded the Lord of from time to time. Now that I am retired, I gratefully reflect on how He has supplied my needs.

God's blessing on us during the working years enabled Marge and me to enter this phase of our lives free of debt. My modest but much appreciated pension plus Social Security cover our church and charitable contributions (God still gets the first check of the month!) and our week-to-week living expenses, including utilities, taxes, medical insurance, car maintenance. With the potential of continued part-time work to cover major capital needs (a replacement car, for example, or a new roof on the house), we are in good shape.

There were times when this trim little house in Garner, North Carolina, seemed a little too trim. Now, with the cool, crisp fall nights upon us and the need to run the heat pump, I am thankful that it is small and tight. I feel a sense of well-being not afforded by our former large house.

I realize that many retirees—including some reading this October 30 meditation—are not that well off. Their earnings may have been less, their employers less farsighted, their families larger, their generosity to the Lord's work greater. But The-Lord-Will-Provide (see Genesis 22:14) is their God as well as mine. He can be counted on to meet their needs, too.

Father, thank You for supplying every need. Amen.

OCTOBER 31

Where the Pray-ers?

*Then Jesus told his disciples a parable to show them
that they should always pray and not give up.(Luke 18:1)*

Raymond S. Jarrett, former treasurer of The Alliance Home in Carlisle, Pennsylvania, and a dear Christian man, made it a practice to let new residents know they were there to serve God, not to mark time until they received their upward summons.

"You have not come here to die," he would say. "You have come here to *live*. All your life you have been saying, 'If I only had time.' Now you have time. You've been in school all your life. Now it's time to put out your shingle and start practicing. You came here to live!"

Ray Jarrett is himself now retired (although not from the Lord's work), but his good consel is still followed at The Alliance Home. The residents live their lives the world around in intercessory prayer. If I had to be dependent on the prayers of just one group of people, I would choose the residents of The Alliance Home in Carlisle.

Intercessory prayer is dependent on information. Missionary publications, missionary "prayer letters," ordinary newspapers, church bulletins are all readily-come-by sources of information to assist the pray-er.

I am thankful that there are still intercessors on the scene. I know of several who uphold my ministry—some of them, incidentally, far from the golden-years age bracket.

As the praying saints receive their promotions to heaven, others step in to fill the gap. These praying saints are extremely important to the effective ministry of God's church, whether at home or worldwide.

Father, keep me enlisted in Your roster of pray-ers. Amen.

NOVEMBER 1

Divine Arithmetic

"When I broke the five loaves for the five thousand, how many basketfuls of pieces did you pick up?"
"Twelve," they replied.
"And when I broke the seven loaves for the four thousand, how many basketfuls of pieces did you pick up?"
They answered, "Seven." (Mark 8:19–21)

It is good to know that circumstances have never limited God's power. Five loaves fed 5,000—with 12 basketfuls left over. Seven loaves fed 4,000—with seven basketfuls left over. The less God has to work with, the more abundant His provision!

How do I translate this truth into these years of retirement? Jesus asked His questions in the face of His disciples' concern because they "had forgotten to bring bread" (Mark 8:14). Twelve hungry men were on a several-hour trip across the Sea of Galilee, and for food they had one pancake-size "loaf."

Only hours before, these same disciples had participated in the feeding of the 4,000 (Mark 8:1–8). And, before that, in the feeding of the 5,000 (6:35–44). Surely they should have understood that Jesus could multiply that one lone loaf into enough bread to sink their boat.

Today inflation has eviscerated the buying power of fixed-income pensions. And the next 20 years could be as bad. But God is with me in the boat. God can still stretch what may be my inadequate supply. His promise stands: He "will meet all [my] needs according to his glorious riches in Christ Jesus" (Philippians 4:19).

Father, my confidence will continue to be in You. Amen.

NOVEMBER 2

The Crowd

They could not get him to Jesus because of the crowd. (Mark 2:4)

Not just the bearers of the paralyzed man had trouble getting their friend to Jesus "because of the crowd." Zacchaeus wanted to see Jesus but "he could not, because of the crowd" (Luke 19:3). Exactly who was this "crowd" that kept getting in the way of people who needed Jesus?

Well, it was the twelve disciples. It was other close followers of Jesus. It was possibly some or all of the seventy whom He sent out to preach. And then there were the hangers-on, attentive to His words, impressed by the miracles—eager, faithful people. They, too, were His followers, the "crowd."

And this "crowd" kept people from reaching Jesus.

I have been a part of the "crowd"—often. There are row upon row of us in the church I go to. We sing. We praise. We worship. We pray. We listen to good preaching. We congratulate ourselves that we can have such good fellowship.

At that very moment, on the streets of our town and in the homes surrounding our church are people who desperately need Jesus. *We* hinder them from discovering Him.

To be sure, the church doors are unlocked. There are some unoccupied seats. But to the uninitiated a church is a formidable place. *Will someone be collecting tickets? Must I know the password? Are the seats reserved?* We on the inside, by our insensitivity, are keeping people from Jesus.

Father, it is not enough to beckon from the church door. Help me say, "Won't you come with me?" Amen.

NOVEMBER 3

Faith First to Last

"The righteous will live by faith." (Romans 1:17)

I confess to a troubling tendency within me that I must counter at all cost. I tend to become critical of God.

Maybe it is the cynical streak I have battled all my life. Or my logical bent that says two plus two must equal four.

I am in the Chronicles in my Bible reading. When David sinned by numbering Israel's fighting men, why did God kill 70,000 "men of Israel" (1 Chronicles 21:14)? Why did He not mete out the punishment to the king, who had committed the sin?

Or, in the wisdom God lavished on Solomon, why could it not have kept him from the stupid blunder of following his pagan wives into idolatrous practices? That very unwise course was catastrophic for Israel. The nation never recovered.

A critical attitude toward God is tell-tale in questions like these:

"Why did You let this happen to me?"
"Where is the needed hundred dollars I prayed for?"
"Why haven't You healed my arthritis?"
"Why are You silent when I ask You to direct me?"

God is sovereign. That fact I must accept. God expects me to trust Him, no matter what. The Christian life is to be a walk of faith—"faith from first to last," as Paul told the believers in Rome (Romans 1:17). Therefore, I *will* believe. God is true and God is truth. Whether or not it makes sense. Whether or not there is light at the end of the tunnel.

Father, I commit myself to trust You to the end. Amen.

NOVEMBER 4

"Disputable Matters"

Accept him whose faith is weak, without passing judgment on disputable matters. (Romans 14:1)

Several years ago I had lunch with business associates in Wheaton, Illinois—the evangelical "Mecca." The restaurant was large and open. My hosts identified table after table of well-known Christian leaders involved in publishing, broadcasting and other services to the church.

What impressed me as a lifetime teetotaler was the number of people at those tables who drank wine. If someone from those tables had been identifying *me*, I hope I of weaker faith—with no wine—would be accepted.

I think I have good rationale for abstaining from alcoholic beverages. But that is not the point. The point is this: alcohol falls under the heading of "disputable matters." And as I age, I find it easier and easier to take a hard line against those who do not conform to *my* ideas of appropriate behavior.

In New Testament times, the disputable matters were holy days, the eating of food offered to idols and the eating of any meat. Today disputable matters can range from clothing styles to music styles to worship styles. Whatever the issue, the principle is unchanged. If the other person is a believer, I am to accept him or her without passing judgment.

Does this mean I should not attempt to convince the other person? Not necessarily, if I do so tactfully, appropriately and in a spirit of love. What if he or she is not persuaded? Then the "accept him" rule is still in force.

Father, give me a generous mind and a loving heart. Amen.

NOVEMBER 5

Respect

"Rise in the presence of the aged, show respect for the elderly." (Leviticus 19:32)

I am no longer young. In my eyes I hardly qualify as "old," and even "older" does not yet quite sit well. But soon enough those terms will fit me.

The tell-tale signs are appearing. My motions are slower, my reflexes less sharp. I note that my joints are stiffening. I can still do a full day's work, but I end up more fatigued than I used to.

Researchers tell me my heart has lost nearly a third of its pumping efficiency. My lung capacity is only half what it was at age 30. The death of brain cells explains why I find it ever more difficult to recall names. My thymus gland, which controls the manufacture of infection-fighting white-blood cells, has shrunk almost to invisibility. I am a ready target for diseases such as arthritis and pneumonia.

In a bizarre switch of cultural mores, Americans have turned God's command concerning respect for the elderly into worship of youthfulness. Americans dread the prospect of old age. The sight of feeble oldsters evokes pity, even revulsion, rather than respect. The attitude is not likely to improve as a shrinking population of young and middle-aged bear the financial burden of an enlarging population of the elderly, whose lengthening life spans are costing the general public more and more.

I can only hope that when I arrive at old age, my way of life and my love for people will be such that the younger will find it easy to respect—and even love—me.

Father, bless the elderly in this world. Amen.

NOVEMBER 6

Simeon

There was a man in Jerusalem called Simeon, who was righteous and devout.... The Holy Spirit was upon him. (Luke 2:25)

There is nowhere in Luke's brief recounting of Simeon's meeting with Mary and Joseph and the Baby Jesus where Simeon is specifically referred to as old. But the words "that he would not die before he had seen the Lord's Christ" (2:26) and his own "Sovereign Lord, as you have promised,/ you now dismiss your servant in peace./ For my eyes have seen your salvation" (2:29–30) lead me to that conclusion.

What qualities about Simeon caused God to put His "Holy Spirit . . . upon him"? Why did God single out Simeon for that special glimpse of His Holy Son? To be sure, Simeon was "righteous and devout." He was "waiting for the consolation of Israel." But statements like that could have been made of many Jews in that politically unsettled time.

Was it Simeon's sensitivity to God's Spirit that caused God to single him out? Luke says, "Moved by the Spirit, he went into the temple courts" just in time to see Mary and Joseph and the Holy Baby arrive. Or was it that Simeon was a praiseful man? Luke says he "took [the Baby] in his arms and praised God" (2:28). God delights in the praise of His people.

I would press to have all of these good qualities that Simeon had: righteousness, devotion, sensitivity, praise. Who knows? Jesus, whom Simeon saw as a helpless Baby, is scheduled to reappear as a conquering Sovereign. Like Simeon, I may be allowed to live to greet His coming!

Even so come, Lord Jesus! Amen.

NOVEMBER 7

Anna

There was also a prophetess, Anna. (Luke 2:36)

It is unlikely that I will attain Anna's age. Luke calls her "very old." Whether she was a widow for 84 years after being married for seven years, or whether her total age was 84, she had defied the 80-year span of Psalm 90:10.

Anna's exact routine was one that is hardly possible today, even if we substitute church building for Jerusalem temple. Luke says "she never left the temple but worshiped night and day, fasting and praying" (2:37). Granted a touch of hyperbole in Luke's words—after all, Anna had to sleep at least once in a while, and even prophetesses occasionally need food—Anna comes across in Luke's account as a very devout, very committed woman. Presumably the priests, motivated by her piety, had provided living quarters for her in the temple complex and saw to it that she had the necessities of life.

Drawn by God's Spirit to the approaching couple, Joseph and Mary, with eight-day-old Jesus in their arms, Anna "gave thanks" to God and "spoke about the child to all who were looking forward to the redemption of Jerusalem" (2:38).

Simeon, the subject of yesterday's meditation, addressed his praise to God. Anna praised God, too, but she went on to speak of God's Son "to all" who looked for God's intervention in those days of national bondage. The prophetic message of this aged saint must have been an encouragement to many oppressed, anxious people as well as to Mary and Joseph.

Father, let my words be a source of encouragement to those who are yet in bondage to the adversary Satan. Amen.

NOVEMBER 8

Nicodemus

"How can a man be born when he is old?"
Nicodemus asked. (John 3:4)

I wish I knew more about Nicodemus.

The Scriptures provide but three glimpses of this unusual, up-in-years member of the Jewish ruling council. The first is the inconclusive, after-dark interview with Jesus when Nicodemus asked his well-known question, "How can a man be born when he is old?" He appears briefly again in John 7. The Jews wanted to arrest Jesus on the spot. Nicodemus urged a moderate, reasoned approach (7:45–52). The last glimpse is just a mention. Nicodemus was with Joseph of Arimathea when Joseph asked Pilate for Jesus' dead body. John reports, "Nicodemus brought a mixture of myrrh and aloes, about seventy-five pounds" (19:39).

Was Nicodemus in the end just an unusually moral man concerned because he felt the young Prophet from Nazareth was receiving unfair treatment? Or had Nicodemus discovered how to be born anew after a person "is old"? Had he experienced the Spirit's new life that remarkably transforms a person?

Tradition says Nicodemus died a believer. Tradition says that Nicodemus, once one of the three richest men in Jerusalem, became penniless as a result of the persecution he suffered for having embraced Christianity. Tradition is not very reliable. I must await heaven to learn the details of his life.

I will be disappointed if he is not there.

Father, I want to be in—not just close to—Your kingdom. Amen.

NOVEMBER 9

Annas

*Annas sent [Jesus], still bound,
to Caiaphas the high priest. (John 18:24)*

There are lessons to be learned even from the "bad guys" who walk across the pages of the Bible. Annas is a case in point.

I wonder what forces bore upon Annas to steer him in the course he took. His years of priestly activity almost surely spanned Jesus' entire earthly life. Josephus, the Jewish historian, says Annas (the name is a contracted form of *Ananias)* was appointed high priest in A.D. 7 by Quirinius, proconsul of Syria, only to be removed seven years later by Valerius Grattus, procurator of Judea, in favor of Annas's son-in-law, Caiaphas. Although Caiaphas had the political title, the elderly Annas still had the recognition of the Jews.

How different history might have been had Annas taken a different attitude toward Jesus Christ. Obviously, his action in condemning Jesus to death played into God's sovereign plan of redemption. At the same time, it earned him history's universal disapproval and God's eternal condemnation.

If only Annas could have forgotten politics. If only he had been sensitive to God's will, to God's great redemption plan! If only he had stopped to examine Jesus' point-blank assertion that He was the Son of God (Luke 22:70–71).

Paul speaks of "the god of this age" having "blinded the minds of unbelievers" (2 Corinthians 4:4). It happened to Annas. Satan has even been known to blind the minds of believers. May it not happen to me.

Father, keep me ever sensitive to spiritual things. Amen.

NOVEMBER 10

Gamaliel

A Pharisee named Gamaliel, a teacher of the law, who was honored by all the people, stood up in the Sanhedrin.... His speech persuaded them. (Acts 5:34, 40)

Gamaliel was a man of sterling reputation. A Pharisee and a teacher of the law, he managed to rise above the narrow prejudices and the tedious semantics that characterized his party. He was held in high esteem by "all the people."

Gamaliel made at least two significant contributions to Christianity. He provided the Apostle Paul his thorough training in Old Testament law. Paul said, "Under Gamaliel I was thoroughly trained in the law of our fathers" (Acts 22:3). Without that training, Paul could hardly have written as persuasively as he does in Romans and Galatians. But Gamaliel made a second contribution. He dissuaded the Sanhedrin when that body was bent on dealing a death blow to Christianity.

Gamaliel's argument on the latter occasion was logical enough: Causes are fueled by opposition. Leave these men alone. If their cause is human, it will quickly burn out. On the other hand, if it is of God, you do not want to be fighting God.

But it was more than Gamaliel's logic that made this elder statesman so persuasive. It was his reputation for fairness. It was the esteem in which he was held by his fellows. A lesser man could not have carried the day.

Age still carries weight. But only if it is backed up by solid reputation.

Father, may the words of my mouth and the meditations of my heart be pleasing in Your sight. Amen.

NOVEMBER 11

Tabitha/Dorcas

In Joppa there was a disciple named Tabitha (which, when translated, is Dorcas), who was always doing good and helping the poor. (Acts 9:36)

Her name, both in Aramaic and Greek, means "female gazelle." The Greeks used the word as a term of endearment for their women.

Dorcas lived up to her name. The unalloyed love she evoked from the Joppa community went beyond people's gratitude for the "robes and other clothing" (9:39) she made and distributed to the poor. It was a response to her gracious, caring personality. Grouches do not sew for destitute widows.

When Tabitha became sick and died, people were devastated—until God's miracle through the apostle Peter restored her to life and vigor.

The fact that Tabitha, although herself widowed, could freely engage in charitable work implies she had been left in financially comfortable circumstances. Could she have been tempted, upon her husband's passing, to withdraw into herself, to hoard her resources, to let the world go by as best it could? Many people do.

But Tabitha was a "disciple." Jesus had touched her life. She no longer belonged to herself but to God. And God had work for her to do. Likely it was the same kind of employment to which she was accustomed as a wife and mother. God does not necessarily demand of His people something unfamiliar, untried.

What a miracle the church would have missed had Tabitha not made herself so indispensable!

Father, help me overcome the temptation to turn inward. Amen.

NOVEMBER 12

Conformed to Jesus

In all things God works for the good of those who love him, who have been called according to his purpose. (Romans 8:28)

God has one ultimate purpose for all His spiritual children. He wants each one to be "conformed to the likeness of his Son" (8:29). He intends for this conformity to be through a means that many believers neglect: prayer.

In Romans 8:26–27, God draws back the veil to let me glimpse the machinery of this heavenly process: "The Spirit helps us in our weakness. We do not know what we ought to pray for, but the Spirit himself intercedes for us with groans that words cannot express. And he who searches our hearts knows the mind of the Spirit, because the Spirit intercedes for the saints in accordance with God's will."

It is staggering to realize that when I drop to my knees to pray, the whole Trinity springs to action. The Holy Spirit assists by turning my imperfectly framed utterances into petitions that conform to the Father's will. And the Searcher of Hearts—Jesus (John 2:24–25; 6:64; 13:11)—relays those petitions to the Father's very presence (Hebrews 7:25).

When I thus pray in God's will, and because of this divine assistance as I pray, God is free in all things to work for my good. But the good is not an end in itself. It is to the end that I might be "conformed to the likeness of his Son." This is God's ultimate objective for me. It is my crowning glory.

In view of God's eternal purpose for me and the one means by which it can be accomplished, how little I pray!

Father, make prayer my major occupation. Amen.

NOVEMBER 13

Patience

You need to persevere so that when you have done the will of God, you will receive what he has promised. (Hebrews 10:36)

The New Testament abounds with references to patience.

Patience is to characterize the Christian. Paul prayed for the Colossians that they might have "great endurance and patience" (Colossians 1:11). It was patience that was to be exercised toward those within the fellowship: "Bear with each other" (3:13). It was to extend as well to those outside the church: "Be patient with everyone" (1 Thessalonians 5:14).

A believer who patiently endures when he or she suffers for doing good pleases God (1 Peter 2:20). It is conduct patterned after Jesus' own, who when He was insulted "did not retaliate; when he suffered, he made no threats" (2:23).

Patience is especially important in respect to the return of Christ Jesus. "Be patient, then, brothers, until the Lord's coming," James advises (James 5:7), citing the farmer who waits patiently for "the land to yield its valuable crop."

Paul urged the Galatians not to "become weary in doing good, for at the proper time we will reap a harvest if we do not give up" (Galatians 6:9).

Perhaps at no time is patience more necessary than when I pray. Like George Mueller, I may be in eternity before some of my prayers are answered. But "this is the confidence we have in approaching God: that if we ask anything according to his will, he hears us. And if we know that he hears us—whatever we ask—we know that we have what we asked of him" (1 John 5:14–15).

Father, I am impatient. Please make me patient. Amen.

NOVEMBER 14

Death Has Purpose

The righteous perish,
and no one ponders it in his heart;
devout men are taken away,
and no one understands
that the righteous are taken away
to be spared from evil.
(Isaiah 57:1)

The note that arrived with Esther Hansen's Christmas card was a shocker to Marge and me. Arthur, her husband, had died of cancer back in September. Art Hansen, our good friend and fellow member at Simpson Memorial Church in Nyack, New York—now gone.

Outgoing, effervescent, up-beat Art, the indomitable salesman, generous in his financial support of the church, a true friend—gone. If only we had received the note Esther said she addressed to us in Pennsylvania. If only some of our mutual friends had thought to mention Art's passing.

We had known of Art's illness and his long process of therapy. When pain began to recur in his back, he was relieved to learn that it was "only" arthritis this time. And now, so quickly, he is gone. Despite our prayers.

The "whys?" are not easy to sort out. Art and Esther seemed always so happy in their Apple Valley, California, retirement home near their son. Now, there is a bereft widow. And a grieving son. And a church that could profit from Art's continued support. Our arguments multiply. But they are essentially selfish; God has ordained a higher mercy for Art. God has spared him from evil. Today he is enjoying eternal pleasures.

Father, even in the matter of death, Your will be done. Amen!

NOVEMBER 15

Widowed

"Do not take advantage of a widow." (Exodus 22:22)

Four out of five people reaching the age of 65 are married, says Tim Stafford in *As Our Years Increase*. Since married couples seldom die together, the death of a spouse awaits most retired people.

Because women, on average, live seven years longer than men, and are four years younger than their husbands, women are much more apt than men to face that devastating trauma.

That it is not reversed is God's mercy to men. Men tend to find the adjustment more difficult than women do. They are apt to be strangers to housework, including cooking. Often they are poor socializers; loneliness can be overwhelming.

Widowhood not infrequently comes as the climax to debilitating illness. Spent from the care of a critically ill mate, the widow must face funeral arrangements, money matters, car registration, yard and house maintenance—things her husband might normally care for. She likely will have a significant drop in monthly income. At no other time does she have a better opportunity to demonstrate her God-given resiliency.

There is life after bereavement. The widow needs to take time to mourn. Although she may wish to flee the scene of past fond memories, she should make decisions slowly and burn no bridges behind her. She may wish to visit children, but she should resist their well-intentioned appeals to live permanently with them.

Beyond the mourning God may have a bright new beginning. God has a special concern for widows.

Father, let Your concern be my concern, too. Amen.

NOVEMBER 16

Deceived

*Satan himself masquerades as
an angel of light. (2 Corinthians 11:14)*

The published research of thanatologists (those who study death and dying) such as Elisabeth Kubler-Ross, Robert Monroe and Raymond Moody has generated sustained interest in the experiences of those who have returned from apparent death.

Hundreds of collected testimonies have common elements: a "dark tunnel," a sensation of being outside one's own body, great peace, an absence of all pain, and telepathic communication with others who are dead. Frequently there is a barrier that these persons dare not cross and from which they turn back to reenter their own bodies.

Central to many of the experiences is a "being of light" which the religiously oriented identify as Jesus Christ. But—and here is the warning flag—this being of light seems strangely unconcerned about the person's previous morality. Regardless of how the man or woman had lived, all is peace and brightness in this euphoric, out-of-body state just beyond death.

Therein the Adversary may have shown his hand.

When these experience-based stories of light and peace and nonaccountability run counter to the Bible, I had better return to the clear teaching of the Scriptures. I should expect Satan, that prince of deceivers, to attempt to personify Jesus Christ, the Light of the World—especially if in so doing he can undermine mankind's need for the atonement made possible by Christ's death and resurrection.

Father, Your Word is a light for my path. Amen.

NOVEMBER 17

Life after Life

Jesus answered, "I am the way and the truth and the life. No one comes to the Father except through me." (John 14:6)

The Scriptures speak of nine specific persons who died and rose from the dead:

- The widow of Zarephath's son (1 Kings 17:17–23)
- The Shunammite woman's son (2 Kings 4:32–37)
- A young man whose body was hastily pushed into Elisha's sepulcher (2 Kings 13:21)
- The widow of Nain's son (Luke 7:12–15)
- Jairus' daughter (Luke 8:49–55)
- Lazarus (John 11:43–44)
- Jesus
- Tabitha/Dorcas (Acts 9:37–40)
- Eutychus (Acts 20:9–12)

The Bible says nothing about what these may have experienced during their "out-of-body" experience. Even Paul, "caught up to the third heaven" (2 Corinthians 12:2), was extremely judicious in what he shared. What he heard was "inexpressible."

But Paul elsewhere affirms his confidence on one point: "Away from the body . . . at home with the Lord" (2 Corinthians 5:8). His hope of seeing God and enjoying Him forever rested squarely on Christ's achievement at Calvary, when He "was delivered over to death for our sins," and at the garden tomb, when He "was raised to life for our justification" (Romans 4:25).

Jesus Christ is the way, the truth, the life.

Father, all that I need is in Jesus! Amen.

NOVEMBER 18

Sight on the Goal

"Set your hope fully on the grace to be given you when Jesus Christ is revealed." (1 Peter 1:13)

If heaven is such a wonderful place, why are Christians so reluctant to go there? Why am *I* so enamored with earthly things and this mortal life?

I was impressed by the perceptive answer my sister-in-law, Evelyn Putnam, gave to the question. Evelyn is an astute observer of human nature. As a resident of The Alliance Home in Carlisle, Pennsylvania, she has had ample opportunity to observe the final struggle that is pandemic to our race.

"It is not that Christians do not want heaven," Evelyn says; "they do not want what they have to go through to get there."

Death is not beautiful. All too frequently it is painful for the person going through it. Always it is painful for the caring ones who must helplessly stand by and watch the uneven struggle. Death is a conquered foe; nevertheless, it looms as a formidable monster poised between the Christian and heaven.

We want heaven; we do not want death.

If I read aright the feelings of the Bible saints—people like Jacob, Moses, David, Elisha, Stephen, Paul, Peter—they were not apprehensive about death. They were so in touch with God that being in His presence made even death tolerable.

I must admit that I have not yet achieved that attitude. For me, death remains formidable. The Jordan is still at flood-stage, and I am not a strong swimmer.

Father, help me set my sights on the grace when Jesus is revealed, and not on what lies between. Amen.

NOVEMBER 19

Heaven

*My soul yearns, even faints,
for the courts of the Lord. (Psalm 84:2)*

The "courts of the Lord" that the Psalmist so intensely longed for are best described in the New Testament. Jesus speaks of a place of "many rooms" (John 14:2) that He would be preparing for His followers. Stephen glimpsed Jesus *standing* "at the right hand of God" (Acts 7:55–56)—as though cheering His faithful first martyr. Paul, caught up to the "third heaven" (2 Corinthians 12:2–4), got a glimpse of the throne, but the overriding impression was not visual but auditory, and even what he heard was too sacred for him to repeat.

It remained for the apostle John to actually describe heaven—to the extent that terrestrial words can depict the celestial (Revelation 4–5). John's description is surrealistic: the throne, the emerald rainbow, the 24 surrounding thrones with their gold-crowned, white-robed "elders," the lightning and thunder, the seven lamps, the glassy sea, the four "living creatures," the "Lamb looking as if it had been slain."

Like Paul, John was captivated by what he heard. I thrill to hear 300 semi-professionals singing Handel's "Hallelujah Chorus." Imagine what it will be like to hear 100 million angels encircling the heavenly throne singing:

> Worthy is the Lamb, who was slain,
> to receive power and wealth and wisdom and strength
> and honor and glory and praise.

Father, I too long for Your courts. Amen.

NOVEMBER 20

Heavenly Citizenship

Our citizenship is in heaven. (Philippians 3:20)

Paul said it, and Christians repeat it, but their lives generally betray them. The sad fact is that my generation—including most of the Christians in my generation—are for all intents citizens of this world. Their preoccupation with its creature comforts and its entertainment puts a "This World" stamp upon those who profess to be citizens of heaven.

Retirement is a "continental divide." Either I become more engrossed than ever in the interests of this world or I allow myself to be drawn to the world to come. I have known some who, upon retirement, abandoned God's house and God's interests for the open road and a life of self-centered play and pleasure. Others have made retirement an occasion to draw closer to God and to serve Him and His church more devotedly.

"Our citizenship is in heaven." Those students from Zaire in our church, though they appreciate America, make it clear that they are Zairians. Marge and I lived for nearly a decade in the Philippines, a land now foreign to Americans. Although we delighted in its people and the natural beauty around us, we cherished our American citizenship.

"This world is not my home;/ I'm just a-passing through," the old song puts it. If I am truly a citizen of heaven, I need to think about heaven, I need to read the literature of heaven, I need to talk to the King of heaven.

I need to plan my trip home.

Father, ready or not, the next life is coming. Please—please—do not let me be deluded by this-world tinsel. Amen.

NOVEMBER 21

Why Pray?

"When you pray . . ." (Matthew 6:6)

Why pray? The question could be posed despairingly—by those, for instance, who have failed to get what they asked for. Impatient in their frustration, they throw up their hands and announce that prayer is a waste of time. It achieves nothing.

Such people, of course, have yet to learn the "patience of unanswered prayer," as the hymn puts it. They have yet to discover the importunate asking and asking that Jesus stressed (see Matthew 7:7). They have yet to experience the wrestling that those schooled in prayer know so intimately.

But the question can be asked as well—and often is—by the religious theoretician. If God is God—sovereign, merciful, loving, all-knowing—what is the point of prayer? My petitions do not inform God; He already is aware of everything. My prayers are not necessary to stir God; He is already compassionate, more solicitous for me than I am for my children (Matthew 7:11). My pleas neither strengthen God's resolve nor reinforce His power. His arm "is not too short to save"; His ear is not "too dull to hear" (Isaiah 59:1). My feeble words are hardly necessary to insure God's will on earth.

God may delight in my prayers. To the extent that I worship Him when I pray I return to Him something He altogether deserves. But does God *need* my prayers? Might not my prayer time be better used in serving God overtly and directly, in personally furthering His kingdom work on earth?

It sounds so plausible, but it comes up short.

Father, You need me to pray; therefore, I will pray. Amen.

NOVEMBER 22

Why, Indeed, Pray?

"When you pray, go into your room, close the door and pray to your Father, who is unseen." (Matthew 6:6)

Why, indeed, pray?

First, because *I* need to pray. I need to know that my dependence is on God, not on myself. My prayers do not move a reluctant God to action; they do prepare this very stubborn, self-centered pray-er for what God has all along wanted to do for him and through him. Prayer, therefore, conditions me for the answers God intends to give.

Second, I am commanded to pray. Even if there was no perceived logic to such an exercise, even if there was never pleasure in the trysting time with Almighty God, even if there were no evident answers before a waiting world, in obedience to God's Word I would still be compelled to pray.

Third, prayer is an essential element in my spiritual battle with Satan. "Our struggle is not against flesh and blood, but against the rulers, against the authorities, against the powers of this dark world and against the spiritual forces of evil in the heavenly realms" (Ephesians 6:12).

For reasons best known to Him, God has chosen to match His strength to my willingness in intercession. In the divine mystery God *does* need my prayers because He has ordained that His work on earth shall be done in partnership with His church.

Intercessory prayer is my part in world evangelization. God's work languishes, relatives and friends remain unsaved, mission fields continue unevangelized if I fail to pray.

Father, teach me to pray. Amen.

NOVEMBER 23

Thankful Today

*Praise the Lord, O my soul,
and forget not all his benefits.
(Psalm 103:2)*

I tend to be so concerned about tomorrow that I fail to be thankful for today. I can still recall the evening in Nyack, New York, when that truth hit me.

I had stepped out of the house just at dusk, rushing to make a hospital call before visiting hours were over. It was one of those rare, smog-free evenings in the metropolitan New York area. Crickets chirped their rickety end-of-summer dirge. The air was crisp, as though bracing itself for autumn, and the Hudson River, visible from my house, reflected the blinking lights of historic Tarrytown, opposite me, on its placid surface. The faint fragrance of the hydrangea by the front steps competed with the aroma of embers from a neighbor's charcoal fire. *And I was so preoccupied with the soon-to-be that I almost missed the blessing of the now-is.*

How often I am guilty of postponing my giving of thanks! Tomorrow—when the washer is paid for, when the disagreeable interview is behind me, when I can think more clearly after a night's sleep—tomorrow I will be thankful. But tomorrow comes, and the washer develops a dismaying noise, or the interviewer wants me to return, or I awake from sleep with a headache. So I put off my thanksgiving.

Ingratitude is an astringent that will shrivel my spirit. It is an implication that God who rules my life and directs my path could not or did not act in my best interest.

Father, forgive me for my lack of gratitude! Amen.

NOVEMBER 24

Negative Thanks

[The Lord] will never let the righteous fall. (Psalm 55:22)

Along with the many positive blessings I can and do thank God for, there are an even greater number of "negative" blessings for which I should be thankful.

I thank God for the accidents that *did not* happen in the many miles of driving I do. I thank Him for the fingers that *did not* get seriously cut or smashed as I sawed and pounded boards. I thank Him for cities that *have not* been destroyed by nuclear war. I thank Him for fires that *did not* get out of control, for bones that *did not* get broken, for disease that *did not* strike, for sickness that *did not* visit us.

No train has ever hit my car as I crossed railroad tracks. No overhead beams, unlodged by earthquake, have pinned me to the ground. No rabid dog has threatened my health. No power mower has sheared off my toes or fingers.

Even in those instances when misfortune has struck, it could have been much worse. I thank God for seeing that it was not. I have only to look around, to read the newspaper, to listen to the newscasts to realize how much God has spared me from.

God has been good to me, and He continues to be good to me. He has given salvation to me and my household. He has Himself walked with me these past more than fifty years. He has loaded me with spiritual and material benefits, meeting my needs, frequently supplying even my wants. I am a living testimony to the goodness of a great and wonderful God!

Father, thank You for sparing me from so very much. My heart is full of praise for all Your benefits to me. Amen.

NOVEMBER 25

Good Times and Bad

When times are good, be happy;
but when times are bad, consider:
God has made the one
as well as the other. (Ecclesiastes 7:14)

Not every bit of advice given by the "Preacher" of Ecclesiastes should be followed. The man regards life from a jaundiced viewpoint, and I need to weigh his words critically. But here is a golden nugget that assays 100 percent pure.

First, the preacher is saying I should expect to find my days an alloy of good and bad. As Annie Johnson Flint put it, "God hath not promised skies always blue,/ flower-strewn pathways all our lives through."

Second, the preacher sees a sovereign Providence in charge of all my days—the prosperous days when it is easy to be happy and the lean days when it is not.

If I believe in God's sovereign care of me (and I do), then I need to "be happy" not only "when times are good" but "when times are bad," not only when I am in health but when I am not.

As a seasoned missionary, Carolyn Eckman made this discovery in Irian Jaya, Indonesia. Everything seemed to be wrong. "There was no joy in my life," she admitted. At that critical point, God asked Carolyn, "Will you praise Me anyhow?" Reluctantly, Carolyn obeyed—with astonishing results. Sick husband, discouraged coworkers, a stalling passport official—all discovered their attitudes changing. Carolyn says, "I was delivered from the depths of despair through the gates of praise."

Father, in "good times" and in "bad" I will praise You. Amen.

NOVEMBER 26

A Pleasant Place

*The boundary lines have fallen for me
in pleasant places. (Psalm 16:6)*

The longer Marge and I occupy this little house in Garner, North Carolina, the more impressive it is.

It is a "tract" house, put up by a builder aiming to construct and sell a maximum number of houses in the minimum amount of time—not usually associated with quality housing. To be sure, there are a few tell-tale signs of haste.

But it was built in the 1970s, before developers had turned totally to cheap substitutes for real wood. Double-glazed windows are not only a solid investment against summer warmth and winter cold, but they eliminate the perennial hassle of storm windows. The brick-veneer exterior should mean low maintenance.

The inside layout is also impressive, maximizing the 1,200 square feet of floor space. The ample living room can be closed off, if necessary, as an extra sleeping room. The dining room is visually separate from the adjoining kitchen. An under-roof screened area beyond the carport and a picturesque front porch are definite pluses.

But a house, no matter how appealing, depends on its setting. Location, as any realtor will say, is everything. Ours is in a development of established, well-kept homes of approximately the same age. It is one of the less expensive houses in the subdivision (another plus when it comes time to sell).

And since Marge and I do not intend to stay here forever, resale value is an important factor.

Thank You, Father, for this comfortable house. Amen.

NOVEMBER 27

"All Your Anxiety"

Cast all your anxiety on [God]. (1 Peter 5:7)

As we left Pennsylvania for North Carolina after a visit with relatives, we prayed for protection on the highway. But a lost handbag? Who could have anticipated *that*?

If only the tables in that delicatessen south of Washington where we lunched had not been so small. Then Marge could have put her bag on the table instead of on the floor by her chair. If only she had left her bag in the car—after all, *I* paid for the sandwiches. If only I had not bought a bulky *Washington Times*, which Marge carried from the table, she might have realized she did not have her handbag. If only—

Afterwards, it is easy to think of the "If onlys." At the moment, there is only that sinking feeling as the extent of the loss begins to penetrate. Call our credit card service to alert them. Call the Motor Vehicles Office about Marge's driver's license. If only we could remember the name of the delicatessen. If only we could remember the *town* it was in—or the exit number on Interstate 95. If only—

"Cast all your anxiety on [God]." Does that include anxiety about a lost handbag? Assuming it did, we prayed that we might recover Marge's missing bag. We also did what we could. We called Frank and Jean Porter, cousins of ours in the Washington area, describing the circumstances. Bless their hearts and bless the Lord! They got in their car, found the exit and the deli and recovered the missing handbag, which had been turned in intact by another customer at the restaurant.

Father, thank You, and thank You for Frank and Jean. Amen.

NOVEMBER 28

Love, Faithfulness

Let love and faithfulness never leave you;
bind them around your neck,
write them on the tablet of your heart.
(Proverbs 3:3)

When Marge left her handbag in the delicatessen south of Washington, D.C., one of our first thoughts was for the charge cards. Charge cards can be both a convenience and a protection, but woe if they fall into the wrong hands!

Love and faithfulness, like credit cards, need to be as jealously guarded. If I let either of them get away from me, I am in serious straits.

Why? Because love and faithfulness are the *sine qua non* of societal life. God has put people into families and neighborhoods and schools and churches and work teams and geo-political entities. When love and faithfulness ebb from these units, they disintegrate. Marriages break up. Neighborhoods become dangerous. Schools, churches, work teams become riddled with mistrust. Geo-political entities can exist only by iron-fisted fiat.

I deplore the swift erosion of faithfulness and love in our national society. Like my fellow-retirees, I am old enough to recall better days. Short of God's omnipotent intervention, the disintegration cannot be reversed.

But that should not leave me wringing my hands. I can make sure *my* love and faithfulness are intact in my family, in my neighborhood, in my church and in the societal entities I belong to. Is that not why I am here? And beyond that, I can pray for God's will to be done on earth.

Father, this troubled society needs Jesus Christ. Amen.

NOVEMBER 29

Succession

*The things you have heard me say ... entrust
to reliable men qualified to teach others. (2 Timothy 2:2)*

I guess it is only natural for me to want to hold on as long as possible, whether it is a neighborhood responsibility or a church ministry. That is good in one sense: I need to be doing. As I have said before, God still expects service.

But I have seen too many hold on too long to believe this whole matter of service is not without problems. For instance, I have seen aging church musicians (I mention musicians because I am one—of sorts) who tenaciously hold to their jobs despite the superior ability of younger talent. Not only has the congregation been denied the best possible accompaniment to its worship, but frequently the able younger person has gone to work elsewhere, leaving the church without succession.

The same observation applies to Sunday school teachers and other people in leadership positions within the church (though in most churches today there is no clamor from gifted teachers waiting to be placed). My objective, as an older person, should be to encourage, to train and then to pass on the torch to a qualified younger person who can perpetuate my ministry. If I do my work well, the church will not lack leaders.

Someone well observed that it is better when a person steps down that people should exclaim, "So soon?" than that they should sigh in thankful relief, "At last!"

Service is a privilege. Preparing another to take my place is also a privilege—and a responsibility.

Father, give me grace to step down when I should. Amen.

NOVEMBER 30

A Little Neglect

*Consider what a great forest is set
on fire by a small spark. (James 3:5)*

It was a costly lesson. I hope I have learned it well.

I was surprised when my power lawn mower began using excessive amounts of oil. I was adding oil as often as gasoline. So after the mower's seasonal tour of duty, I carted it off to the repair shop for an overhaul.

I now have the sad news. Not only did the motor need new rings, but the piston itself was badly scored and had to be replaced. The problem? A simple air filter, which I had neglected to service as frequently as specified. Dust had penetrated the defenses of that filter, doing damage to the precision inner parts of the engine.

I am now back in business, ready for the first mowing of the new season. But it was a costly repair. And an unnecessary one—had I replaced the air filter on schedule.

And that is where my "lesson" comes in.

By nature, as I have admitted elsewhere, I tend to put things off—usually to my hurt. The dripping faucet not only wastes water but it discolors the sink. The squeaking hinge, deprived of oil, may ultimately need to be replaced. Caring for these little things in a timely way can save me both money and aggravation, not to mention domestic tranquility.

The lesson is transferable. It is applicable to my spiritual life as well. The cost of neglecting prayer and the Word of God can be staggering. *That* neglect I especially want to avoid.

Father, now that I have time, I am without excuse. Amen.

DECEMBER 1

God Has Spoken

All your words are true;
all your righteous laws are eternal.
(Psalm 119:160)

When Satan intruded on Eve in the Garden of Eden, he first questioned God's word: "Did God really say . . . ?" (Genesis 3:1). That first subtle questioning of God's established word quickly progressed to a denial of His truthfulness: "You will not surely die" (3:4), Satan said.

This progression takes place whenever people begin to question God's Word. They start subtly with something in the Scriptures that seems in conflict with current scientific or archaeological premises. Once the admission is made that some part of the Bible may be inaccurate or in error, it is an irresistible temptation to broaden the inquest to other parts of the Bible. Suddenly the questioner finds that he has set himself up as an arbiter of what is and what is not God's true Word.

The only viable alternative to this kind of existential chaos is the reasoned conclusion that a Book which claims to be totally inspired by God is as error free as the perfect God who inspired it. Either I can pick the Bible apart, lift out what I want and end up an impoverished semi-Christian, or I can accept it all and be governed by all it has to say.

Admittedly, there are some parts of the Bible that await more light. Other parts may be forever obscure. But I shall not allow either that which is obscure or that which is empirically unprovable to rob me of the total impact of God's total Book.

Father, I accept the truth of Your Book, the Bible. I set myself to meditate daily on what You have to say to me in it. Amen.

DECEMBER 2

Guarded by Peace

The peace of God, which transcends all understanding, will guard your hearts and your minds in Christ Jesus. (Philippians 4:7)

This is a day when I can make use of some of God's peace. I never expected to be so backed up with work once I was retired. This book is a major, continuing project. I also have two or three editing projects. And there are the reports that I evaluate for our denomination's Office of Alternative Education. At church several of us have been working to finish off two Sunday school classrooms. Like the fellow in the fairy tale, I chop through one tree root and two others take its place.

God's peace is the answer. And He promises it. But the promise actually begins with an *And*—attaching it to what Paul has just said. "Rejoice in the Lord always. . . . Let your gentleness be evident to all. . . . In everything, by prayer and petition, with thanksgiving, present your requests to God. *And* [my emphasis] the peace of God, which transcends all understanding, will guard your hearts and your minds in Christ Jesus."

As usual, my problem is of my own making. I have overlooked the by-the-numbers sequence. I am to (1) rejoice in God, (2) evidence gentleness to all and (3) present my requests with thanksgiving to God. Once those matters are obediently cared for, I am eligible for the peace transcending all understanding that God has promised me.

The work load may not diminish, but without the inner turmoil I will accomplish more in far less time. That, I would guess, is why God's peace transcends understanding!

Father, help me today to be eligible for Your peace. Amen.

DECEMBER 3

Numbered Days

*Teach us to number our days aright,
that we may gain a heart of wisdom.
(Psalm 90:12)*

Am I ready for another reminder from the Scriptures that life will not go on forever? Of course, I *know* that death ultimately is coming—just like the young athlete knows that he cannot play football forever. But death tends to be always somewhere off in the future. I am reluctant to acknowledge that it could be right around the corner.

Moses, the probable author of Psalm 90, had a longer, more vigorous life than I can anticipate. He was 15 years beyond the magic 65 number when he reluctantly agreed to lead Israel from Egypt to the Promised Land. As a result of the people's disobedience, what might have been a two- or three-year migration stretched into a 40-year ordeal.

But as his days, so was Moses' strength. If the 120-year-old veteran evidenced any halting as he made his solo climb from the plains of Moab to the top of Mount Nebo, the Scriptures do not mention it. There on the lofty peak of Pisgah, overlooking the Jordan's West Bank and the land of promise, Moses was "gathered to his fathers" and buried by God Himself.

It was this man, head and shoulders above the Old Testament's other great individuals, who prayed that God would teach him to number his days that he might gain a heart of wisdom.

Like it or not, my days *are* numbered. I need to keep that fact in mind lest I let them slip by unused, irretrievably lost both to me and to God.

Father, I dedicate all my days to You. Amen.

DECEMBER 4

Pray

"Ask and it will be given to you." (Luke 11:9)

Prayer is Jesus' present occupation. He is in heaven interceding for those who come to God through Him (Hebrews 7:25). Prayer should be my present occupation, too. It is one task from which I never need step down. As long as mind functions, I shall never grow too old to pray.

No task is more important. No occupation has the potential for greater influence on this world and its inhabitants. When I pray, I harness the limitless resources of heaven. My prayers can impact people, churches—even nations.

There is personal reward as well. Prayer draws me close to God, and He in turn draws close to me (James 4:8). I bask in the warmth of His presence. Like Peter, James and John, I become a member of God's inner circle.

My life and work over the years have been enhanced more than I will know down here by praying saints who took time to intercede for me. Many of them were elderly—retired from the pressures of earning a living. Many have been promoted to higher service, and I mark their passing with personal regret, knowing I am bereft of their intercession for me.

But God continues to replenish His ranks of intercessors—men and women who will be serious about prayer, who keep apprised of needs, who make a difference in this world by their occupation. The time has come for me not simply to be thankful for such intercessors. I now have the time and the high privilege of joining their ranks.

Father, keep me diligent in prayer. Amen.

DECEMBER 5

Judgment Coming

Man is destined to die once, and after that to face judgment. (Hebrews 9:27)

Standing between death and eternity is a judgment appointment. Everyone, saint and sinner, faces judgment.

It seems clear that God keeps a divine listing in what the Bible calls "the book of Life" or "the Lamb's book of life" (Psalm 69:28; Revelation 13:8; 21:27). Names once in the book may be "blotted out" (see Exodus 32:33).

The Bible speaks of other "books" at the "white throne" judgment (Revelation 20:12). The context leads me to suppose these are ledgers describing the good and bad deeds of the dead while they were alive on earth. "The dead were judged according to what they had done as recorded in the books."

One declaration is especially sobering: "If anyone's name was not found written in the book of life, he was thrown into the lake of fire" (Revelation 20:15). That "fiery lake of burning sulphur" is called "the second death" (Revelation 21:8).

And the believers? They too shall "stand before God's judgment seat" (Romans 14:10). The purpose? "That each one may receive what is due him for the things done while in the body, whether good or bad" (2 Corinthians 5:10). Rewards? Yes. But may there also be punishments?

The Scriptures, as I said earlier (see August 23), do not answer all my questions concerning this upcoming judgment for believers. But what they do say greatly sobers me. As a Christian, I should walk very carefully.

Father, judgment is coming. Let me face You unafraid. Amen.

DECEMBER 6

Paul - I

What has happened to me has really served to advance the gospel. (Philippians 1:12)

If I could have one wish for retirement, it would be to have the Apostle Paul's mind-set.

Paul, under Roman house arrest, might justifiably have felt that God had abandoned him. He might have thought that God had failed to answer prayer. He might have supposed that God was not concerned about the people of Rome and Spain whom he wanted to reach with the gospel of Jesus Christ.

But Paul was a mixture of dogged determination and pure optimism. His normal ministry might have been cut short by imprisonment, but Paul did not sit back and wait for a better opportunity. He aggressively served the Lord *right where he was*. Therein is a valuable lesson for me.

Paul conveyed greetings to the Philippians from the "saints . . . who belong to Caesar's household" (Philippians 4:22). It is unlikely that there were saints in Caesar's household before Paul's arrival in Rome. Paul's aggressive witness while a Roman prisoner accounted for those saints.

Moreover, Paul's untiring witness had emboldened the other Christians in Rome "to speak the word of God more courageously and fearlessly" (1:14).

"What has happened to me has really served to advance the gospel," Paul said to the Philippians. He added, "Because of this I rejoice" (1:18).

Father, what an indomitable man! No wonder he accomplished so much. Help me to follow his example. Amen.

DECEMBER 7

Paul - II

*Rejoice in the Lord always. I will say
it again: Rejoice! (Philippians 4:4)*

Indomitable! How else can I describe the Apostle Paul? Under house arrest in Rome, his chief concern was for the churches he had founded. Hindered from the missionary ministry that was his calling, he nevertheless advised his friends in Philippi to "rejoice in the Lord always."

I feel most like rejoicing when everything is functioning optimally. Adequate money for my expenses. Good food on the table. A sound roof over my head. No aches or pains. A car (at least one and preferably two) on good behavior. Appreciative friends. Nothing threatening to tip the boat.

How is it that Paul can see the silver lining in every rain cloud, the right-side-out pattern in every disheveled tapestry? Here is a person, possibly not much different in age from me when he wrote to the Philippians, who has a perspective that I cannot quite seem to gain. What was his secret?

Perhaps it was not a secret at all. He says earlier, "I will continue to rejoice" (1:18). Paul made up his mind not to be put down by circumstances. He determined in his mind that rejoicing would be his attitude.

Paul also said to the Philippians, "Join with others in following my example" (3:17). He was determined to be a good model of Christianity. He wanted others to be attracted to Jesus and to the gospel he was commissioned to proclaim. He knew that a dour, pessimistic attitude would attract no one.

Father, I too am a model. Make me a rejoicing Christian. Amen.

DECEMBER 8

Paul - III

I have fought the good fight, ...
I have kept the faith. (2 Timothy 4:7)

History's assessment of the Apostle Paul is so towering that I am tempted to think of his physical appearance in those dimensions. Actually, he was uncommonly short of stature, even for those times. Like some other short men, he made up in combativeness what he lacked in stature.

In his letters he mentions having "fought wild beasts in Ephesus" (1 Corinthians 15:32). He speaks of the "conflicts on the outside" (2 Corinthians 7:5) during his mission to Macedonia. He told the Corinthians that he fought to win: "I do not fight like a man beating the air" (1 Corinthians 9:26). He counseled young Timothy, "Fight the good fight of the faith" (1 Timothy 6:12). Yes, Paul was a fighter.

I, too, have fought the good fight and kept the faith. Perhaps not with the intensity with which Paul fought. But I have given God full measure, and if I were doing it all over again, there are not many things I would want to change.

So much for my past. What about now? Am I still fighting? Am I still giving God 100 percent? Do I still "contend for the faith . . . entrusted to the saints" (Jude 3)?

Paul never slacked off. Even in chains he was still working for the "crown of righteousness, which the Lord, the righteous Judge, [would] award to [him] on that day" (2 Timothy 4:8). It was a crown, Paul declared, that would go not only to him but "to all who have longed for [Jesus'] appearing."

Father, give me Paul's longing—and his constancy. Amen.

DECEMBER 9

Luke

Since I myself have carefully investigated everything from the beginning, it seemed good also to me to write an orderly account for you. (Luke 1:3)

Luke's age qualification to be among the Bible's senior achievers is admittedly circumstantial. He was a missionary colaborer with Paul right to the end (2 Timothy 4:11), and if that implies a similarity of age, then Luke was at least in his 60s when he undertook his "orderly account"—his Gospel—and older yet when he followed up with the Acts.

Luke probably was a Gentile. He was well-educated and well-versed in Greek culture. A physician by profession, he was eminently equipped to become the Spirit's communicator of the good news about Jesus Christ to the secular, non-Jewish mind.

Perhaps he began the project during those lonely days of Paul's second Roman imprisonment. Other associates of necessity had left to minister elsewhere. One had abandoned them. Only Luke and Paul were together, and Paul was in chains.

Be that as it may, Luke used his time and skills to create, under God's inspiration, a two-part record of the life and ministry of Jesus Christ for and in the church. Luke's endeavor has left the world in his debt.

"What is that in your hand?" God asked 80-year-old Moses (Exodus 4:2) when Moses worried about his ability to lead Israel out of Egypt. God used Moses' shepherd's rod and He used Luke's pen. What do I have that God can use?

Father, in these retirement years I put my education, my skills, my experience, my time at Your disposal. Amen.

DECEMBER 10

Peter

*Just as he who called you is holy,
so be holy in all you do. (1 Peter 1:15)*

For Peter, the rough-hewn fisherman whom Jesus called to discipleship, holiness was an exciting prospect. It also would be for him both a process and a crisis.

The crisis came at Pentecost, when, as he recalled many years later, his heart was "purified" (Acts 15:9). But the process had begun when he first met Jesus and had to admit, "I am a sinful man!" (Luke 5:8). It continued through Gethsemane (John 18:10–11), the courtyard of the high priest (Luke 22:54–62), the post-resurrection breakfast beside Galilee (John 21:15–22), the encounter with Paul in Antioch (Galatians 2:11–14).

Now an older man, Peter writes to "scattered" Christians, urging them to be holy. He offers 10 steps to a holy life:

1. Obey the truth (1 Peter 1:22).
2. "Crave pure spiritual milk" (2:2–3)—God's Word.
3. Be part of God's "spiritual house" (2:5)—the church.
4. "Abstain from sinful desires" (2:11).
5. "Submit . . . to every authority" (2:13).
6. "Die to sins and live for righteousness" (2:24).
7. Submit to your husband; be considerate of your wife (3:1, 7).
8. "Live in harmony with one another" (3:8).
9. "Set apart Christ as Lord" (3:15).
10. Let physical suffering be the death-blow to sin (4:1).

Who, reading First and Second Peter, can doubt that Peter achieved the holiness God called him to?

Father, You are holy. I also would be holy. Amen.

DECEMBER 11

John

Dear friends, let us love one another, for love comes from God. (1 John 4:7)

Am I the only one who finds it difficult to love *everyone* in God's household? There are certain Christians who seem to defy my best efforts to genuinely love them.

John earned the name "the apostle of love." He came from an affluent Galilean family who owned a fleet of fishing boats and employed servants to man them. It was not the kind of background guaranteed to produce progeny who would be bubbling over with love for everyone. Jesus chose John and his brother James to be His disciples. Together with Peter (a fellow fisherman), they became Jesus' "inner circle."

John refers to himself as the "disciple whom Jesus loved" (John 13:23; 19:26; 20:2; 21:7, 20). For anyone else, it might have sounded like braggadocio; for the guileless John it was a statement of fact. And one who was so much an object of his Lord's divine love in turn found it easy to love others—and to urge them to be evangels of love.

Love, John notes, is not self-generated. True love "comes from God." I may be naturally drawn to some people, either by their personalities or by common interests. But that sort of love falls short of what John is urging. The love John speaks of has its source in God's divine love that He has "poured out . . . into our hearts" (Romans 5:5). It is as a receptor of that divine love, and not through any self-generated effort on my part, that I am able to love the hard-to-love.

Father, let Your love flow freely through me to others. Amen.

DECEMBER 12

A Birthday

You crown the year with your bounty. (Psalm 65:11)

"Birthdays," remarked Raymond J. Jeffreys in *Life Begins at 100*, "steal away a little more of our youth each year, but they add much more of the things worth while."

Tomorrow is my birthday.

In my much younger years, I regarded a December birthday as a mixed blessing. By then, stores could be expected to have an unsurpassed pre-Christmas selection of toys (good). But with the holiday expenses just ahead, my would-be benefactors had to exercise restraint in their birthday spending (bad). Now that 29-cent gifts have inflated to as many dollars, a December birthday is still a drain on family members.

Birthdays are a good occasion for reflection. I think of the loving parents who made extraordinary preparations for my safe entry into life and sacrificially nurtured me through Depression years to adulthood. I think of my faithful wife, Marge, who has stood by me all these years, through the good times and the difficult. I think of my four children—a delight to me as they grew and a continued blessing in adulthood. I think of God's mercy through numerous crises and how He has directed my life, allowing me to serve Him in a number of capacities. Surely God has been bountiful—this year and all the others.

And now that it is evident I will not die young, I can thank God as well for long life, above-average health and the blessing of useful activity even in retirement.

Father, as I enter an uncharted new year of life, my commitment to You is unchanged. Amen.

DECEMBER 13

New Wood Every Year

*He is like a tree planted by streams of water,
which yields its fruit in season
and whose leaf does not wither. (Psalm 1:3)*

Today, as I announced yesterday, is my birthday. There was a time when I would have considered someone this old *old*!

I thank God for the years He has meted out to me. I praise Him for permitting me another anniversary. Not that I am unready or unwilling for the fantastic alternative, but I like to think that my family still needs me. Perhaps God wishes me to complete this book of devotional meditations.

How special it will be to have Rebecca and Sarah here for dinner! Rebecca guesses it must be 20 years since she has celebrated my birthday with me; it will be Sarah's first time. (Tooth extractions have forced John to cancel.)

I thank God that I can still "yield . . . fruit in season." I like what Longfellow once said:

> To those who ask how I can write so many things that sound as if I were as happy as a boy, please say that there is in the neighboring town a pear tree, planted by Governor Endicott 200 years ago, and it still bears fruit not to be distinguished from that of a young tree in flavor. I suppose the tree makes new wood every year, so that some parts of it are always young.

Perhaps this is the way with some men when they grow old. I hope it is so with me.

Father, please make it so with me, as well. Amen.

DECEMBER 14

Many-Sided

"Any of you who does not give up everything he has cannot be my disciple." (Luke 14:33)

I am reminded of the question a woman once asked me in the days before Communism became so universally discredit. "Is it fair," she asked, "to compare the dedication of a Christian with that of the Communist?"

Her point was reasonable. The Communist has one loyalty: the party. I as a Christian am called to a number of loyalties: to God, to family, to community, to church, to job. But how can those loyalties be reconciled with the dedication Jesus spoke of when He talked about my giving up everything in order to be His disciple? More specifically, what in practical terms does discipleship mean now that I am retired?

Quantitatively, my dedication has to be total. God must have all of me. There can be no equivocation there. *Qualitatively*, my dedication has to be spread much more thinly than does the loyalty of the Communist zealot.

I have known Christians whose service to the church was unparalleled in intensity. But their children languished for a parent's love. There are others whose zeal for foreign missions was tireless. But the needs of people a few blocks away did not seem to concern them.

As with the past, so with what is left of my life: My first call is to love God with heart, soul, strength and mind. Second, I am to love my neighbor as myself (Luke 10:27).

Loving God is the key. It is easy to serve a God whom you love. And to love the people He loves.

Father, in these retirement years give me a good sense of balance as I seek to love both You and neighbor. Amen.

DECEMBER 15

Reward in Kind

One man gives freely, yet gains even more; another withholds unduly, but comes to poverty. (Proverbs 11:24)

If I seem to be always returning to the theme of giving, it may be because the Bible emphasizes it so much. And many of the references have the same message: God not only rewards the generous giver, but *He rewards the generous giver in kind*.

With this first year of retirement drawing to a close, I am looking closely at the year's financial picture. It was not easy to establish a budget for this calendar year. With a probable move mid-year, housing expenses had to be "guesstimated." I was not even sure what earnings I might have in addition to Social Security and pension.

I should not be amazed at the outcome, but I am. In spite of some substantial gifts to God's people and God's work in addition to my church tithe, Marge and I are going to end the year with a small surplus. Our retirement reserves, still untapped, can continue to appreciate against older age.

I am thankful for physical health and mental ability to continue working part-time. Without that income, the situation would be different. That work has in fact done triple service: in addition to benefiting my employer, it has both supplied some of our financial needs and contributed to my self-worth.

As long as God gives me mind and strength, I want to be doing. Most of all, I want to be doing in work that benefits the kingdom of my Lord and Savior, Jesus Christ.

Father, You have more than supplied our needs! Amen.

DECEMBER 16

Run for the Prize

Run in such a way as to get the prize. . . . I do not run . . . aimlessly. . . . I . . . make [my body] my slave so that . . . I . . . will not be disqualified. (1 Corinthians 9:24–27)

Paul was writing to Christians of Greek descent in the Grecian city of Corinth. Not surprisingly, he turned to the idiom of Greek foot races to depict the Christian life.

As the celebrated runners competed for the laurel, their every thought was on the prize awaiting the winner. Every motion was concentrated on the goal. Their bodies, already well practiced, were slaves to the wills of the runners.

Paul says that should be my attitude as I strive for the prize awaiting me at the end of my earthly course. "Everyone who competes in the games goes into strict training" (1 Corinthians 9:25). I should prepare myself by diligent Bible study, by prayer, by reading, by seeking the counsel of seasoned believers.

"I do not run aimlessly." My every effort must be with the goal in mind. "I do not fight like a man beating the air" (9:26). Every motion must count.

"I . . . make [my body] my slave." What a contrast to the average person—even the average Christian—who is a slave to his or her body!

This sounds very unlike contemporary Christianity. It should not. Paul has set forth a biblical standard to be followed. A person can only surmise—sadly—that many flabby, undisciplined Christians in the contemporary church are in for a shock when they stand before Christ's judgment seat.

Father, You are my goal. I shall press on for the prize. Amen.

DECEMBER 17

Stand Firm

Stand firm. Let nothing move you. (1 Corinthians 15:58)

When Paul advised the Corinthians to stand firm, it was not a whistling-in-the-dark psychological ploy. His counsel was based on a Christian verity that he had just taken great pains to prove: *Jesus has risen from the dead; He is alive.* That fact makes all the difference.

What is the worst-case scenario I may face these next years?

The death of Marge, my wife? "Away from the body . . . at home with the Lord" (2 Corinthians 5:8). Though temporarily separated, we shall see each other again!

Cancer or some other devastating personal illness? Disease has power only over my physical body. "After my skin has been destroyed,/ yet in my flesh I will see God" (Job 19:26).

Loneliness? The resurrected Lord Jesus Christ lives within me, and I have His promise: "Never will I leave you;/ never will I forsake you" (Hebrews 13:5).

Financial reverses and loss? The One who lives within me says, "Do not worry, saying, 'What shall we eat?' or 'What shall we drink?' or 'What shall we wear?' . . . Your heavenly Father knows that you need [these things]. But seek first his kingdom and his righteousness, and all these things will be given to you as well" (Matthew 6:31–33).

War? Civil disturbance? A threat to my own life? God says, "When you pass through the waters,/ I will be with you. . . . When you walk through the fire,/ . . . the flames will not set you ablaze" (Isaiah 43:2).

If Jesus is with me, I will fear no evil.

Father, in light of Your promises, I will take heart. Amen.

DECEMBER 18

The Time Is Short

The time is short. (1 Corinthians 7:29)

Probably the Apostle Paul was alluding to the return of Jesus Christ when he made the statement. To the cynic who observes that 19 long centuries have gone by since then, I reply, "Think how much shorter the time is *now*!"

As a retired person, I have a second reason for believing the time is short. I am drawing ever closer to my final summons. What I do for God must be done now or never. Exactly how should this shortness of time affect me?

First, since I have a wife, I should live as if I did not (1 Corinthians 7:29). Does this mean to abandon her, pay her no attention? No. It means that the two of us, in partnership with God, should be striving together to do God's work.

Second, if I mourn—and there will be times when I do—I should not appear to be in mourning (7:30). Why? Because God's work goes on, and the time is short.

Third, if I am happy, my celebration should not infringe unduly on my work for the Lord (7:30).

Fourth, if I make a purchase—whether something substantial, such as a car, or something minor, such as a pair of socks, I am to look upon such an acquisition as temporary and tenuous (7:30), acquired so I can better pursue my work for the Lord.

Finally, if I have occasion to use "the things of the world"—anything material from ballpoint pens to houses—I am not to be too enamored with them (7:31). They and the world supporting them are destined to pass away.

Father, let all my activity be with eternity in view. Amen.

DECEMBER 19

Families for the Lonely

God sets the lonely in families. (Psalm 68:6)

Probably few people, earlier in life, intended to spend their mature years living alone. For some, circumstances may have pointed them in the direction of solitary living and they found it tolerable, if not indeed satisfying. In retirement, they see no good reason to change.

Others have been forced into a solitary life by bereavement or divorce. Some of them may have had—and may have—other options, such as living with children, but they prefer to live alone. Some long for fellowship but cannot seem to find it.

Unfortunately, some elderly single adults have chosen to turn inward. They lack the initiative to mix easily with others and to take their place in the Lord's work. Deep down inside they may be miserable. They need help.

The church is especially fitted to offer what Harriet Labarre, a widow and author of a book on living alone, has called "the one vital ingredient missing in the lives of those who live alone": emotional relationships on an adult level. "They want to have someone to share things with," she says.

These individuals may have special qualifications that equip them to serve the church. A retired office worker, for instance, may be able to assist in the church office. A retired florist may maintain the church's plantings. The very elderly (as well as younger adults) pray.

"God sets the lonely in families." For no one should the words be more prophetic than for the retired Christian single.

Father, lead me to a single who needs my friendship. Amen.

DECEMBER 20

"Do Not Slouch!"

Put on the full armor of God, so that when the day of evil comes, you may be able to stand your ground, and after you have done everything, to stand. (Ephesians 6:13)

In his premed days at Cornell, noted physician and teaching surgeon Carleton Campbell was a member of the university's rowing team.

Competition between the eight-man shells was intense, each school's team hoping to best the other in races that stretched as long as four miles up beautiful Cayuga Lake. The oarsmen crowded all the effort they could muster into every stroke.

Dr. Campell recalled the shout of the coxswain as they neared the finish line: "Add ten more with all you've got!" and—after the ten strokes—"Now, another ten!"

But even when the last measure of strength was drained out of the boatmen as they skimmed across the finish line, they were not permitted to slump in exhaustion.

"Our coach, Charles E. Courtney, never allowed us to slouch at the end of a race," the doctor remembered. "If you looked at the Cornell team at the finish of their races, you would see each man sitting erect in the shell."

It was an important bit of philosophy Coach Courtney hammered home, and the doctor, for one, never forgot it. Dr. Campbell was his own best illustration. Into his 80s, long after he had retired from active medicine, he busied himself with civic and national interests. He read widely and remained at heart a teacher, anxious to build into the lives of younger people his own Christian principles.

"Do not slouch!"

Father, give me the fortitude to finish on my feet. Amen.

DECEMBER 21

Christmas Is Family

*... the Father, from whom his whole family
in heaven and on earth derives its name. (Ephesians 3:15)*

I am very grateful to God for my biological family: Marge, my wife these past 42 years; and our children, Rebecca, Deborah, Daniel and Esther. Marge and I thank God for bringing each of our children into His heavenly family through Jesus Christ. We have no greater blessing than that.

We are thankful, too, for our spiritual family here in Garner, North Carolina. A year ago, we barely knew any of them; today they are as dear to us as the spiritual family we left in New Cumberland, Pennsylvania, or in Nyack, New York, or in the Philippines, or in our home towns. And—this is the wonderful part—these in Garner are not exchanges but additions. The others are still within our spiritual family. We have not lost them; we have simply gained others.

Marge and I are grateful to God for the high privilege this year of having all of our biological family together once again—around our table—for Christmas. There have been many Christmases past when it was not possible. Two weeks ago, it did not seem possible this year. But God intervened in ways that still leave us incredulous. In this first year of our retirement, in a locale where on occasion we still feel a bit "foreign," God has heaped blessing upon blessing. We praise His name.

We are undeserving of these gifts, but out of God's great love and grace He has given them to us.

Father, I thank You for Jesus, Your matchless Gift, and the blessings made possible through Him. Amen.

DECEMBER 22

Bethlehem's Price

*"But you, Bethlehem Ephrathah, ...
out of you will come for me
one who will be ruler over Israel."*
    (Micah 5:2)

Bethlehem.

The picture is the warp and woof of Christmas. Bethlehem bathed in starlight bright as moonbeams. The stable, embellished a thousand times over from the smelly, nondescript original. A serene Mary gazing at her newborn Baby in the manger. Joseph standing stalwartly by her side. Shepherds. cattle.

I do not completely comprehend the miracle, but I know that in that straw-filled manger lay the Son of God, a dependent, peaceful, glowing bit of Humanity—*Humanity* spelled with a capital "H" because He was also Deity, God enfleshed.

Therein lies the awesome cost of Bethlehem.

Enfleshment for Jesus Christ was not simply a 33-year ordeal—a relatively brief hiatus during which He temporarily set aside the insignia of His Deity in order to live among His creation and ultimately die for them, after which He would rise again from the dead and eventually revert to His Spirit-status.

Enfleshment was a *permanent* encumbrance. Forever He will bear the impediment of humanity.

Jesus' body is a glorified body, to be sure. But it is a body. Never again will He be pure spirit. And He agreed to that permanent restriction so that I might be redeemed.

Only in the light of that revelation can I begin to understand the price of Bethlehem.

Father, I bow humbly before You in worship and praise. Amen.

DECEMBER 23

Alone

*[Mary] wrapped [Jesus] in cloths
and placed him in a manger. (Luke 2:7)*

As a finite earthling, I have not the imagination to describe the feelings of the Father God as His Son, Jesus Christ, entered the human stream to be born in Bethlehem.

For God the Son it must have been frustrating. He who had known nothing but the instant mobility of Deity was suddenly restricted by three-dimensional human existence—and as a helpless babe besides. He must have found it lonely, too. He who was accustomed to the royal excitement of the heavenly Throne Room, with its legions of worshiping angels ready to respond at God's slightest command, was suddenly isolated amid the very people He had created.

Nothing in the annals of human experience—not missionaries in strange lands or prisoners in solitary confinement or space-walking astronauts—is analogous to that which Jesus must have felt as He became man.

The paradoxes of that entry and sojourn in this world are many. Jesus became poor that I might through His poverty be enriched. He bore my sins that I might be forgiven my sins. He carried my sicknesses that I might through His life be healed. He died that I might live—live abundantly.

And in the loneliness of His existence on earth, He effected reconciliation and fellowship. Jew, Gentile—they have been made one in Christ Jesus.

That is what His Advent means.

Father, thank You for sending Jesus. Amen.

DECEMBER 24

He Gave Community

You are ... fellow citizens with God's people and members of God's household. (Ephesians 2:19)

Although I entered the Christian faith by means of an individual decision, Christianity is not a religion of isolation. It is a religion of community. Salvation opens the door to an unfolding company of people called the church.

As a Christian I can go anywhere, crossing boundaries of culture and language. Yet whenever I encounter another Christian there is instant fellowship. Becoming a child of God through the new birth creates a mutual kinship that the uninitiated know nothing about. The widening camaraderie I have experienced over the years is one of Christianity's happiest aspects.

This sense of community, however, is more than just a by-product. It is part of Christianity's essence. "None of us lives to himself alone" (Romans 14:7). Christianity was never intended to be practiced in isolation. Most of the New Testament is directed specifically to communities of believers—churches—and must be understood in such a context.

This community is expandable. Christianity is contagious. It is intended to be shared. Only as I spread the good news am I fulfilling my communal responsibility. "Go and make disciples," Jesus said (Matthew 28:19).

The Prince-Leader was rejected by His people, forsaken by His followers. Even God the Father turned away when Jesus hung, a sin offering, on the cross. Yet out of the loneliness of His Passion Jesus has effected community.

Father, at this Christmas season I worship You. Amen.

DECEMBER 25

Present

The Word became flesh and made his dwelling among us. (John 1:14)

On this Christmas Day I stand in awe at what God did.

I can barely begin to understand all it meant for God's Son to take on Himself the restrictions of human flesh, to endure the impotency of babyhood and the loneliness of planet Earth. John says it so simply: "The Word became flesh and made his dwelling among us." Paul details it more fully, declaring that Jesus,

> . . . being in very nature God,
>> did not consider equality with God something to be grasped,
>
> but made himself nothing,
>> taking the very nature of a servant,
>> being made in human likeness.
>
> And being found in appearance as a man,
>> he humbled himself
>> and became obedient to death—
>>> even death on a cross! (Philippians 2:6–8)

One painting of Jesus as a boy has Him working in His father's carpenter's shop. As a bright Nazareth sun streams through the open doorway, it picks up objects in the room that cast the shadow of a cross where Jesus is standing. At no time in His earthly sojourn was Jesus far from Calvary's shadow.

Jesus came willingly and died willingly. What amazing love He demonstrated for His wayward, undeserving creation! How thankful I am for such a great salvation.

Father, Your love overwhelms me. Amen.

DECEMBER 26

Missionary

God was reconciling the world to himself in Christ. . . . And he has committed to us the message of reconciliation. (2 Corinthians 5:19)

It was an amazing, glorious act whereby Jesus Christ enfleshed Himself with humanity in order to redeem His creation. Amid my wonder and my gratitude, I need to remember that my own existence on earth also has redemptive aspects—or at least it should have. To paraphrase missiologist Allen Tippett, God created us and put us in a context. I do not exist in isolation, segregated from my fellow beings, concerned only for my own needs and welfare. I live in the context of other people.

Jesus said to His first disciples, "As the Father has sent me, I am sending you" (John 20:21). I who follow in that tradition must understand that God has placed me in my context also for a redemptive purpose.

Even in "Christian" America, I may be my neighbors' only means of hearing the gospel. The insurance broker, my auto mechanic, the clerks at the hardware, my barber—to each of them also I am "one sent"—a missionary.

Christmas is once a year. Missionary responsibility is every day of the year. Was that not Jesus' commission to all His followers? "Go and make disciples of all nations, baptizing them in the name of the Father and of the Son and of the Holy Spirit, and teaching them to obey everything I have commanded you" (Matthew 28:19–20).

Father God, may I not let the wonder of the Incarnation blind me to the responsibility You place on me to proclaim it. Amen.

DECEMBER 27

Under Construction

You . . . are being built into a spiritual house. (1 Peter 2:5)

PBPGIFWMY—Please Be Patient, God Isn't Finished With Me Yet—is more than a clever little slogan proposed by Bill Gothard in his Basic Youth Conflicts seminars. It is the Christian truth.

Peter likens the construction of the saints to a building being erected: "As you come to him, the living Stone—rejected by men but chosen by God and precious to him—you also, like living stones, are being built into a spiritual house."

Saints do not automatically become a living building any more than cement and window glass automatically become a physical building. Physical buildings require planning, design and effort. So does the building of the saints.

It is a ministry that each Christian is to be absorbed in. If I am "caught in a sin," those who "are spiritual should restore [me] gently" (Galatians 6:1). Christians are to "be kind and compassionate to one another, forgiving each other, just as in Christ God forgave [them]" (Ephesians 4:32).

Customarily, God uses the church—the local body of believers instructed by pastors and teachers—for this building ministry (Ephesians 4:11-13). He uses ordinary Christians to "carry each others' burdens, and in this way . . . fulfill the law of Christ" (Galatians 6:2).

"Built on the foundation of the apostles and prophets, with Christ Jesus himself as the chief cornerstone," believers in Him "are being built together to become a dwelling in which God lives by his Spirit" (Ephesians 2:20-22).

Father, thank You for giving me a place in Your temple. Amen.

DECEMBER 28

Why Little Progress?

Grow in the grace and knowledge of our Lord and Savior Jesus Christ. (2 Peter 3:18)

Knowledge continues to increase geometrically—just as Daniel the prophet intimated (see Daniel 12:4). Someone has calculated that total knowledge doubled in a century and a half from 1750 to 1900. It doubled again between 1900 and 1950. And again between 1950 and 1960. Now it doubles every five years or less!

The communications technician, for instance, leapfrogs over the painful days of clicking telegraph keys and uncertain party lines to begin with fiber optics, digital transmissions and powerful computer circuitry. He builds on past progress.

But when we look at the average Christian—even the average "committed" Christian—we see correspondingly little spiritual progress. The church of Jesus Christ is still in the era of Morse Code and crank-to-ring telephones.

Can it be the nature of Christianity? It is both experiential and experimental. New converts cannot build their Christian lives on the spiritual achievements of other believers. They have to start from zero. True, they will find instruction and guidance in the experiences of others, but their own advancement depends on the time and effort they are willing to expend in working out their own salvation.

As another year end approaches, I must inquire whether I am seeing in my life the personal spiritual progress that I should. If not, there is no time like now to formulate an appropriate resolve for the new year. Better yet, for today!

Father, I hereby commit myself to spiritual growth. Amen.

DECEMBER 29

Reassessment

Examine yourselves. (2 Corinthians 13:5)

In almost all human endeavor, from such mundane activity as walking in a straight line to such complex activity as flying an airplane, it is necessary to assess performance against objectives and make corrections accordingly. Why is it, then, that in the spiritual realm so many Christians go year after year without attempting to evaluate past performance?

There is no better time than year's end to take a backward look to see how the last 12 months stacked up. Especially is it important at the end of Year One of Retirement!

- Exactly what did I accomplish during the past year?
- Was it worth five to 10 percent of my retired years?
- In what ways could I have increased or improved my service for my Heavenly Father?
- Did I make any serious mistakes that should be guarded against in the future?
- In what way or ways can I intensify my own personal devotion to Jesus Christ?
- How and where can I best make my contribution to God's kingdom during the ensuing year?
- What shall be my goals or objectives for the new year?

These are soul-searching questions. But if in the next year I am to be the person God wants me to be, I shall have to discover the answers to them.

Father, thank You for walking with me this past year. Let me live the New Year on an even higher plane—for Your glory. Amen.

DECEMBER 30

No Retrogression

*Let us live up to what we have
already attained. (Philippians 3:16)*

"You were running a good race," Paul told the Galatian believers (Galatians 5:7). "Who cut in on you and kept you from obeying the truth?" A basketball team can rack up a comfortable lead but lose the game in the final quarter. A businessman, doing well, allows himself to coast, only to face sudden new competition that drives him into bankruptcy.

It can happen in the Christian life, too. Not all who begin well follow through to the end. Not all the 45-year-old saints are still saintly at 70.

Christianity is not a lifetime glide once Jesus lifts me from sin's mire. Paul speaks of the righteousness in the gospel being "by faith from first to last" (Romans 1:17). The Lord declares through Habakkuk that "the righteous will live by his faith" (Habakkuk 2:4), and the writer to the Hebrews expands on the expression to say that the one who "shrinks back" from a by-faith lifestyle earns God's displeasure (Hebrews 10:38).

How can I best assure myself of this continuity of faith so essential to my heavenly goal?

I must diligently maintain my relation to Jesus Christ, the Head of the body.

I must remain immersed in the Word, letting it live in me in all wisdom.

I must watch and pray, lest I enter into temptation.

I must do good to all men.

Father, I am a year closer to heaven. Help me not to slack off now. Amen.

DECEMBER 31

On to Year Two!

My cup overflows.
Surely goodness and love will follow me
all the days of my life.
(Psalm 23:5–6)

I am very thankful. God has brought me safely through this first year of retirement. The money has not run out. The transplant from Pennsylvania to North Carolina was successful—with no signs as yet of rejection. Marge and I are in a caring church where we feel accepted. Our children still love us.

My cup truly overflows.

Ahead of me lies the anticipation of continued productive work. Book editing. Other writing projects. Voluntary work at the church.

In the coming year I want to know God better. I want also to enter more fully into the lives of people God has put along my path: neighbors Marge and I can introduce to Jesus, church members who need the concern and love we can show them, other contacts whose wounds from life's blows are masked by a courteous smile or a perfunctory "Have a good day!"

"Unknown" is stamped in bold letters across the title page of the New Year. But Marge and I enter it with confidence because God will continue to be our Shepherd.

> Surely goodness and love will follow me
>   all the days of my life,
> and I will dwell in the house of the Lord
>   forever.

Father, thank You for every step of the way thus far. You know the future, and I know You. That is enough. Amen.

BIBLIOGRAPHY

Boyer, Richard, and Savageau, David, *Retirement Places Rated*. (Chicago: Rand McNally, 1987).
An extremely interesting compendium for the five percent who are looking to retire elsewhere than in their home territory. The authors rate 131 places or areas by cost of living, climate, personal safety, services, housing, leisure living. Secular and admittedly not foolproof, the book is nevertheless thorough enough to be helpful. Recommended.

Drakeford, John W., *Growing Old—Feeling Young*. (Nashville: Broadman, 1985).
The thesis: A person can stave off the growing old process by mental, physical, social and spiritual effort. En route to his objective, the author offers an abundance of practical advice.

Dychtwald, Ken and Flower, Joe, *Age Wave*. (New York: St. Martin's Press, 1989).
Subtitled "The challenges and opportunities of an aging America," the book takes a generally positive look at what may be in store for Americans in the next 30–50 years, be they currently "boomers," middle-aged or over 65. The Age Wave is coming, the authors insist, and "no American alive today, nor for generations to come, will be left untouched by [it]."

Ellison, James W., *et al, Retiring on Your Own Terms*. (New York: Crown Publishers, Inc., 1989).
The front half of the book is taken up with financial preparation for retirement and therefore comes too late for the person already retired. The latter half is filled with statistics and counsel that should encourage and motivate any retiree.

Friedman, Roslyn and Nussbaum, Annette, *Coping with Your Husband's Retirement*. (New York: Simon and Schuster, Inc., 1986).
Secular, but excellent in its insights, the book is based on interviews with 75 retired women. At the end, to stimulate mutual discussion, the authors ask several pages of detailed "His/Her" questions covering the subjects of the chapters.

Fromme, Allan, *60+: Planning It, Living It, Loving It*. (New York: Farrar, Straus & Giroux, 1984).
The viewpoint is strictly secular, but upbeat and practical. "A happy life after sixty is more a product of *attitude* than of opportunity and luck. . . . How is the right attitude developed? . . . By getting out and *doing* things, by forcing yourself." The author, a psychologist and himself sixty plus, has good, practical insights. His text, rich in metaphor, is a delight to read.

Hess, Bartlett and Margaret, *Never Say Old*. (Wheaton, IL: Victor Books, 1984).
A popularly written, mild polemic against retirement (the authors, with a combined age of 142 years at the time, were both active in public ministries. Autobiographical in style, the book, largely written by Margaret, explores such topics as attitudes, goals, friends, children, money, death. Especially helpful are chapters on nutrition and coping with stress through rest and exercise. Recommended.

Hutchinson, James H., *Ten Steps to Successful Retirement*. (Nashville: Desktop Communications, 1989).
A practical treatise covering such subjects as goal setting, the value of a sense of humor, adult education, travel, hobbies, fitness and nutrition, volunteerism, locale and positive thinking. Helpful.

Janis, Martin A., *The Joys of Aging*. (Dallas: Word Publishing, 1988).

Martin Janis, from Toledo, Ohio, served for eight years as Director of the Ohio Commission on Aging, the state's first official program in behalf of its older citizens. As the title implies, his outlook is positive. Mildly Christian.

Jeffreys, Raymond J., *Life Will Begin at 100*. (Columbus, OH: Capitol College Press, 1955).
A by-now very dated, very rose-colored and—in retrospect—very naive look at old age. Based on a column the author wrote for the St. Petersburg (FL) *Independent*. Despite the book's drawbacks, Jeffreys has succeeded in cramming a wealth of good adages into 226 pages of text.

Kaplan, Lawrence J., *Retiring Right*. (Wayne, NJ: Avery Publishing Group, Inc., 1987).
Helpful forms for tracking everything from investments to funeral arrangements. Much of the book, however, is slanted more to 40-year-olds planning for retirement than to the already retired. And some of the information is already outdated. The perspective is secular.

Mustric, Peter, *The Joy of Growing Older*. (Wheaton, IL: Tyndale House Publishers, 1979).
An easy-to-read advice book to and about seniors by the Minister to Senior Citizens at Scott Memorial Baptist Church, San Diego, CA. Mustric covers such topics as Christian service, finances, children, housing, health, hobbies and vacations. A mixture of Scripture and anecdote observed by this pastor to 600 seniors.

Smith, Tilman R., *In Favor of Growing Older*. (Scottdale, PA: Herald Press, 1981).
Subtitled "Guidelines and Practical Suggestions for Planning Your Retirement Career," this Christian approach, while helpful, tends to be very sectarian. Nearly all the author's illustrations are from a Mennonite context, and the Mennonite ethic is prominent throughout. But the author has collected (and included) a wide selection of

commentary on aging and the aged which spices the book and adds immeasurably to its value.

Stafford, Tim, *As Our Years Increase*. (Grand Rapids: Zondervan, 1989).
Overlook the author's incongruous days-of-the-week-analogy ("Monday," a vigorous 65; by "Friday," in need of assistance; "Sunday," at rest in the grave) and his scattershot approach—sometimes addressing the aging individual, sometimes the care-givers—and this volume by the editor of Campus Life Books is full of helpful insights on coping with the aging process.

Stokell, Marjorie and Kennedy, Bonnie, *The Senior Citizen Handbook*. (Englewood Cliffs, NJ: Prentice-Hall, Inc., 1985).
An exhaustive compendium of data, alphabetically arranged, from *A*bsent-mindedness through *H*ome health care and *T*axes to *Z*eal, *Z*est, *Z*ing and *Z*ip. Very practical, even if somewhat dated.

Willing, Jules Z., *The Reality of Retirement*. (New York: Wm. Morrow and Co., Inc., 1981).
Subtitled "The Inner Experience of Becoming a Retired Person," this book focuses on the psychology of retirement—how a person reacts to the experience. Slanted to the business executive, for whom money is not normally a problem, the book nevertheless is a valuable—almost unique—contribution to retirement literature. Definitely recommended.

INDEX OF MEDITATION TITLES

Aaron 4/19
Abandoned 6/17
Abiathar 8/14
Abraham 2/24
Adam 1/16
Add-On Years 5/22
Adventure 6/8
Agent of Change 2/7
Ahithophel 8/13
All My Needs 9/23
All My Sins 9/20
"All Your Anxiety" 11/27
Alone 12/23
Amram and Jochebed 4/17
Anna 11/7
Annas 11/9
Another Transition 10/10
Antiques 9/08
Anything, Everything 6/19
Assets 9/4
Awaiting a Savior 6/15
Back to Work? 4/14
Bad Ending, A 6/29
Balance I Need 6/11
Barzillai 8/15
Bathsheba 8/16
Be Still 4/28
Bear With, Forgive 4/29
Being Content 5/30
Being Realistic 9/29
Bethlehem's Price 12/22
Beyond Sacrifice 6/4
Bible Literate 5/25
Birthday, A 12/12
Broken Cycle 4/9
Broken-down Walls 7/15
Brother Passes On, A 4/23
By Prayer 6/20
Caleb 5/16
Children 6/03
"Childrenized" 3/13
Christmas Is Family 12/21
Clearing the Air 4/7
Close Inspection 1/26
Closed Mind, A 8/28
Commit, Continue 7/22
Communicating 7/17
Confidence 3/12
Conformed to Jesus 11/12
Contentment 10/14
Continuing Education 1/13
Courage 7/23
Credit Cards 2/12

Cremation? 5/12
Cross!, The 3/24
Crowd, The 11/2
Crowned! 2/2
Cutting Back 8/30
Cyrus the Great 10/6
"D. V." 7/7
Daniel - I 10/4
Daniel - II 10/5
Daniel Dreamed 9/10
Darius the Mede 10/7
David 7/9
Death Has Purpose 11/14
Deceived 11/16
Dependent Giving 5/5
Depression 10/18
Destiny: Death 2/17
Devotional Life, The 5/21
Dillens, The 8/11
"Disputable Matters" 11/04
Divine Arithmetic 1/1
"Do Not Slouch!" 12/20
Doing Good 10/1
Done with Sin 7/21
Down Payment 8/22
Eleazer 5/15
Eli - I 6/22
Eli - II 6/23
Eliphaz & Co. 2/4
Elisha 9/15
Encounter with Death 5/10
Enoch 1/18
Esau 3/18
Eve 1/17
Even to Old Age 8/4
Exclusive Friends 8/9
Exclusive Privilege 1/2
Faith All the Way 2/15
Faith Is Obedience 2/29
Faith First to Last 11/3
False Economies 10/15
Families for Lonely 12/19
Fasting 6/25
Finding a Friend 8/7
Four Rules 1/10
Fruitful to the End 9/30
Gad 7/11
Gamaliel 11/10
Gambling 9/2
Generosity/Fairness 4/10
Gideon 5/19
Giving, Receiving 8/19
God Bears My Burdens 4/24

Title	Date
God Still Leads	5/7
God Has Spoken	12/1
God Will Supply	8/31
God Cares	8/5
God's Strength	1/14
God's Will and Mine	10/27
God's Temple	4/6
Good Name, A	6/18
Good Times and Bad	11/25
Gospel, The	7/18
"Gotcha!"	7/31
Gray Matter, Power	3/8
Guarded by Peace	12/2
Haggai	10/21
Halfway Christians	10/9
Harvest Coming	7/30
Have a Minute?	2/8
He Endured	3/27
He Gave Community	12/24
Heaven	11/19
Heavenly Citizenship	11/20
Hiram	8/18
Holding on Too Long	5/31
Hollow, Hollow	4/2
Hosea	9/16
How Fleeting Life	3/26
How Describe It?	2/18
How Long?	9/27
Husbands, Wives - I	1/7
Husbands, Wives - II	1/8
"I Pray for You"	9/21
If I Should Die	5/11
"If It Is to Be"	2/6
Imitating God	6/26
Important Census	4/1
In Favor of Old Age	9/26
In the Name of Jesus	10/16
In Writing	4/3
Is This My God?	3/2
Isaac	2/28
Isaiah	9/17
Ishmael	2/27
It Is in Your Head!	9/11
Jacob	3/19
Jehoiada	9/14
Jehu	9/13
"Jesus Loves Me"	1/4
Jethro	4/22
Joab	7/10
Job	2/3
John	12/11
Joseph	3/22
Joshua	5/17
Joyous Long Life	2/20
Judah	3/21
Judgment Day	8/23
Judgment Coming	12/5
"Keep Looking Down!"	5/29
Laban	3/20
Lasting Mark	7/14
Leadership	4/15
Let Down	7/13
Life after Life	11/17
Little Neglect, A	11/30
Living Carefully	2/5
Living Wisely	2/19
Living Bodies	3/3
Living for Jesus	9/5
Lord of Every Area	3/4
Lot	2/26
Love, Faithfulness	11/28
"Love Your Wives"	1/9
Luke	12/9
Making Friends	8/6
Making Ends Meet	10/30
Manasseh	9/19
Manoah	5/20
Many-Sided	12/14
Marge	8/1
Mercy Triumphs	5/1
Micah	9/18
Mind over Heart	3/17
Mind for Others, A	7/28
Miriam	4/18
Misplaced Affection	9/3
Missionary	12/26
Modifying	6/13
Momentary Trouble	4/13
Money Enough	8/29
Mordecai	10/23
Moses - I	4/20
Moses - II	4/21
Mother	5/14
Moving Ship, The	1/27
Musical Praise	1/30
My Ever-Present Help	2/9
My Choice	8/3
My Partner	6/9
My Will and God's	10/28
Naomi	6/21
Nebuchadnezzar	10/3
Necessities, The	2/11
Needed Then?	10/25
Negative Thanks	11/24
Nehemiah	10/22
Never Lack Zeal	1/6
New Attire	5/23
New Wood Every Year	12/13
New House	8/21
Next Transition, The	10/11

Title	Date
Nicodemus	11/8
Night Ministers	10/19
Night School	6/30
No Retrogression	12/30
No Empty Days	1/5
No Place like Home	1/22
No Favoritism	1/31
Noah	1/19
Not the White House	10/2
Not Over Yet	4/4
Numbered Days	12/3
Of Some Value	3/1
Old Age? Me?	9/28
"Older Men"	3/28
"Older Women"	3/29
On Wisdom	10/8
On to Year Two!	12/31
Open Door	4/16
Othniel	5/18
Path of Life	2/16
Patience	6/16
Patience	11/13
Patriotism	6/14
Paul - I	12/6
Paul - II	12/7
Paul - III	12/08
Paul's Goal	7/20
Peace and Quiet	8/2
Perfection	5/8
Perpetual Joy	9/12
Persevering Prayer	9/6
Peter	12/10
Plain Talk	3/10
Planning Ahead	5/2
Pleasant Place, A	11/26
"Plentycost"	5/27
Practical Atheism	6/1
Praise Wins	6/7
Pray	12/4
Prayer	9/25
Present	12/25
Preserving the Past	10/24
Priceless Treasure	1/12
Procrastination	6/5
Productive Lives	3/30
Project Finished!	9/22
Promise, A	9/7
Proving Ground	3/16
Ransomed	2/22
Real Miracle, The	3/31
Reassessment	12/29
Receive Graciously	6/6
Remember the Poor	2/13
Remember Mercy	7/4
Renewed Identity	5/28
Respect	11/5
Retired. Day One.	1/1
Retirement Center?, A	10/13
Reward in Kind	12/15
Reward Time - I	8/24
Reward Time - II	8/25
Rewarded	6/10
Rich Provision	7/2
Right Spirit, The	7/5
Rise and Shine!	2/14
Rule of Peace	4/8
Rules for Good Days	5/4
Run for the Prize	12/16
Sacrifice, Sacrilege	7/16
Samuel	6/24
Sarah	2/25
Satisfied	1/29
Saul	7/8
Second Wind	3/9
Second Residence	4/11
Seizing Opportunity	7/6
Self-Discipline	2/1
Senior Achievers	1/15
Serving the Lord	6/28
Shimei	7/12
Shut Mouth, A	5/24
Sight on the Goal	11/18
Simeon	11/6
Slave or Master?	1/28
Solomon	8/17
Spirit Power	3/5
Spiritual Leaders	8/10
Stand Firm	12/17
Staying Put	1/23
Stoke the Fire	3/15
Stumbling Blocks	6/12
"Submit" - I	7/25
"Submit" - II	7/26
Succession	11/29
Sunday School	4/27
Sunset Law	6/27
Tabitha/Dorcas	11/11
Thankful Today	11/23
They Walked with God	11/20
Things God Cannot Do	4/26
Throne Room Help	8/27
Through Generations	5/13
Time for Revival	7/3
Time	7/1
Time to Houseclean	3/7
Time Is Short, The	12/18
To the Work!	9/9
To Be Continued	3/23
To Go or to Stay?	10/12
To Live Is Christ	4/25

Title	Date
Today	2/21
Transformed	7/24
True Riches	3/11
Truth on Trial	10/17
Truthful People	8/20
Two Worlds	5/9
Two More Miracles	4/5
Ultimate Submission	7/27
Unashamed Giving	2/10
Under Construction	12/27
Undeserving	5/6
Uneven Exchange	2/23
Unfailing Promise	4/12
Unknown Influence	7/29
Up and at it!	3/14
Uplook Is Good, The	9/24
Wake Up!	8/12
Walking Temples	3/6
Wayward	6/2
Wealth	9/1
Weighing a Move	1/24
What Quality Life?	10/29
What Counts	5/3
When Two Retire	1/3
Where the Pray-ers?	10/31
Where to?	1/25
Where? Why?	1/21
Why Serve Christ?	5/26
Why Pray?	11/21
Why Suffering?	7/19
Why Little Progress?	12/28
Why, Indeed, Pray?	11/22
Why I Give Thanks	8/26
Widowed	11/15
Wills	10/26
Wives, Husbands	1/11
Work Rushes In	4/30
Younger Friends	8/8
Your Counsel	3/25
Zerubbabel	10/20

SCRIPTURE TEXTS FOR THE MEDITATIONS

Genesis
1:11 .... 4/7
4:1 .... 1/16
4:25 .... 1/17
5:21–24 .... 1/18
5:24 .... 1/20
6:9 .... 1/20
6:9, 13–14, 22 .... 1/19
12:1 .... 1/24
13:8-9 .... 1/25
13:12 .... 2/26
16:11 .... 2/27
17:5 .... 2/24
17:15–16 .... 2/25
24:1 .... 10/10
25:26 .... 2/28
31:26 .... 3/20
32:28 .... 3/19
44:18, 34 .... 3/21
49:22-26 .... 3/22

Exodus
4:14 .... 4/19
6:20 .... 4/17
15:20–21 .... 4/18
18:5 .... 4/22
20:12 .... 5/14
22:22 .... 11/15
33:13 .... 4/20

Leviticus
19:32 .... 11/5

Numbers
8:25 .... 5/31
12:1 .... 4/18
13:17–18 .... 1/26
20:23–26 .... 5/15
20:26 .... 4/23

Deuteronomy
8:1 .... 9/1
31:6 .... 1/3

Joshua
1:6–7 .... 7/23
7:7–11 .... 7/13
14:6, 10–12 .... 5/16
24:15 .... 5/17

Judges
3:9 .... 5/18
8:32 .... 5/19
16:31 .... 5/20

Ruth
4:15 .... 10/13
4:16–17 .... 6/21

1 Samuel
2:30 .... 6/22
4:18 .... 6/23
12:1–3 .... 6/24
16:7 .... 2/5
28:15, 19 .... 7/8

2 Samuel
17:23 .... 8/13
18:33 .... 6/2
18:33 .... 6/2
19:37 .... 1/23
21:15–17 .... 9/29

1 Kings
1:17–18 .... 8/16
2:8–9 .... 7/12
2:27 .... 8/14
2:30 .... 7/10
5:12 .... 8/18
11:4 .... 8/17
10:31 .... 9/13
13:17 .... 9/15

1 Chronicles
17:26 .... 5/6
21:9–10 .... 7/11
29:2 .... 10/28
29:14 .... 5/5
29:26–28 .... 7/9

2 Chronicles
6:9 .... 6/8
7:14 .... 7/3
20:21 .... 6/7
24:15–16 .... 9/14
33:16 .... 9/19

Nehemiah
2:18 .... 9/9
6:15 .... 9/22
13:6–7 .... 10/22

Esther
4:12–14 .... 10/23

Job
2:11 .... 2/4
5:7 .... 7/19
14:5 .... 9/27
42:12 .... 2/3

Psalms
1:3 .... 12/13
14:1 .... 6/1
16:6 .... 11/26
16:7 .... 6/30
16:11 .... 2/16
23:1-2 .... 5/7
23:4–5 .... 4/12
23:5–6 .... 12/31
27:10 .... 6/17
31:15 .... 9/24
32:8 .... 3/25
33:18 .... 10/11
37:25 .... 10/30
39:4–5 .... 3/26
42:6 .... 10/18
46:1 .... 2/9
46:10 .... 4/28
48:14 .... 10/12
55:22 .... 11/24
57:8 .... 1/6
65:11 .... 12/12
68:6 .... 12/19
68:19 .... 4/24
71:9 .... 9/28
73:24 .... 1/27
78:32–33 .... 6/29
84:2 .... 11/19
86:8 .... 4/26
90:10 .... 10/29
90:12 .... 12/3
90:14 .... 2/14
90:17 .... 7/14
91:1, 16 .... 9/7
92:12-14 .... 9/30
100:5 .... 5/13
103:2 .... 11/23
119:160 .... 12/1
127:3 .... 8/19
134:1 .... 10/19
136:1 .... 8/26
144:12 .... 1/12

Proverbs
2:8 .... 9/4
3:3 .... 11/28
3:27 .... 10/1
5:18–19 .... 8/1
5:21 .... 7/31
9:10–11 .... 5/22
11:14 .... 12/15
11:15 .... 8/11
12:22 .... 8/20
12:25 .... 6/11
16:31 .... 2/2
17:1 .... 8/2
17:5 .... 2/13
17:9 .... 5/24
17:22 .... 9/11
18:24 .... 8/9

22:1 .... 6/18
25:28 .... 7/15
Ecclesiastes
3:1 .... 7/1
4:13 .... 10/8
5:4 .... 6/5
7:14 .... 11/25
9:10 .... 4/30
Isaiah
6:8 .... 9/17
40:30–31 .... 3/9
44:28 .... 10/6
46:4 .... 8/4
46:9 .... 10/24
57:1 .... 11/14
57:15 .... 4/11
Jeremiah
26:18–19 .... 9/18
51:59 .... 10/15
Lamentations
1:1, 10 .... 9/8
Daniel
4:37 .... 10/3
5:31 .... 10/7
6:5 .... 10/5
6:28 .... 10/4
7:1 .... 9/10
Hosea
1:1 .... 9/16
6:6 .... 6/4
Micah
5:2 .... 12/22
Habakkuk
2:4 .... 2/29
3:2 .... 7/4
Haggai
1:3–4 .... 10/21
Zechariah
4:6 .... 3/5
4:9 .... 10/20
Malachi
2:14 .... 1/10, 6/9
2:15 .... 1/8
Matthew
4:3 .... 4/2
4:3-4 .... 4/3
6:6 .... 11/21, 11/22
6:16 .... 6/25
10:8 .... 7/16
20:15 .... 4/10
20:28 .... 1/28, 2/22
Mark
2:4 .... 11/2

8:19–21 .... 11/1
10:21 .... 10/25
Luke
1:3 .... 12/9
2:7 .... 12/23
2:25 .... 11/6
2:29 .... 5/11
2:36 .... 11/7
4:13 .... 4/4
6:38 .... 6/6
11:5 .... 8/6, 8/7
11:9 .... 12/4
14:33 .... 12/14
18:1 .... 10/31
23:46 .... 4/5
John
1:14 .... 12/25
3:4 .... 11/8
3:7 .... 10/9
3:16 .... 5/26
14:6 .... 11/17
18:24 .... 11/9
19:30 .... 3/31
Acts
2:1 .... 5/27
4:35 .... 2/11
5:34, 40 .... 11/10
7:54 .... 10/17
9:36 .... 11/11
20:33 .... 9/2
20:34 .... 6/13
Romans
1:17 .... 11/3
1:25 .... 2/23
4:3 .... 2/15
8:28 .... 11/12
12:1 .... 3/3, 3/4
12:2 .... 3/8
12:11 .... 6/28
12:12 .... 9/6
12:13 .... 4/16
13:8 .... 2/12
14:1 .... 11/4
14:7 .... 7/29
14:8 .... 9/5
1 Corinthians
6:19 .... 4/6
6:19–20 .... 1/2
7:29 .... 12/18
8:9 .... 6/12
9:24–27 .... 12/16
15:3–5 .... 7/18
15:55 .... 5/10
15:58 .... 12/17

2 Corinthians
3:18 .... 7/24
4:1 .... 9/26
4:16 .... 8/3
24:17 .... 4/13
4:18 .... 5/9
5:1 .... 8/21
5:5 .... 8/22
5:10 .... 8/23
5:15 .... 5/28
5:19 .... 12/26
6:10 .... 3/11
6:16 .... 3/6
8:12 .... 2/10
9:8 .... 8/29
9:10 .... 8/31
11:14 .... 11/16
11:28 .... 4/15
12:9 .... 1/14
12:14 .... 10/27
13:5 .... 12/29
13:9–11 .... 5/8
Galatians
3:6 .... 1/15
5:6 .... 5/3
5:22 .... 6/16
6:9 .... 7/30
6:14 .... 3/24
Ephesians
2:6 .... 5/29
2:19 .... 12/24
3:15 .... 12/21
4:13 .... 12/28
4:23 .... 2/7
4:26 .... 6/27
4:28 .... 10/2
4:29 .... 3/10
5:1-2 .... 6/26
5:15 .... 2/19
5:16 .... 2/8
5:18 .... 7/5
5:19–20 .... 1/30
5:21 .... 7/25, 7/26
5:22, 25 .... 1/11
6:2–3 .... 2/20
6:9 .... 1/31
6:13 .... 12/20
Philippians
1:6 .... 3/12
1:12 .... 12/6
1:20 .... 5/12
1:21 .... 3/7, 4/25
2:4 .... 7/28
2:12 .... 3/23
3:10 .... 7/20

3:16	12/30
3:18–19	3/2
3:20	6/15, 11/20
4:4	12/7
4:6	6/19, 6/20
4:7	12/2
4:11	8/30
4:11–12	5/30
4:19	9/23

Colossians

1:9	9/21
2:14	9/20
3:2–3	9/3
3:9–10	2/6
3:12	5/23
3:13	4/29
3:15	4/8
3:16	5/25
3:17	10/16
3:19	1/9
4:5	7/6
4:12	9/25

1 Thessalonians

4:11	10/26
4:12	4/14
4:17	2/18
5:12	8/10
5:14–15	3/14
5:16–17	9/12
5:18	1/1
5:19	3/15
5:21	3/16

1 Timothy

4:8	3/1
5:8	6/3
6:6–8	10/14
6:17	7/2
6:18	1/5

2 Timothy

1:2	8/8
1:7	2/1, 3/17
1:12	8/28
2:2	11/29
2:15	4/27
3:1–4	3/13
4:7	12/8
4:13	1/13

Titus

2:2	3/28
2:3	3/29
3:14	3/30

Hebrews

2:14–15	4/9
3:7	2/21
4:16	8/27
9:27	2/17, 12/5
10:36	11/13
11:24–27	4/21
12:2	3/27
12:16	3/18
13:5	1/29

James

2:13	5/1
3:5	11/30
4:7	7/27
4:15	5/2, 7/7

1 Peter

1:13	11/18
1:15	12/10
2:5	12/27
2:16	1/22
2:17	6/14
3:7	1/7
3:10–11	5/4
3:15	7/17
4:1	7/21
4:19	7/22
5:7	8/5, 11/27

2 Peter

3:18	5/21

1 John

3:18	1/4
4:7	12/11

2 John

8	8/25

3 John

4	6/10

Revelation

3:1–2	8/12
3:8	1/21
11:18	8/24
21:27	4/1